Challenge and Opportunity

Edited by John D. Dennison

Challenge and Opportunity: Canada's Community Colleges at the Crossroads

UBCPress / Vancouver

Printed in Canada on acid-free paper ∞

ISBN 0-7748-0516-1

Canadian Cataloguing in Publication Data
Main entry under title:
Challenge and opportunity

   Includes bibliographical references and index.
   ISBN 0-7748-0516-1

   1. Community colleges – Canada. 2. Postsecondary education – Canada.
I. Dennison, John D., 1929-   LB2328.C52 1995   378'.052'0971   C95-910106-3

UBC Press gratefully acknowledges the ongoing support to its publishing program from the Canada Council, the Province of British Columbia Cultural Services Branch, and the Department of Communications of the Government of Canada.

Set in Stone by Irma Rodriguez, Artegraphica Design Co.
Printed and bound in Canada by D.W. Friesen & Sons Ltd.
Copy-editor: Joanne Richardson
Proofreader: Anne Webb

UBC Press
University of British Columbia
6344 Memorial Road
Vancouver, BC V6T 1Z2
(604) 822-3259
Fax: (604) 822-6083

Contents

Acknowledgments

This book could not have been written without the generous assistance of a number of colleagues who gave freely of their time and expertise to ensure that the final product would be an important addition to the literature on community colleges in Canada. First, however, I wish to acknowledge the support of the Canadian Studies Directorate of the Secretary of State. This organization supplied the initial impetus for a project designed to document the performance of a uniquely Canadian educational enterprise – its public community colleges.

To report accurately and comprehensively on the wide range of developments in the community college sector in each province and territory since 1985, it was crucial to draw upon the expertise of a cadre of individuals in each region of Canada. The following willingly contributed their time and knowledge:

British Columbia: Kerry Jothen and Shell Harvey, Ministry of Skills, Training and Labour

Alberta: Bill Workman and Larry Orton, Ministry of Advanced Education

Saskatchewan: John Biss, Ministry of Education; Andrew Mirlin, Northwest Regional College

Manitoba: Tony Knowles, Red River Community College

Ontario: Ian Calvert, formally at the Association of Colleges of Applied Arts and Technology of Ontario; Robert (Squee) Gordon, Humber College; Patricia Groves, George Brown College; Glen Jones, Brock University

Québec: André Le Blanc (who provided the entire section on Québec), Champlain Regional College

Nova Scotia: Jack Buckley and Dermot Mulrooney, Nova Scotia Community College

Prince Edward Island: Chris Bryant and Archie MacFadyen, Holland College

New Brunswick: Jim Cromwell and Jack Syroid, New Brunswick Community College

Newfoundland: Doug Fowlow, Westviking College; Andrea Dicks, Department of Education
Yukon: Aron Senkpiel, Yukon College
Northwest Territories: Mark Cleveland, Arctic College

As a consequence of reviewing college development region by region, a number of common and significant issues emerged which seemed destined to dominate the role of Canada's community colleges during the next decade. A number of these issues were referred to individuals who had both the expertise and the experience to deal with them. To those who willingly and enthusiastically contributed chapters on these issues, I owe a deep debt of gratitude and wish to acknowledge each one individually.

John Levin, a former college instructor and administrator, is now a professor of higher education at the University of Arizona. He represents a new generation of scholars, which is directing its attention to the many issues facing postsecondary education in Canada and elsewhere.

Starr L. Owen also has extensive experience as a college teacher and is now pursuing a new career as a scholar in the field of higher education.

Janet Knowles has worked in several provinces developing links between postsecondary education and the business sector. She is now manager of contract services at Douglas College. Her chapter on entrepreneurship was written with the able assistance of Colleen Hawkey.

Douglas Baker has been involved in the college sector in many capacities in many provinces and was formerly the president of Nicola Valley Technical Institute, a predominantly First Nations college in British Columbia. He is now at Northwest Community College.

Charles W. Joyner has extensive experience and expertise in competency-based education. He is now engaged in international activities with the Association of Canadian Community Colleges in Ottawa.

Paul Gallagher has dedicated most of his professional life, as an administrator, scholar, writer, teacher, and critical observer, to the promotion and advancement of the community college concept in Canada. He is the author of innumerable articles dealing with many aspects of Canadian education and is, above all, a valued friend and colleague.

Finally, although their names appear above, there are three people who deserve special mention. Paul Gallagher served as a critical reviewer for many chapters and provided a great deal of helpful comment; Douglas Baker gathered a good deal of the material on several regions and wrote some of the early drafts; and André Le Blanc was, as always, an invaluable resource on colleges in Québec.

Introduction

John D. Dennison

Given their creation in the 1960s and 1970s and their attainment of maturity twenty-five years later, Canada's community colleges may be described as having grown old quickly. Although the idealism of their early years has been replaced by pressures to maintain relevancy and stability in a difficult political and fiscal environment, the colleges continue to play an important role in the social and economic life of this nation. The 1994 statistical profile of the college sector is impressive. In all, the approximately 150 institutions which fall under the rubric of community colleges deliver education and training through more than 700 satellite campuses and other centres. Although variations in instructor classification occur among the provinces and territories, approximately 25,000 full-time and over 150,000 part-time personnel teach in the college sector. The student population is even less well defined, but the most recent statistics from the Department of the Secretary of State (Canada 1991) indicate that about 500,000 students are enrolled in credit programs in colleges. However, it is estimated that an additional 1.5 million students are enrolled in credit-free continuing education. Two-thirds of the credit program enrollees are full-time students, while the remainder attend on a part-time basis.

In some provinces, colleges offer both pre-university or university-equivalent courses as well as academic upgrading and technical/career preparation. About one-third of all students, both full- and part-time, are enrolled in university-related courses. While the majority of full-time students in the college sector are women (54 per cent), males outnumber females by a ratio of two to one among full-time instructional staff.

In fiscal terms, the community college sector has grown into an enterprise with an annual operating budget of $6 billion, while its capital assets are valued at $30 billion. The return from investment in Canadian colleges is partly reflected in an estimate which states that 25 per cent of the nation's workforce holds college credentials (Price Waterhouse 1993). In terms of employment, almost 80 per cent of those with a college diploma or certificate are active in the workforce. In 1991, unemployment rates for college graduates (8.9 per cent) were lower than those for people over the age of twenty-five who had not graduated from college (10.4 per cent) (Price Waterhouse 1993).

Impressive as it may be, the foregoing simply documents a statistical profile which provides only minimal insight into the complexities of community college development, particularly since the mid-1980s. Canada's colleges must now contend with a far different environment than that which characterized their first two decades. As described in an earlier work (Dennison and Gallagher 1986), community colleges were born in an optimistic atmosphere of growth and expansion (in both human and economic terms). Popular ideas and predictions (e.g., the democratization of educational opportunity, the numerous rewards from investment in human capital, the imperative of a skilled workforce, an unprecedented wave of high-school graduates seeking further education, and the largely unchallenged role of the federal government with respect to financing education and training) all contributed to a massive expansion of the non-university alternative in postsecondary education.

But the era of expansion was brief. In fact, the fiscal consequences of extraordinary growth in the college sector became more than the public treasury could bear. Optimistic expectations of returns from investment in human capital, especially in the postsecondary education sector, were reduced to a debate about unemployed and underprepared graduates. To be fair, it must be acknowledged that similar concerns over the predicted virtues of investment in higher education have occurred in all advanced technological societies. Teichler (1988:97-8) notes that, in the late 1970s, there was a 'shift from optimism or euphoria regarding the needs and virtues of education expansion [to] pessimism or renewed skepticism.' Doubt began to emerge as to whether the expansion of higher education did actually increase opportunities for traditionally disadvantaged groups (Smith 1993). A deliberate slowing in the growth of institutions ultimately meant that many of the optimistic goals set in the 1960s and 1970s were not going to be realized.

In the 1980s, issues arose which were characteristic of higher education systems in all countries. Teichler (1988) outlined a list which included an emphasis on the need for quality improvement; increased support for diversity; attention to more efficient management of institutions; growth in the use of performance indicators to measure quality and efficiency in resource allocation; greater interest in the utility of higher education to the private sector; and the internationalization of higher education. Each of these issues attained prominence in Canada and, to a greater or lesser extent, had an impact upon its various college systems. Again, consistent with observations made by Teichler (1988), one of the most pervasive problems for Canada's postsecondary educational institutions concerned the debate over the relative advantages of 'diversified' vis-à-vis 'integrated' models: 'Whereas proponents of the former model are in favour of quite distinct educational provisions in a not clearly segmented system, but rather in a system of blurred boundaries and overlapping clienteles, advocates of the latter want to limit differences in educational provision through individual units in higher education serving relatively heterogeneous student bodies' (p. 97).

Since 1960, provincial higher education systems have clearly favoured the growing diversity within and between the university and the non-university sectors. This diversity is based upon grounds advanced by Stadtman (1980), who argues that it increases the range of choices available to learners, makes higher education available to virtually everyone, matches education to the needs and abilities of individual students, enables institutions to select their own missions and to limit their activities accordingly, and constitutes a precondition for college and university freedom and autonomy. Nevertheless, it is important to recognize that diversity has various forms (Goedegebuure et al. 1992), and provinces have adopted one or more of the following:

- systematic diversity (differences in institutional type, size, and control)
- structural diversity (whether institutions exist as a single unit or as an integrated part of a multicampus system)
- programmatic diversity (level of credential offered, comprehensiveness, mission, and emphasis)
- procedural diversity (delivery systems, administrative processes)
- regulational diversity (selectivity of students)
- constitutional diversity (backgrounds, abilities, values, goals of students and other personnel)
- values and climate diversity (differences in institutional cultures and subcultures).

All of the foregoing forms of diversity can be found in Canada, stemming primarily from public policy decisions made during the 'golden age' of development in postsecondary education during the 1960s. The creation of Ontario's College of Applied Arts and Technology, Québec's collèges d'enseignement général et professionnel, Alberta's and British Columbia's comprehensive institutions, the community-based colleges of Saskatchewan, and the centralized models of Manitoba and New Brunswick, were all products of specific policy goals and objectives. Furthermore, the relationship of colleges to both the established and the emerging universities in each region was a consequence of a particular form of diversity.

In recent years, new policy initiatives, although increasingly restrained, have further enhanced the diversity of the postsecondary system. The growth of distance-learning opportunities, measures to extend access to disadvantaged groups such as First Nations peoples, and the provision of new educational credentials under alternative administrative arrangements, have all added to system diversification.

Diversity, particularly as exemplified in Ontario, with its distinctively separate 'parallel' college and university sectors, is not without its critics. Studies by Anisef et al. (1982) and others suggest that developing an alternative college sector preserves inequality of educational opportunity by diverting lower middle-class youth in that direction, while preserving the prestige and high-return programs of the universities for the socioculturally advantaged. The Ontario model is in dramatic contrast to the Québec model, in which *all* students are exposed to pre-university programs as a mandatory precursor to continued participation in advanced education.

While diversity has long been the guiding principle behind the organization of Canada's higher education systems, a different initiative has become evident during the 1990s. As described in detail later in this book, governments in several provinces have begun to argue that current realities, both financial and human, are such that the drastic restructuring of postsecondary education is necessary if it is to remain effective and efficient. Faced with massive changes in the requirements of the workplace (associated with technological advances and a new economic order), many individuals now seek retraining and further education. In turn, educational institutions are being challenged to provide flexible and accessible programs; to ensure maximum mobility of graduates as well as full recognition of previous learning, wherever it was obtained; and to allow for the appropriate transfer of program credits. To meet this challenge, institutions are expected to collaborate in their planning and to develop improved learning partnerships, not only among themselves, but in concert with the private sector (particularly with management and organized labour). All of these initiatives lead towards a more integrated, rather than a more diversified, institutional structure. This approach prescribes a need for restructuring and carries with it a clear government message, at both the federal and the provincial level, that future financial support will be targeted to that end.

Indeed, it is the financing of postsecondary education which has begun to dominate public-sector debate over the sector's continued health. This topic is by no means confined to Canada, and, again, much can be learned from experience in other highly industrialized jurisdictions. While many of the latter's postsecondary systems are national, involving massive intervention by central governments (e.g., the United Kingdom, New Zealand, and the Netherlands), other countries (e.g., Germany, Australia, and the United

States) utilize their federated political structures to influence the direction of their educational systems. Smith (1993) argues that two broad policy strategies have emerged in recent years. The first requires increasing government control over planning and resource utilization; the second involves 'a stepping back by government from detailed centralized control by encouraging higher education institutions to be more autonomous, self regulating and market oriented in their operations, albeit within an overall framework of government priorities' (Kogan 1988, cited by Smith 1993:31). While the first option has been the trend in many countries, there is increasing evidence that a move towards the second option has been developing over the last few years. The dismantling of the binary system in Australia and the United Kingdom has been accompanied by greater government encouragement of institutional endeavours to seek alternative funding sources. In the United States and Japan, large private-sector involvement in postsecondary education has ensured competition and has encouraged innovative efforts to attract and maintain students.

In this context, Canada provides an interesting case which defies easy comparison. Skolnik (1991) attributes the lack of national planning in higher education to the stringent constitutional reality which places higher education firmly under the aegis of provincial governments. However, he also notes the latter's unwillingness to intervene in the management of institutions under their jurisdiction. While this observation applies more accurately to the universities, colleges have also been awarded a reasonable measure of autonomy. Skolnik draws attention to the provinces' ambivalence regarding whether to move towards a free-market model of postsecondary education or to tighten public control over it. Again, directing his comments primarily to the university sector, Skolnik concludes that,

> while some modest steps toward deregulation in higher education would produce moderately beneficial results, the present balance between public and private in Canadian higher education is quite likely more a source of strength than of weakness. In the medium to long run, a little bit of insulation of universities from either or both the immediate instrumental designs of government and the transient faddishness which often characterizes private market demand will likely – even if perhaps paradoxically – protect the capacity for more solid and more lasting contributions to the economy than a strategy which involves capitulation to either of these pressures. (p. 6)

While Skolnik's comments are instructive, the future of Canadian colleges will assuredly rest, not upon an optimistic expectation of continuing fiscal support from provincial governments, but upon their ability to adapt to

changing priorities and to demonstrate their contribution to economic renewal. It seems, too, that government funding will be aimed at programs
that demonstrate cooperation in the planning and delivery of education
and training. Furthermore, colleges will be expected to ensure improved
access to groups such as First Nations peoples, those unemployed as a result
of structural changes in the economy, and those seeking new skills to increase their employability.

Inevitably, the issue of privatization will become more and more prominent in the lexicon of college education. Those gaining the advantages of
further education will be expected to bear an increasing proportion of the
cost of their training. In some areas, these will be students; in other areas,
they will be employers, unions, and private-sector agencies which share in
the benefits that accrue from advanced education programs. In Canada, in
particular, the burden of fiscal support for all forms of education has been
borne largely by the public purse. It has become evident that this policy
will change, partly due to the inability of provincial governments to regain
their financial health and partly due to the realization that public support
of advanced education often results in subsidizing those most able to support themselves.

There is also every indication that provincial governments are increasingly concerned about the complex relationships between postsecondary
education, economic restructuring and renewal, and those forms of employment available in the new global economy. As documented in the chapters which follow, almost every provincial government since 1990 has commissioned reports which have the potential to set new priorities and new
directions for college sectors.

Smith (1993) notes that comparable concerns have arisen in all highly
industrialized countries, particularly those which have invested heavily in
public higher education. In the European community, a recent report (Kaiser et al. 1992) indicates that the average cost per student has been declining in wealthy countries while increasing in poor countries. In part, this
trend is the result of wealthy countries attempting to improve the delivery
of educational services (e.g., distance learning). Inevitably, innovative
schemes are challenged over questions of quality – and here there are conflicting views.

Within the current policy environment, Smith (1993) poses three questions relating to the impact of market forces upon postsecondary education:

> How are differences in collective and individual interests to be managed?
> How can social, economic and demographic realities be taken into ac-
> count in managing the 'intangible capital' which is now inextricably linked
> to economic prosperity?

What are the best ways of ensuring opportunities for recurrent education, training, flexibility, and varied access and mobility within higher education systems? (p. 34)

These are complex problems which may be addressed in a number of ways.
Much of what follows in this book is intended to examine such questions
from the perspectives of those involved in Canadian community colleges.
While colleges play a major role in the sociocultural and economic life of
this country, very little systematic effort has been made to document their
contributions, to analyze the changes that are occurring within them, or to
examine the issues which must be addressed if they are to continue to play
a viable role.

Chapter 1 provides an account of significant activities, initiatives, and
related literature respecting the college systems in each province and territory since 1986. Comparable events, including historical accounts of college development, were the subject of *Canada's Community Colleges: A Critical Analysis* (Dennison and Gallagher 1986). These reports from various
jurisdictions are factual (in that they record the substance of the events)
and analytical/critical (in that the author comments upon the particular
structure, function, and future role of the colleges in each region). Chapter
1 concludes with an overall view of the common themes of college activity
across Canada, what problems and issues seem to be shared, and which
priorities and scenarios will determine how they will develop in the next
decade.

The rest of this book contains a number of essays which focus upon the
critical issues and challenges which community colleges (and, indeed, the
entire spectrum of postsecondary education in Canada) will have to accommodate if they are to maintain their relevance in the future. Few would
argue with the assertion that education in general, and education and training beyond high school in particular, faces a crisis in public confidence. In
consequence, there are increasing government concerns over how institutions should respond to the needs of both individuals and of the country.
Clearly, it is time to reassess, to take account of what must be preserved and
of what is no longer relevant, to set clear priorities for the future, and to
evaluate new and perhaps more efficient ways of delivering services – particularly to those who were not well served in the past.

Leadership is widely regarded as critical to setting the course most likely
to enable colleges to regain the confidence of both government and the
public. In Chapter 2, John Levin develops a case for a kind of leadership
which will reflect the nature of society in the third millennium.

As described in my discussion of how Canada's postsecondary systems
have moved from diversified to integrated models, a principal challenge

has to do with bringing traditionally disparate institutions into a cooperative working relationship. In part, cooperation at this level involves the seeking of an acceptable compromise in areas long regarded as integral to institutional autonomy (including recognition of academic credits earned in other institutions and/or under unconventional arrangements; cooperative development of curricula for programs offered jointly by one or more colleges or universities; acknowledgment of prior learning gained in formal and informal settings; and the recognition of credit banks [i.e., an individual learner's accumulated record of accomplishment]). In Chapter 3, I critically examine a number of arrangements for institutional cooperation, ranging from credit transfer policy to a sophisticated approach to the idea of a system.

In order to understand why some organizations work effectively while others appear to be in a constant state of crisis, it is necessary to analyze organizational culture. Community colleges are complex organizations in which internal and external forces combine to exert constant pressure upon management to maintain stability and a common sense of purpose. In Chapter 4, using a number of examples from the college sector, Starr Owen offers an analysis of how current theories about organizational culture may be used to understand the sources of institutional conflict and/or harmony characteristic of the community college.

Another fundamental question which is rarely addressed in the literature on community colleges concerns their underlying values. In Chapter 5, I propose four basic value sets which are applicable to the college concept and which provide the bases for setting operational policies. As a practical exercise, a number of value statements are offered, together with some case studies. At a time in which colleges will be forced to decide which activities are essential to their mandates and missions, these four value sets provide a blueprint for how such decisions may be made.

Faced with the reality of declining financial support from both federal and provincial governments, many community colleges are actively pursuing new sources of revenue, utilizing approaches consistent with their mandates. In Chapter 6, under the general heading of 'entrepreneurship,' Janet Knowles analyzes the theory behind this strategy, describes a variety of cooperative arrangements with private-sector agencies, and discusses the inherent risks and the potential advantages for colleges should they adopt an entrepreneurial approach to education.

In spite of continuing efforts by community colleges to broaden access to disadvantaged societal groups, their success in meeting the needs of aboriginal peoples has been, at best, inconsistent. In Chapter 7, Douglas Baker, a former president of an institution devoted to First Nations students, offers critical insight into the challenges which community colleges face if they are to effectively serve Canada's aboriginal peoples. Baker describes the major barriers to participation and the factors which contribute to aboriginal learners succeeding in educational and training programs. He also documents examples of successful approaches to policy development as well as the implementation of aboriginal postsecondary education, including a variety of organizational models which are utilized across Canada.

When considering how colleges are expected to justify their receipt of public dollars, few terms are used more frequently and with less precision than is 'accountability.' In Chapter 8, I discuss the various uses of this term, the problems involved in its application, and the challenges involved in defining measures which accurately reflect the complexity of a college's performance.

Questions regarding the increasing costs of maintaining public colleges in a growing climate of fiscal restraint have often focused upon ways to increase productivity, particularly in the delivery of instruction. In Chapter 9, Charles Joyner describes a Canadian-designed teaching model which has been widely adopted by other countries. The DACUM technique and the individualized competency-based technique of instruction has earned both support and criticism. Joyner outlines the unique history and organization of this teaching model.

Finally, in Chapter 10, Paul Gallagher offers a critical review of Canada's colleges, focusing on past accomplishments and future promises. He then provides a detailed list of priorities which, if met, will revitalize their role in the next decades. A long-respected practitioner and advocate for the community college sector, Gallagher leaves little doubt as to the realities of a new economic environment – an environment in which colleges will have to compete for their share of resources.

References

Allen, M. 1983. *The Goals of Universities*. Milton Keynes: Open University Press

Anisef, P., N.R. Okihiro, and C. James. 1982. *The Pursuit of Equality: Evaluating and Monitoring Accountability to Post-Secondary Education in Ontario*. Toronto: Ministry of Colleges and Universities

Canada. Department of the Secretary of State. 1991. *Profile of Higher Education in Canada*. Ottawa: Ministry of Supply and Services

Dennison, J.D., and P. Gallagher. 1986. *Canada's Community Colleges: A Critical Analysis*. Vancouver: University of British Columbia Press

Goedegebuure, L., F. Kaiser, P. Maassen, L. Meek, F. van Vught, and E. de Weert. 1992. *Higher Education Policy in International Comparative Perspective*. Enschede, The Netherlands: Centre for Higher Education Policy Studies

Kaiser, F., R. Florax, J. Koelman, and F. van Vught. 1992. *Public Expenditure on Higher Education*. London: Jessica Kingsley

Kogan, M. 1988. 'Government as the Management of Higher Education.' *International Journal of Institutional Management in Higher Education* 12:5-15

Price Waterhouse. 1993. *Human Resource Study of Canadian Community Colleges and Institutes.* Ottawa: Association of Canadian Community Colleges

Skolnik, M. 1991. 'Odd Country Out: A Speculative Commentary on Possible Causes and Consequences of the Absence of a National Policy toward Higher Education in Canada.' Paper presented at the Annual Meeting of the Association for the Study of Higher Education, Boston

Smith, R.T.H. 1993. 'The Transition from Elite to Mass Higher Education.' *Conference Proceedings.* Canberra: Higher Education Division, Occasional Papers Series

Stadtman, V.A. 1980. *Academic Adaptation: Higher Education Prepares for the 1980s and 1990s.* San Francisco: Jossey Bass

Teichler, V. 1988. *Changing Patterns of the Higher Education System: The Experience of Three Decades.* London: Jessica Kingsley

1

Community College Development in Canada since 1985

John D. Dennison

During the past decade, Canadian community colleges have undergone a period of change, reassessment, and, in some cases, fundamental restructuring in an attempt to maintain relevance in a political environment quite different from the one in which they were originally created. In many respects, the forces of change which bear upon college systems merely reflect a much wider confluence of economic, sociopolitical, and cultural events which have helped to reshape this nation, perhaps forever.

While many of the most noteworthy national debates (e.g., efforts to reform the Constitution, the advent of the North American Free Trade Agreement (NAFTA), and the increasing significance of the Charter of Rights and Freedoms) have had only a peripheral impact upon college development, there are other events whose influence has been more direct. In particular, the federal government's change of policy, as seen in such programs as Canadian Jobs Strategy (CJS), has resulted in vocational training being supported by the private sector rather than by the public sector and, thus, has forced colleges to become entrepreneurial in ways never anticipated at the time of their establishment. But of even greater significance to colleges has been the growing concern at all levels of government with escalating deficits and the accompanying efforts to curtail spending on social programs, particularly education. Initiatives to limit expenditures in the public sector have concentrated on such areas as tighter control over collective bargaining; demands for an increase in productivity; funding support being targeted to specific programs; and, inevitably, reductions in services.

As described later in this chapter, community colleges are particularly vulnerable in a climate of fiscal restraint. In part, their relationship with provincial governments allows the latter a good deal of direct control over funding and program support. Furthermore, colleges do not usually benefit from powerful lobbying interests, such as those enjoyed by universities and school boards. University graduates tend to occupy influential positions in society, while public schools are the concern of a large segment of the population. Unfortunately, technical-vocational and developmental education is seen as being of low status when compared with academic and professional programs – a perception often reinforced by the media and by others who influence public opinion. In consequence, colleges have difficulty promoting their role in the economic and social future of the nation.

The stability, mandates, and missions of Canadian colleges vary considerably. In Alberta, British Columbia, Ontario, and Québec, for example, they have long been established, and their role and relationship with respect to other sectors of the education system are generally clearly understood by both the government and the public. As a result, attempts to reform them are based upon a well-established format. On the other hand, colleges in Newfoundland, Nova Scotia, and the two territories are relatively recent creations and are still attempting to establish stable identities. In the difficult economic climate of the 1990s, this process has become even more uncertain and disruptive. Yet another scenario is apparent in Saskatchewan, where college-sector changes have reflected quite dramatically different directions in public policy. Here, colleges may be returning to the model upon which they were first established.

The following pages document the development of Canadian colleges in each region of the country during the last decade. The discussion focuses upon the most significant changes which have occurred, the factors which produced those changes, and the major issues which either remain unresolved or which are topics of debate regarding the future. The chapter concludes with an analysis of the common themes which confront Canadian colleges and which seem likely to underscore their role as they enter the next millennium.

British Columbia

The extended period of fiscal constraint in public-sector expenditures between 1983 and 1985 had a significant impact upon the postsecondary education sector in BC. With the introduction of formula funding and changes in their governing structure (Mitchell 1986), community colleges were brought more firmly into a provincial system. While the Pacific Vocational Institute (PVI) was amalgamated with the BC Institute of Technology (BCIT) and the Open Learning Agency (OLA) was created through the melding of the Knowledge Network of the West (KNOW) with the Open Learning Institute (OLI), all other colleges and institutes survived – albeit with some downsizing.

The period between 1986 and 1990, however, might be described as the period between recessions. The Social Credit government of Bill Vander Zalm directed its attention to a policy of 'recovery' and, in response to numerous expressions of concern, placed the issue of access to higher education near the top of its priority list.

Access to Advanced Education and Job Training in British Columbia
In 1987, the minister of advanced education established a provincial access committee charged with 'undertaking a review of the current state of participation in, and accessibility to, the various forms of advanced education and job training' (Provincial Access Committee 1988:7). A series of papers and reports dealing with retention, transfer, and transition from education to work had been prepared prior to the formulation of this committee. Its members included representatives from every region of the province and from each sector within the postsecondary education system. The final report, *Access to Advanced Education and Job Training in British Columbia,* contained many recommendations which were to have an immediate impact.

It was revealed that BC ranked ninth among the provinces with respect to degrees awarded relative to its population, and it ranked seventh in full-time enrolment with respect to the eighteen- to twenty-four-year-old age group. Given the extensive and diversified system of public postsecondary education in BC (three universities, fifteen colleges, and five specialized institutes, including OLA), these statistics were disconcerting. Furthermore, it was noted that problems of access were particularly evident for certain groups (e.g., First Nations persons, persons with disabilities, and those incarcerated in provincial prisons). Of particular concern was that those living outside the Lower Mainland did not have equal access to degree programs, as the three established universities are located in Vancouver and Victoria.

Inter alia, the report stated:

> If British Columbia is to share in the benefits of the emerging economic and social era, and contribute to the solution of provincial, national and international problems that will inevitably accompany that era, our advanced education and job training efforts must not only allow us to catch up with other parts of Canada but also to keep pace with increases in participation and successful completion rates currently being pursued in other parts of the world. (1988:5)

What followed was a series of recommendations designed to address the issue of access. Recognizing an immediate need to create 15,000 new places in degree programs if the province was to meet comparable national standards, the report recommended that

- priority be given to the use of open learning systems
- cooperative arrangements be made whereby more degree programs would be delivered by colleges and universities through OLA
- there be further exploration of a new university in the north of the province
- colleges by allowed to grant associate degrees
- a council on admissions, credit transfer, and articulation be created to facilitate mobility of students within the system
- in densely populated regions outside the Lower Mainland, colleges should offer degree programs through a university-college arrangement.

In effect, the clear message contained in the report was that BC should encourage more creative and cooperative arrangements within its postsecondary education system in order to provide expanded access, enhanced mobility, and better delivery of its services. Better utilization of the present system was assumed to be the key to the accommodation of more students, particularly those for whom access was restricted.

The Access Report received a positive reaction throughout the system, and many of its recommendations were implemented. The University of Northern British Columbia became a reality. Following the reports of two advisory committees, one on provincial literacy and the other on postsecondary education for Native learners, action was taken to address the problem of illiteracy and to develop strategies to better serve the needs of First Nations peoples. A quasi-independent provincial council on admissions and transfer was created, which had representatives from all segments of postsecondary education as well as a permanent secretariat. The council quickly began the process of formalizing arrangements for the transfer of academic credit for students who progressed from college to university – an issue which will receive greater attention in Chapter 3 of this book.

But perhaps the most radical of initiatives which followed the publication of the Access Report was the establishment of university-colleges, initially in three institutions – Malaspina College in Nanaimo, Okanagan College in Kelowna, and Cariboo College in Kamloops. The university-college was a new concept in postsecondary education in that, in offering degree-completion programs, it attempted to introduce into one institution characteristics of both the university and the community college. The university-college has not been tried in other parts of Canada as it entails numerous problems. Given the complexity of the university-college idea, these problems will be addressed in detail in Chapter 3.

Meanwhile, the newly formed OLA pursued its expanded mandate as a flexible, distance-learning, degree-granting alternative to conventional universities. Under its flexible academic organization, OLA was able to create a credit-bank (through which students could accumulate credits previously earned in one or more institutions and apply them towards a degree), thus pioneering the recognition of prior learning. Furthermore, through co-operative planning with OLA, a number of colleges, including BCIT, were able to provide degree-completion programs in areas such as health sciences, fine arts, and business.

The Advanced Education Council of British Columbia

For many years, two separate agencies represented the management of colleges and institutes; these were the BC Association of Colleges and the Council of Principals (Presidents). The former represented the trustees of college and institute boards and, as such, conducted professional development seminars on issues such as collective bargaining; it also served as an advocate for the non-university system. The Council of Presidents was the collective voice of the chief executive officers (CEOs) of the colleges and provincial institutes, which advised government on policies affecting the postsecondary system. In 1989, these two organizations merged to form the Advanced Education Council of British Columbia (AECBC). Despite its name, however, the council's constituency did not include the universities.

Under its new title, the AECBC became an even more outspoken advocate for the colleges and institutes, and, in August 1992, it issued a public report, *Access for Equity and Opportunity* (British Columbia 1992a), which documented the serious problems created by the limited number of education and training spaces in postsecondary education. The report provided examples of the frustration faced by potential consumers of the college and institute system. It also identified the 'neglected majority' (i.e., the two-thirds of Grade 12 graduates not eligible for admission to BC universities, the 40 per cent of students who do not graduate from high school, and the 20 to 40 per cent who fail basic standards of literacy and numeracy).

In summary, the report recommended that:
- the system be expanded to include an additional 28,000 funded Full-Time Equivalent (FTE) spaces over the next five years
- priority be given to the expansion of technical and vocational training programs in areas of documented need
- attention be given to regional inequities and to places for disabled, special-needs, and multicultural communities.

The public presentation of this report indicated that the council was prepared to enter the political arena. Its publication placed additional pressure upon a government faced with many fiscal problems as well as with a declining capacity to support public services.

Partners for the Future: The Ministry Plan

Since the early 1980s, the Ministry of Advanced Education, Training and

Technology has produced five-year planning frameworks upon which each college and institute was required to base its own multi-year plan. These frameworks reflected the ministry's designs for the college and institute system, while the respective multi-year plans indicated how each college would contribute to the overall realization of these designs.

In July 1991, the ministry produced a new planning framework, *Partners for the Future* (British Columbia 1991b), which, for the first time, addressed all elements of the system – universities, colleges, institutes, and the private sector. The plan emphasized synergy (which implied partnership, integration, and articulation), greater diversification, excellence and accountability, and expansion of applied technology in order to support economic growth. The remainder of the plan was devoted to attempting to mould education, training, and research so that they would produce a more highly skilled workforce, address outstanding deficiencies in areas such as literacy training and lifelong learning, and stimulate the economy within a competitive, knowledge-based environment. The Ministry of Advanced Education, Training and Technology expressed its mission as follows: 'To promote the development of knowledge and skills to enable British Columbians to achieve their potential, and to provide leadership in anticipating and responding to the needs of the dynamic economy and society' (p. 7).

Adult and Continuing Education
From its earliest beginnings, British Columbia has placed a high priority on the provision of educational programs for adults. Most of these activities have been credit-free and have been provided through a multitude of agencies, both public and private. One long-standing issue has been the relationship among the major public providers of adult programs (i.e., school boards, colleges, institutes, and universities) with respect to overlap, competition, and funding policy.

During the period of fiscal restraint after 1983, adult continuing education received no targeted funding in the allocation formula which was applied to the colleges. Consequently, these programs were placed upon a full-cost recovery basis. There were some strong advocates of adult education in both the Ministry of Advanced Education and in the institutions, and, being concerned about serious erosion, these people initiated and prepared reports on the status of adult education.

One such study was *Lifelong Learning for the 21st Century* (Faris 1992). The objective was to make recommendations regarding the policy framework and delivery of adult/continuing education in BC. Among the many recommendations were the following:

• Government should present a clear policy statement advocating the adoption of the lifelong learning concept as an organizing principle and a social goal throughout all ministries as well as throughout the total education system.

- Interministerial coordination of adult/continuing education should be assured by appropriate policies and mechanisms.
- Comparable access and fee structures should be created in all agencies providing adult and continuing education, while adult basic education to high school completion should be tuition-free.
- A common credential should be developed for all adults who complete high-school level education.
- Community learning councils should be established on a pilot basis in several communities.

Faris's observations were reinforced in a subsequent report, *Continuing Education in British Columbia's Colleges and Institutes* (Day 1992). The purpose of this study was to assess continuing education in the colleges after the years of restraint. A dramatic change in the composition of such programs was evident. Between 1984 and 1990, enrolment in general interest courses dropped from 100,000 to 65,000, while part-time vocational registration grew from 40,000 to 100,000. Over a third of the students were registered in three areas – business management, office administration, and computer science/data processing. The demand for English language training, citizenship education, and First Nations programs was high. Both the BC Federation of Labour and Employment and Immigration Canada continued to be involved in upgrading the workforce through continuing education activities offered in the postsecondary sector.

English as a Second Language
Largely because of its location, climate, and historical pattern of immigration, BC continues to be the preferred location of large numbers of new Canadians, primarily from countries in which English is not the dominant language. Many adults in this population seek language skills as a prerequisite to obtaining employment. The community colleges, particularly those in large urban areas, are under constant pressure to provide the language training which so many immigrants seek. Alister Cumming (1991) undertook a study to assess the need for English as a second language (ESL) instruction in BC. The results of this study clearly indicate one of the major challenges which will confront community colleges in this province during the next five years.

According to Cumming's study, as a consequence of current patterns of immigration (together with a continuing pool of residents with limited English), over 140,000 adults will need language instruction, the bulk of which will inevitably fall upon the college sector. A further factor in the equation is that more than 80 per cent of those requiring ESL training do not have a high-school education. At the time of the study, over 14,000 adults were receiving ESL instruction in BC, but only about one in five had their tuition and other costs covered by government sponsorship. The community colleges were the largest single providers (almost half) of ESL instruction. Given the range of training needed and the increasing pressure for seats, the requirement for training will undoubtedly exceed the college sector's capacity to provide it.

In a subsequent study conducted by the Ministry of Advanced Education (British Columbia 1993c), additional information was obtained about students seeking both adult basic education (ABE) and ESL. It was apparent that upgrading basic skills (including languages) and obtaining jobs were paramount reasons why people enrolled in these programs. These priorities were the same for all age groups, regardless of socioeconomic status and/or gender.

Despite continuing problems, such as lack of financially accessible child care and concern about obtaining adequate government assistance to enable them to continue their education, students were positive about their experiences and held optimistic views about how these programs would improve their futures. The results of this study left little doubt that many disadvantaged individuals held high expectations for the contribution which a college education could make to their future lives.

College Student Outcomes

Since 1988, with the support of the Ministry of Advanced Education, each college has conducted follow-up studies of its graduates. The purpose of these projects is to determine the success of graduates of both occupational programs (e.g., did they get jobs?) and academic programs (e.g., are they doing well at university?). Response rates vary considerably by program area. In 1992, about 40 per cent of a potential pool of 21,000 students provided information. Their responses give some indication of how well colleges are meeting their objectives.

The 1992 *College Student Outcomes Report* (British Columbia 1993a) contained the following highlights:

- Although placement rates had declined slightly since 1988, the great majority (87 per cent) of job-seeking graduates from career and vocational programs obtained training-related employment after leaving college.
- Employment rates varied by program area and were highest in health related areas, lowest in fine arts and communication arts.
- A majority of graduates in occupation fields reported their training as 'definitely worthwhile' (73 per cent) and indicated that their main objec-

tives upon enrolling in college had been 'definitely' realized (56 per cent).
- Graduates found employment throughout the province, and over 85 per cent were employed in the region in which their respective institutions were located.
- Of the students from arts and science programs, 84 per cent of those intending (and qualified) to transfer to another institution did so – of these, 59 per cent went to a BC university.
- Reported gains in the cognitive skills of academic students were high, particularly for those who considered themselves deeply involved in a variety of college activities.

In general, while respecting the inevitable caveats that follow-up studies tend to generate, it may be said that BC's colleges are achieving their primary goals with respect to student outcomes.

The Client Survey Project

Another study designed to shed light upon the role of postsecondary education in BC is the *Client Survey Project* (British Columbia 1992b), which was commissioned by the Ministry of Advanced Education. The project was intended to assess what high-school seniors, apprentices, and postsecondary students expected from their education and how they rated the importance of career goals as opposed to intellectual goals. Furthermore, employers were asked what they expected to find in graduates from postsecondary programs. Responses were obtained from more than 5,000 individuals – about 40 per cent of the population surveyed.

The data revealed that virtually all Grade 12 students intended to eventually continue their formal education, and 75 per cent intended to do so immediately. Students placed the highest importance upon career preparation (70 per cent) and the development of potential (56 per cent). These results were consistent across all socioeconomic levels but varied slightly by program. The greatest concern expressed by these students was over lack of information about sources of financial assistance.

Among employers, there appeared to be an interesting contradiction in that, while they were more supportive of applied than they were of academic programs, almost all required that graduates have good communication and organizational skills. Responses from apprenticeship students revealed that they waited an average of eight years before entering their respective trades, which suggests that these programs are either too unattractive or too inaccessible to high-school students. Overall, client response indicated that a balanced, accessible system of post-high-school education was essential to the future plans of most young people in the province, and that it was equally important to their potential employers.

The Human Resource Development Project

In early 1991, on the initiative of the deputy minister of advanced education, the British Columbia Human Resource Development Project (HRD)
was formulated. Its charge was 'to develop a policy framework for the future of all forms of education, training and learning for adults in our province' (British Columbia Human Resource Development Project 1992:2).
The project adopted a stakeholder approach to its organization, whereby a
steering committee was formed to plan and execute its development. This
committee was widely representative of labour, business, and public and
private education as well as of students, First Nations, and government.
Over an eighteen-month period, it met with over 3,000 individuals and
organizations.

The steering committee's final report covered three areas. It summarized
the long and extensive history of human resources development in the province; it outlined in detail the economic, sociocultural, and educational
changes which demand new strategies to address current deficiencies in the
system; and it offered a policy framework for future action. The primary
thrust of the proposed new policy framework was to reinforce the interdependence and interrelationship among the various sectors of education and
training. Collaborative planning and the offering of programs by business,
labour, and educational institutions was vital if the province's human resources were to access the learning opportunities so necessary in the new,
competitive economic environment. In was made clear that programs could
no longer stand alone; that individuals must be given the opportunity to
upgrade credentials and to pursue educational mobility with appropriate
transfer of credit; and that much greater liaison between government agencies, labour, business, and the education sector was necessary in order to
ensure program comprehensiveness and responsiveness.

In one respect, the HRD project was unusual – it prepared a report which
was addressed to its own stakeholders. In so doing, it avoided a long list of
government recommendations and/or calls for action. The report provided
an extensive framework for policy initiatives, including values and goals,
the challenges in creating a new education and training strategy, the elements of that strategy, and an appeal for stakeholder groups to immediately
begin the process of implementation.

The Private-Training Sector

Although in recent years private training schools have been established in
growing numbers in all regions of Canada, the BC experience has been
extraordinary. By 1994, over 800 such schools were registered in the province, offering a wide range of programs from training in ESL, computers,
hairdressing, and cooking to advanced technologies, graphic design, and

religious education. There are numerous factors which contribute to growth in the private-training sector, not the least being (since the mid-1980s) federal government funding initiatives – initiatives which supported training outside the public sector. In consequence, a major task for the provincial New Democratic Party (NDP) government is to regulate or to accredit private colleges in the interest of the general public. Under the Private Postsecondary Education Act, 1990, private colleges are registered, but the formal process for accreditation is not yet complete. It is expected that by early 1995, legislation will be enacted and accreditation will become a formality.

Current government policy respecting education and training presumes a much more expanded partnership between the public and private sectors than has been the case in the past. Inevitably, as community colleges rationalize their offerings on the basis of cost and demand, private colleges will expand their programs where the need exists. Given the large number of such institutions in BC, the task of planning an integrated system will be a major challenge for both government and the public and private education sectors.

The Skills Now Initiative
Following advice received from representatives of business, labour, education, and community groups at the Premier's Summit on Skills Development and Training in June 1993, the BC government announced a new initiative in its report *Skills Now: Real Skills for the Real World* (British Columbia 1994b). This multifaceted program was supported by an overall investment of almost $200 million worth of public funds.

The primary objective of *Skills Now* is familiar in all regions of Canada; that is, to establish a skills training plan which could ensure that high school leavers and adults (both employed and unemployed) would be appropriately prepared for new jobs in a rapidly changing economy. This was a challenge faced by all provincial governments, but few were able to commit a level of funding support comparable with that offered in BC. The success of this program will rest in large measure upon the willingness of all key partners in business, labour, and the education sectors (both public and private) to cooperate in its planning and execution.

Skills Now has four major thrusts:
(1) Linking high schools to the workplace. This initiative involves an expansion of work experience opportunities for students, provision for the accumulation of postsecondary credits in vocational programs while at high school, the creation of alternative education programs aimed at encouraging more students to stay in school, mandatory career planning, and upgrading of vocational and technical training at the secondary level.

(2) Provision of more seats in college and university programs. *Skills Now* will triple spaces for new students in the public postsecondary sector, award degree-granting status to the four university-colleges as well as to BCIT and the Emily Carr College of Art and Design, and offer training opportunities through the ten new community skills centres across the province (the latter to be linked by computer and telecommunications).

(3) Retraining workers closer to home. The newly established BC Labour Force Development Board, involving business, labour, government, and education and training providers, will be expected to offer advice on job market and training needs at the regional level. Furthermore, partnerships with small businesses will provide retraining programs for those in the forest industry who have become redundant as a result of government policies in that sector. Community-based training courses will be established in cooperation with the community skills centres.

(4) Moving from welfare to the workforce. An investment of $78 million is allocated to provide counselling, retraining, and support for local business in order to provide training seats for skills oriented to those who are unemployed and dependent upon social assistance.

While *Skills Now* is a formidable program, public postsecondary institutions, particularly community colleges, will also be challenged to mount programs which will meet expectations to be innovative, cost efficient, and accessible. It is a challenge which will require strong leadership from college administrations as well as flexibility from faculties and staff. While the college sector may be seen as part of the solution to the skills training and retraining issue, government support will not be automatic. Colleges must be prepared to produce programs which go well beyond the status quo such as those which utilize innovative forms of course delivery and interactive technology.

There is little doubt that the results of *Skills Now* will be watched closely by Canadian governments and educational institutions as well as by the private sector. The colleges of BC have an unprecedented opportunity to demonstrate their ability to meet the needs of those adversely affected by social and economic change.

Concluding Comments

While BC's postsecondary institutions faced many of the same problems as did those in other provinces (i.e., an increasing demand for all programs coupled with decreasing resources available to accommodate the student flow), the system has continued to expand and to restructure. However, there is no shortage of issues which need to be addressed. The rapid growth of degree-granting institutions and programs has stimulated the Ministry of Advanced Education to review the mandates of the new university-colleges, the governing structure in all non-university institutions, and the process by which new degree programs are planned and designed. As a consequence of the above, the College and Institute Act was amended in the spring of 1994 to formalize the independent degree-granting authority of the six institutions mentioned earlier and to introduce major revisions to the governing structure of the non-university sector.

Under the revisions to governance, board membership is to be expanded to include representatives from the students, teaching faculty, and support staff. But education councils, composed primarily of instructional faculty, will also be created in each institution. These councils, comparable in some respects to university senates, will have both statutory and advisory powers. Academic decisions (e.g., curricula content, criteria for academic standards, grading, and student evaluations) will be made by the councils. The councils must also advise the board on the institution's educational policies. In effect, the colleges in BC will be under a form of bicameral governance – a first for the community college sector in Canada.

Turning to other issues, although in real terms the number of postsecondary students has increased dramatically in the last six years, participation rates in both colleges and universities continue to compare unfavourably with other provinces. With respect to the number of total full-time postsecondary students, for example, BC's participation rate has grown from 18 per cent to 23 per cent between 1985 and 1991, but comparable national figures are 25 per cent to 29.5 per cent.

Many educators in the province would argue that: (1) the system is not working cooperatively, (2) adult and continuing education has been systematically downgraded, (3) vocational and technical education is given low priority, (4) access is still difficult for several disadvantaged segments of the population, and/or (5) unions and the business community do not fully appreciate the value of investment in education and training. Despite these concerns, and there is some truth in each of them, the performance of BC's postsecondary education and training systems has been impressive. Access, for example, is far easier for many students than was the case twenty years ago. Articulation among institutions is improving gradually, in part because of initiatives taken by the Council on Admissions and Transfer. British Columbians may choose between a public education and training sector and a galaxy of private institutions. Financial aid is available for virtually all deserving students, although some would argue that it is does not provide adequate support to severely disadvantaged groups.

The issue for the future is how well the overall system (including public and private sectors, distance learning and workplace training, unions and employee agencies, federal and provincial governments) can adapt to the reality of a rapidly restructuring economy and the need for a differently prepared workforce to sustain it. The response to this issue will, ultimately, determine BC's position in the marketplace of the twenty-first century.

Alberta

Alberta has maintained one of the most stable provincial postsecondary education systems. While it, like the other provinces, continues to experience the pressures of fiscal restraint along with a rising demand for access by an increasingly diverse student clientele, Alberta has focused on rationalization and long-term planning rather than upon radical restructuring. The productive relationship between the provincial government and the institutions (a relationship administered through the Department of Advanced Education) has continued to be one of interdependent coordination and negotiation rather than one of reactive response to the directives of a centralized administration. In spite of the administrative role of government in setting financial allocation policy and in program approval, there remains a high level of institutional autonomy and diversity. While there have been initiatives to ensure the more effective planning of the system, to develop guidelines to reduce redundancy and duplication of programs, and to increase access to certain vocational and academic programs, efforts have also been made to provide financial equity between various types of institutions.

The Alberta non-university sector has had no institutional additions and only two amalgamations in the period between 1986 and 1992. One amalgamation was that of the Westerra Institute with the Northern Alberta Institute of Technology. The other brought a number of community vocational centres and the vocational college at Grouard together to form a new college at Lesser Slave Lake. The postsecondary system, comprised of eleven public colleges, two technical institutes, four provincially administered vocational colleges, and five hospital-based schools of nursing, represents only one component of the network of agencies responsible for non-university postsecondary education in Alberta. Four very effective community consortia and eighty-five publicly funded further education councils also encourage access throughout all regions of the province. When all of these are combined with the four universities, four degree-granting private colleges (also regulated through a legislated accrediting policy and receiving some public financial support), Banff Centre, and the 400 licensed programs offered by about 90 private vocational schools, there is little doubt that Alberta maintains one of the most differentiated educational galaxies in Canada. Due in large part to the provincial policy of managing change through study, legislation, and coordination, the postsecondary education system, while diverse, is neither highly competitive nor chaotic. Each type of institution has a particular constituency, and students should be able to move easily from one institution to another. The Department of Advanced Education provides direction through the use of coordinating mechanisms, while board governance is limited only by fiscal dependence and mandates approved by the minister of advanced education.

The most recent period in the development of non-university post-secondary education has been characterized by Andrews, Holdaway, and Mowat (1992) as the end of the reductionist era of restrained government funding and the emergence of the current phase of entrepreneurialism. This latter phase includes a greater emphasis upon individual and institutional initiatives in order to secure funding from non-governmental sources. This transition is not an abrupt shift but a slow evolution facilitated by a number of incentives which alleviate the pressure for greater accountability, efficiency, and planning.

As a background to an analysis of higher education policy in Alberta during the last six years, it is helpful to review the deliberations of three major reports: *Postsecondary Operating Grants in Alberta: An Equity Study* (Dupré 1987), *Guidelines for System Development* (Alberta 1989), and *Toward 2000 Together: A Discussion Paper on Alberta's Economic Options and Choices* (Alberta 1991d).

Postsecondary Operating Grants in Alberta: An Equity Study
In this report, Stefan Dupré provided a detailed description and analysis of the entire public postsecondary system in Alberta. From a historical point of view, the report was actually more useful in its cataloguing of the development of institutional types than in its recommendations. Dupré examined program profiles at each institution as well as enrolment characteristics and FTE cost comparisons over time. Furthermore, he analyzed the evolution of base operating grants, supplementary enrolment funding, vocational and manpower grants, and the endowment and incentive fund with respect to their roles in the development of the postsecondary education system. The major conclusion was that few real funding inequities existed but that historical differences between institutional types had created perceived inequities. The recommendations included proposals for some increases in operating grants to selected institutions and greater consideration of the costs of providing educational programs in northern Alberta. The need for more multilateral relationships between government and institutions would, in Dupré's view, help remove the perception of inequities generated by the existing bilateral communication structure.

Guidelines for System Development
System development policy formulation is a continuing process in Alberta. Central to the procedure are the ideas contained in each institution's long-range development plans. It is also supported by quarterly status reports on

the rationalizing process (i.e., eliminating or adding programs over a long time period). This strategy is a tangible example of the government's role in monitoring and coordinating the system while emphasizing increasing efficiency at a time of diminishing financial resources.

Toward 2000 Together:
A Discussion Paper on Alberta's Economic Options and Choices

This position paper on long-term economic planning, produced by an advisory committee appointed by the provincial government, addressed the role of the education system in labour force planning. The report criticizes the lack of employer investment in workforce training and suggested that, in the future, there should be a more equitable balance between government-sponsored and employer-funded initiatives. A policy respecting the promotion of entrepreneurial skills in public postsecondary programs was strongly emphasized. A notable reference was made to the fact that, while the number of Albertans holding educational credentials is higher than the national average (18 per cent postsecondary diplomas and degrees in Alberta as opposed to 16.3 per cent in Canada as a whole), the province also sustained a 30 per cent high-school drop-out rate and a 25 per cent functional illiteracy rate. By the year 2000, it is estimated that 80 per cent of all new entrants into the Alberta workforce will be women, aboriginal peoples, visible minorities, and persons with disabilities. These are issues faced by all Canadian provinces, and they represent a challenge to both training/education establishments and to employers. A downturn in the petroleum and natural gas industry and a national recession left the Alberta postsecondary system with only a 3 per cent increase in operating grants for 1992-3. At the same time, there are increasing demands for more spaces in both academic and vocational training programs. At the other extreme, there was over a 50 per cent drop in apprentices-in-training during the early 1980s, with the biggest losses being sustained at the two technical institutes in Edmonton and Calgary, respectively.

In 1990, the minister of advanced education issued a policy framework entitled *Responding to Existing and Emerging Demands for University Education: A Policy Framework* (Alberta 1990). The institutional response to this document led to adding more first- and second-year transfer places to public colleges and to facilitating transfers to universities. Other suggestions from the colleges and institutes included the creation of degree programs in areas such as the social sciences and criminology as well as in the area of technology.

Reflecting the high level of concern over access issues, another document, entitled *Foundations for Adult Learning and Development Policy,* was published in 1991 (Alberta 1991c). This policy statement was intended to provide some remedies to the access problems experienced by adults with low academic skills. It should be recognized that Alberta's vocational colleges have a primary mandate in this field, although public colleges and further education councils are also increasingly active.

Growth in the System

In the last seven years, the postsecondary system in Alberta has continued to grow. By 1989-90 it included nearly 100,000 full-time credit enrolments (an increase of 17 per cent), of which half were in the non-university sector. Part-time credit enrolments have reached approximately the same number but display a growth-rate of over 80 per cent, three quarters of which is served by the technical institutes (34 per cent), vocational colleges (27 per cent), and public colleges (16 per cent). Apprenticeships showed a slight increase of 5 per cent in the latter 1980s, with enrolments exceeding 12,000. Non-credit enrolments have maintained almost half a million registrations, of which further education councils accounted for over half and public colleges accounted for one-quarter. It is apparent that the growth in participation rates in Alberta has been composed primarily of working adults; that is, part-time students taking upgrading and technical vocational courses.

The growth in expenditure upon the system, which in itself is enrolment-responsive (not directly driven), has generally corresponded to the rate of full-time credit enrolment expansion. In 1991, the postsecondary system received over $900 million dollars, with over half allocated to the universities (including the Banff Centre and Athabasca University) and 45 per cent to the colleges, institutes, and vocational colleges.

Restructuring the System

In spite of its reputation for providing consistently strong support for postsecondary education, Alberta's fiscal condition in the early 1990s was such that the government was giving serious consideration to finding ways to control the escalating costs of that education system. Largely as a consequence of low world prices for petroleum and natural gas products, Alberta faced a deficit projection of $2.3 billion in its 1992-3 provincial budget. Although the percentage of the budget allocated to postsecondary education had fallen from 10 per cent to 9 per cent in the past decade (by comparison, expenditure on health and social services had risen from 30 per cent to 45 per cent), it became apparent that higher education must become more cost-effective.

In September 1992, the minister of advanced education informed all institutions of the fiscal challenges facing the postsecondary education system and noted that it 'will be expected to respond in innovative and flexible ways to such issues and pressures as increasing enrolment, demand for research and technology transfer and the maintenance of an extensive and complex infrastructure' (Gogo 1992). In response to this challenge, the Ministry of Advanced Education is planning a broad public consultation which will include the institutions and will be designed to lead to creative structural change. To date, the institutions have identified the issues which are likely to emerge in the next few years and have proposed strategies to address those which have been given priority.

Strengths of the Alberta Postsecondary Education System

Alberta has shown leadership through a number of initiatives in postsecondary education and continues to provide innovations in the area of system development. The commitment to access remains strong, and is exhibited in the support for rural areas demonstrated by further education councils, community education committees, and satellite centres of the Alberta Vocational Centre (AVC), colleges, and community consortia. In the urban centres, the institutes, AVCs, and colleges have demonstrated that part-time and undereducated adult students have benefited from increased opportunities. The Alberta Council on Admissions and Transfer, the first such council in Canada, continues to encourage mobility between institutions as the demand for higher levels of educational credentials accelerates.

Unlike the recent BC policy of granting authority to award baccalaureate degrees to a number of community colleges, the Department of Advanced Education in Alberta has resisted pressures from several colleges to award them degree-granting status. These pressures are not new, as spasmodic efforts to achieve this goal have been alive for over twenty-five years. However, as some colleges gained greater maturity over the past decade, their interest in degree-granting status escalated. One very strong contender, for example, is Mount Royal College in Calgary, which has advanced a case for offering selected degree programs in response to community needs. There are also similar pressures to extend diplomas in technology at Northern and Southern Alberta Institutes, from a two-year to a three-year program.

Nevertheless, while full authority to award degrees has not been achieved, a number of creative arrangements have been concluded by which Alberta's universities are able to offer degree programs at selected colleges. Examples of such initiatives include business, with Athabasca University and Keyano College (the 'capstone' program) and nursing, with the University of Alberta, Red Deer College, and the hospital schools. Other nursing arrangements have been developed for several major communities.

Alberta has also recognized the role of private institutions by creating the first private accreditation board in Canada and incorporating it in the Universities Act. Private-public partnerships are also recognized in the endowment and incentives fund set aside for capital project support. Furthermore, Alberta has a policy of supporting aboriginal education, which is described in more detail in Chapter 7, as well as equity programs in its public institutions.

The Alberta postsecondary system, while underfunded and facing demands for more spaces in degree programs, more basic education, and more advanced vocational training, continues to be one of the most innovative, functional, and stable in Canada. Nevertheless, recent government announcements regarding fiscal reductions in the public sector will have serious implications for the community colleges. To be specific, a portent of the future of postsecondary education is contained in a departmental White Paper, entitled *Adult Learning: Access Through Innovation* (Alberta 1994), which was released in the spring. Described as a strategic plan for the transformation of the province's adult learning system, the White Paper prescribes a vision and outlines the goals that must be met in order to achieve it.

The White Paper notes that, while the overall budget for advanced education and career development will decrease by 15.8 per cent over the next three years, the number and characteristics of learners seeking access to the system will increase – and they will be seeking more and different types of education, training, and retraining. The four goals set out in the White Paper are:

(1) to foster individual responsibility in a learner-centred system
(2) to ensure responsiveness and accountability to learners and taxpayers
(3) to enable Albertans to participate in a changing economy and workforce
(4) to promote access to affordable, quality learning opportunities.

While a number of strategies are listed as ways to accomplish each goal, some of the more innovative include:

- the capping of tuition fees at 20 per cent of net operating expenditures
- recognition of appropriate prior learning and experience to facilitate student transfer and access within the system
- transfer programs to be redefined as a shared responsibility between colleges and universities, displaying a clear and viable route to degree completion
- changes to the Alberta Council on Admissions and Transfer required to help it more effectively carry out its role
- the establishment of a comprehensive accountability framework which will include an agreed-upon set of expected results for the system, a core set of quantitative and qualitative performance indicators, and mechanism to communicate results to learners and taxpayers
- a new formula for funding postsecondary education and training that focuses on access and performance outcomes, to be devised and implemented by 1996-7

- a $47 million access fund created to finance innovative, cost-effective ways of expanding access
- the promotion of increased employer-based training.

And, of unusual interest in academic circles, the White Paper notes: 'Many postsecondary collective agreements place inappropriate barriers to termination of employment for reasons of fiscal stringency and redundancy. Legislative changes would aim at allowing institutions to respond to changing economic circumstances' (p. 8).

It has become evident that in the future the Department of Advanced Education and Career Development will assume a more direct and responsible role in setting policy for the postsecondary institutions in Alberta. If the community colleges are to maintain viability, courageous and creative leadership will be essential to ensure that crucial, albeit controversial, decisions are made regarding matters such as resource allocation and program reorganization. The greatest challenge yet to confront Alberta's community colleges is about to begin.

Saskatchewan

More so than in other provinces, the mission of the community colleges in Saskatchewan has always been subject to the political priorities of the provincial government of the day (Dennison and Gallagher 1986:52-7). Established in the early 1970s, the colleges were designed to respond to local needs, stimulate community development, and supplement the quality of life in rural regions (Dennison and Gallagher 1986). With respect to program delivery, Saskatchewan's colleges adopted a unique brokerage model, whereby academic and vocational-technical courses were provided under a contractual arrangement with more conventional universities and technical institutes. Renowned for their flexibility, the colleges owned little in the way of permanent facilities and employed few full-time faculty. A change from a New Democratic to a Conservative government and with it a shift to a more market-driven approach to postsecondary education, however, brought with it many dramatic transformations. During the period between 1986 and 1994, there was a reorganization of the Saskatchewan college system which included closures, amalgamations, boundary changes, mandate enhancement, and governance adaptations.

The minister of education issued a policy framework in April 1987 entitled *Preparing for the Year 2000* (Saskatchewan 1987b), which prescribed a new model for non-university postsecondary education in Saskatchewan. The review of the college mandate, which began in 1983, culminated in the Regional College Act, 1988, and its companion legislation, an Act Respecting the Saskatchewan Institute of Applied Science and Technology (SIAST), 1987. These acts formalized changes which were necessary in order to meet the technical, educational, and skill-training needs of the province, and they reflected the political and economic ideology of the government of the day.

The changes transformed the community colleges from local development agencies in the rural communities to regional colleges, which, while retaining many of their previous functions, were to become more traditional providers of education. The four urban colleges in Saskatoon, Regina, Moose Jaw, and Prince Albert merged with the technical institutes in those cities to become campuses of SIAST. This large, urban, multicampus organization became a full community college similar to those in other provincial jurisdictions.

The non-university, adult education system, in addition to SIAST, was now composed of seven enlarged rural regional colleges; a consolidated northern college, Northlands, which was an amalgamation of three colleges; Lakeland, an interprovincial institution; a strengthened Saskatchewan Indian Community College with a province-wide mandate; and the Gabriel Dumont Institute (a Métis language, teacher education, and curriculum development centre). The colleges' mandates and functions were adjusted to reflect less community orientation and greater emphasis on economic values, as were their geographic service regions. One of the primary purposes of colleges now became the delivery of SIAST's technical-vocational programs and academic credit courses offered through the two universities. In each case, a brokerage format was to be utilized as described in Chapter 3. They could also offer their own credits for career programs and continue full-time and part-time remedial and preparatory basic education. An important initiative, placing greater emphasis on literacy training, was included, and the community education function was removed. 'Personal' and 'hobby' courses were, however, to be offered by recreational and service organizations. The authority to acquire permanent educational facilities was enhanced, but emphasis was placed on leasing or sharing facilities with school divisions in preference to purchasing them.

College governance continued to be provided by ministerially appointed boards made up of four to seven residents of the service region, except in the case of Northlands, whose board had a maximum of ten members. The powers of boards were generally increased, but ministerial approval was required for the remuneration of college staff and faculty as well as for the purchase or rental of real estate. The minister of advanced education also retained approval authority over annual operating budgets.

SIAST was designated as a corporate entity and had an appointed board of ten to twenty members. Being governed by a board rather than reporting directly to the minister of advanced education was a significant change in institutional policy. The powers of the SIAST board are more extensive than are those of regional colleges and are comparable to those of community colleges in other provincial jurisdictions. SIAST's mandate embraces all types of educational offerings, including the contracting of credit courses leading to academic degrees under the auspices of the universities. The merger of eight institutions into one multicampus organization was a difficult and complex process and, by 1993, was still incomplete and unresolved. In July 1992, in its final report, the SIAST review committee noted that, in spite of its new comprehensive educational mandate, it was still viewed as a job training agency. Troubled personnel relations and the continuous rotation of CEOs and other administrators, combined with several structural changes, has plagued SIAST since the beginning. The goals of a common curriculum and a high quality of instruction and service, which prompted its creation, have been overwhelmed by the problems presented by such a large merger. The postsecondary education system, as revised by the two acts, essentially creates a two-tiered model with an urban, multicampus, comprehensive institute and small, less autonomous, rural colleges which are expected to broker the programs of the larger agency.

A new distance education system, the Saskatchewan Communications Network (SCAN), contracts with the regional colleges to offer local satellite video/audio receiving sites. The courses are developed and offered by the communities and SIAST, and they are approved by the Provincial Distance Education Programme Review Committee. Computer-assisted literacy programs (IBM-PALS and PLATO) are province-wide projects entailing partnerships with the federal government, industry, and the colleges.

Funding for the revised system is based on different arrangements for regional colleges and for SIAST. The colleges receive a base grant (which amounts to approximately $6 million in total), and targeted funding is available for specific programs (such as skills extension and development, vocational rehabilitation, and the non-status Indian and Métis programs). These targeted program funds constitute from 50 per cent to 70 per cent of the colleges' operating revenues. An enhancement fund (approximately $250,000 per college) is another important source of revenue. The colleges also have program-by-program access to Canadian Jobs Strategy (CJS). Contracts to operate a computer-assisted literacy program is another source of funds. In 1991, the province's operating revenue commitment to the colleges was less than $20 million. SIAST, on the other hand, had a provincial allocation of over $100 million, which constituted 70 per cent of its budget. The remainder of its revenue is derived from tuition, CJS, and training contracts with private-sector employers.

The regional colleges, with multiple sources of revenue and minimal educational autonomy, continue to provide effective service to one out of seven adults in Saskatchewan. In 1990-1, their clientele included over 25,000, of which two-thirds were cost-recovery, non-credit enrolments. The balance consisted of enrollees in institute/university courses and in ABE (2,500 enrolments). Over 2,000 participants benefited from regional college and SIAST literacy programs in 1991. Nine-hundred enrolments were recorded in vocational rehabilitation, of which SIAST served over one-third.

Saskatchewan's service to aboriginal students, through programs funded through the regional colleges and SIAST, amounted to 900 enrolments at an expenditure of $4.5 million. In addition, there were 100 enrolments in urban and northern teacher education programs operated by the universities, the Gabriel Dumont Institute, and the Saskatchewan Indian Federated College. SIAST has discontinued its Native Services Division, as a federated agreement between the latter and the Dumont Technical Institute is soon to be concluded.

In the period between 1986 and 1992, the postsecondary agenda has been dominated by the creation and development of SIAST. The turmoil accompanying its merger, its ongoing operational struggles, and its relationship with the regional colleges has obviously preoccupied those administering and governing the postsecondary system. While SIAST reported over 40,000 full- and part-time enrollees in 1990-1, these were dominated by ABE students (28 per cent), followed by students enrolled in health and business programs. Agriculture and natural resources comprised only 2 per cent of enrolments.

Issues surrounding the operational and structural effectiveness of SIAST were addressed in the review committee's final report. While the reviewers supported the retention of the merged model upon which SIAST was based, they also advocated decentralizing and reorganizing campus administrations in order to improve the level of participation in decisionmaking, to strengthen staff morale, to increase organizational communication, to improve instructional motivation, and to increase job performance and satisfaction. It was suggested that the relationships formerly enjoyed between the campuses and their communities might be restored by the creation of local advisory councils, which would contain representatives from business and industry, aboriginal groups, and so on. These councils would have seats on the governing board of SIAST. Other recommendations included implementing a more formalized relationship with the regional colleges in order to address curriculum and program planning and delivery as well as implementing a course credit transfer system between SIAST, the colleges, and the universities. Issues of governance, professional development, employment equity, and strategic planning were also addressed.

The Saskatchewan college system, particularly as it is manifested in rural institutions which have no long-term commitments to maintaining either facilities (often leased) or staff (usually on sessional contracts), is flexible enough to be effective in difficult economic times. However, the spirit of innovation which created the colleges as instruments of community self-development has been redirected to more individualized training focused on personal and employment goals. The attention to ensuring access for the less advantaged remains a prominent feature of Saskatchewan colleges.

The Regional Colleges Act requires that the mandate and operations of colleges be reviewed every five years. In 1992, the Regional College Committee of Review was established by the minister of advanced education to provide recommendations on governance, accountability, accessibility, and overall coordination. Consistent with the philosophy of the NDP government, the approach of the committee was to include extensive public consultation with private citizens and other educational organizations at the postsecondary and K-12 (kindergarten to Grade 12) levels. The six-month review yielded a wide range of recommendations regarding every aspect of the operations of the colleges. The central theme of the report was the need to re-establish the relationships between the colleges and their immediate communities. Furthermore, colleges were to:

- work in partnership with local and regional communities, business, industry, and agriculture to support rural social and economic development
- strengthen the delivery of university and SIAST credits in response to regionally identified needs
- respond to the learning needs of aboriginal peoples
- coordinate delivery of all educational programs in rural communities for government departments and agencies
- designate a community as the university centre in each region and make sure it contains a library, laboratory, and computer resources
- redraw boundaries to assign the delivery of rural adult education within 50 kilometres of the cities to the SIAST campus
- grant certificates for skills/technical training which other institutions cannot deliver.

In addition to the general themes, the report also paid particular attention to the problems of two institutions, Northlands College and Lakeland College. The former is by far the largest college in Saskatchewan, with ten times the participation rate of other colleges and an enrolment of over 1,200. Funding, however, was not commensurate with these factors. Inter alia, the review committee recommended that three separate regions be created, each reporting to a single board.

Lakeland College is an interprovincial college, although by far the greater proportion of its budget is borne by Alberta. Nevertheless, a large percentage of its students come from Saskatchewan. In response to a brief by the college, the committee recommended that Lakeland be able to broker courses in Saskatchewan and that the interprovincial agreement concerning mandate, governance, funding, and boundaries be reviewed.

Concluding Comments

Saskatchewan's postsecondary education system, after considerable reorganization, mandate redefinition, and comprehensive review, seems to be facing an uncertain future. While they have demonstrated their capacity for efficient delivery of postsecondary services, Saskatchewan's community colleges have long been subject to changing political priorities, and they are entering yet another phase of development. There is little general agreement, even among college personnel, as to which is the most appropriate organizational model for the next decade. The concept of colleges as flexible, adaptable instruments of community development still enjoys widespread support. Others, however, see colleges as more conventional postsecondary institutions, offering their own programs in their own facilities to a more traditional clientele.

The ongoing debate over the future role of Saskatchewan's community colleges is summarized succinctly by Kirkland (1991), of North West Regional College, who makes the following comments regarding the changes which have occurred since 1987:

> However, the system continued with the brokered program/existing facility concept – the colleges remained more a delivery system than an institution. Such a system has many advantages. It is student driven, it is cost efficient, it is flexible, it has the capacity to respond quickly to the needs of the learner and/or the market place and it does maximize use of existing community resources.
>
> What it lacks is image, stability, credibility in some ways, professionalism and security for its employees. A growing trend, led by some community groups pushing for a 'junior college concept' and by an influx of college personnel from more 'institutionalized' provinces is developing pressure to address these issues by establishing independent 'bricks and mortar' campuses, structured, ongoing programs, base funding and permanent staff. In short, creating an institution, rather than a delivery system.
>
> Both systems obviously have distinct advantages. The 'institution' has more prestige, is better for its staff, and if it works, for the economic benefit of the community where it is built. On the other hand, the 'delivery system' is more responsive to community needs and is more cost efficient. It is a system that has been studied and adapted to the needs of many third world countries. It is a system advocated by many of the world's leaders in 'alternative' adult education as best suited to large geographic areas that are sparsely populated and economically limited. (p. 2)

In spite of the best intentions and convictions, Saskatchewan's uncertain financial status suggests that the availability of additional resources to develop any new model will be highly unpredictable. The more likely scenario is that Saskatchewan's colleges will continue to pursue the role which has distinguished them in the past: that of innovative institutions which are highly responsive to the needs of their communities and which provide maximal services with minimal resources.

Manitoba

Prior to 1 April 1993, one characteristic which distinguished the colleges of Manitoba from their counterparts in most other provinces was the absence of boards of governance. However, on that date, Bill 49, the Colleges and Consequential Amendments Act, was implemented; it was assented to in July. The three colleges thus became the responsibilities of their newly appointed boards of governors. Henceforth, they have become conventional board-governed community colleges as opposed to postsecondary branches of the Ministry of Education and Training.

Bill 49 attempted to strike a balance between flexibility and accountability and, at the same time, to create a partnership between institutional autonomy and government control. The move to board governance was also intended to allow colleges to be more responsive to community needs and to forge new relationships with other agencies in both the public and private sectors. In an era of recession, the government undoubtedly expected greater efficiency in the use of public monies from an arm's-length, rather than from a centrally managed, college system. Quasi-autonomous colleges derive more revenue from contract training and tuition sources than do those which are less autonomous. The new act also provides the government with a greater opportunity to demand program performance measures, financial efficiency, and demonstrations of increased service from market-driven training initiatives.

The legislated mandate of the colleges specifies that they will provide
- a comprehensive range of credit programs in trades, vocational, technology, and academic disciplines to full- and part-time students
- access support, through counselling, literacy, basic education, transition, and college preparation programs
- university transfer courses offered through agreements with the universities
- services to government, corporations, or non-profit groups on a partial or total cost-recovery basis.

This mandate provides for a significant expansion of the colleges' responsibilities, given their ability to enter into agreements and contracts without government approval. The authority to offer brokered university courses represents a departure from the Manitoba tradition of having a binary system, characterized by a the separation of vocational/technical colleges and academic/professional universities.

A college board now consists of a minimum of ten and a maximum of twelve government-appointed members, including one selected from the student association and one selected from college employees. The president is an ex officio, non-voting member of the board. Another structure required by the act is a college council, the primary function of which is to advise the board on academic and service delivery issues. At least one-third of each council will be composed of instructional staff, with the remaining members being drawn from other staff groups and students.

The powers and duties of the boards are similar to those in other provinces, with an additional requirement regarding the provision of information. As well as requiring annual, audited, financial reports, the colleges must also provide an annual academic report on enrolments, student retention, graduation, and employment placement. The Colleges and Consequential Amendments Act also specifies that each college must provide its respective board with regular, multi-year plans and evaluations.

The colleges will assume responsibility for their own labour relations, with over one thousand Manitoba Government Employees Association (MGEA) members to receive college-based collective agreements upon the expiry of the MGEA/Government Master Agreement on 1 September 1994. College funding, currently a block-grant system, is expected to be replaced by an allocation formula in 1994.

Manitoba has a unique program, the Access Initiative, which was created in 1972 to increase the participation of disadvantaged Manitobans in basic and career education. These programs are well established in the colleges and will continue under quasi-autonomous college management. The Postsecondary Career Development Branch operates student allowance programs which, in turn, enable Access Initiative candidates to pay tuition and living costs. Student allowance policies were rationalized in 1988 in order to provide all Access Initiative participants with equal access to all educational programs at all institutions, regardless of location or circumstance. This kind of financial aid program increases equity and improves the probability of success in postsecondary education.

The Colleges of Manitoba
The colleges, with their vocational/technical roots, have moved towards the integration of academic education (formerly the sole responsibility of the universities), which, in turn, provides for a more comprehensive program profile. They are committed to economic and social development through career/technical programs tailored specifically to the economies of

their regions. Contracts and partnership training (involving employers and community organizations) play an increasing role in college service delivery. Continuing education is a central function of colleges, and it has enrolments triple those in full-time credit programs. All three colleges have clearly stated commitments to multiculturalism, internationalization, equity of access, and affirmative employment. Red River Community College (RRCC) serves the needs of 750,000 people in the greater Winnipeg region and delivers courses to an extensive rural area. It had nearly 30,000 registrations in 1992-3. Programs are offered at a main campus and at regional centres located at Riverton, Winkler, Portage La Prairie, Selkirk, and Steinbach. Contracted, partnered, and brokered programs are offered off-campus in Winnipeg and at rural sites.

The strategic objectives of RRCC for 1992-3 were
- to enhance the quality of the learning experience based on client/customer service principles of total quality
- to expand support to part-time learners through partnership arrangements
- to support access programs and the retention of students, with emphasis on aboriginal and ethnocultural groups
- to expand cooperative education
- to respond to the training requirements of employers
- to take an active role in supporting the economic, social, and cultural environment for the community and province within a global marketplace
- to participate in international education.

RRCC complements its very strong technology programs with formal partnerships with institutes such as the Toyota Technical Training Centre. Laddered nursing and teacher education programs are supported by an increasing arts and science university-transfer component of the curriculum. The eighty-plus full-time programs are also complemented by numerous part-time certificate offerings, which enrolled 18,579 registrants in 1992-3.

Assiniboine Community College (ACC) emphasizes supporting and maintaining a strong rural economy. Its role as a rural community college is reflected in its program mix, in its strong emphasis on continuing education, and in its establishment of numerous regional centres and partnership delivery sites. Agricultural programs and extension courses are central to a comprehensive program profile, currently featuring such unique offerings as Sustainable Shelter Technology and rural initiatives programs.

ACC served over 8,000 enrolments in 1992-3 from its campuses at Brandon, Dauphin, and Russell. Of the 996 full-time students and 467 graduates in 1992-3, one-third were of aboriginal descent. Equity targets, special access, and First Nations reserve delivery sites account for increasing aboriginal participation. Partnerships with school districts, Yellow Quills (First Nations) College, and Brandon University provide accreditation and credit-transfer opportunities.

Keewatin Community College (KCC) serves a huge region north of latitude 53 from a main campus in The Pas, a campus in Thompson, and a regional centre in Flin Flon. Twenty-eight hundred students (40 per cent of whom are of aboriginal descent) enrolled in over twenty programs. The one- and two-year offerings range from ABE, pre-employment trades, and heavy-duty mechanics courses to computer analyst and university transfer courses. Its northern socioeconomic mix requires specific programs, such as resource management and band and northern community administration. A graduate survey conducted by KCC in 1992 revealed that 81.6 per cent of those surveyed were employed (87.1 per cent of these in their fields of study), and 90.1 per cent had returned to their home communities.

Manitoba's colleges, under their new governing structure, are now more able to create service and program profiles which respond to regional needs. The college system has a history of inclusiveness and sensitivity to the needs of different socioeconomic communities, and it is providing programs compatible with changing employment and lifestyles. To this date, however, the colleges in Manitoba have been viewed as centrally governed agents of the Ministry of Education, focusing primarily upon employment training and adult upgrading. As noted previously (Dennison and Gallagher 1986), the use of the term 'community' as applied to these colleges is a misnomer. The idea of board governance has been discussed for some time, usually under the assumption that full responsiveness to the educational and training needs of regional communities was unattainable under centralized control. Finally, in 1993, board governance was realized. The question which now must be answered is whether this new opportunity will translate into institutions which will more accurately deserve being called 'community' colleges. At a time in which government support will continue to be constrained, public colleges must find alternative sources of funding if they are to continue to respond to ever-increasing demands for their services. The new college legislation in this province provides an incentive for them to seek out innovative sources of financial support. While the opportunity may be there, the future of Manitoba's colleges will depend upon a leadership willing to undertake both the challenges and the risks of change.

Finally, it is necessary to comment upon a recent development in postsecondary education which promises to have significant implications for the future of the college sector in Manitoba. In December 1993, *Doing Things Differently: Report of the University Education Review Commission* (Roblin 1993), also known as the Roblin Report, was made public. Notwithstanding its title, the report includes an extensive section devoted to the future role of the colleges. One of its most relevant recommendations is contained in the section on financial matters. The report states: 'It is recommended that improving the range of programs and increased use of existing facilities for the community colleges be the first system priority for the allocation of new financial resources to the postsecondary education system' (p. 93).

The Roblin Report also drew particular attention to the long-standing lack of any formal relationship between Manitoba's university and college sectors, noting that the two kinds of institutions have 'functioned for the most part at arm's length from each other' (p. 39). Roblin observed that there had been a divide between what is defined as 'academic' and what is defined as 'applied.' The report agreed that there is an urgent need for im-proved program articulation, more reasonable transfer arrangements, and a framework for joint planning between colleges and universities. Responsi-bility for initiating these reforms should be given to a new organization, the Council on Postsecondary Education, which would have authority over both sectors.

With respect to program development in the college sector, Roblin ex-pressed a preference for two- and three-year diplomas in technologies de-signed to create a pool of highly trained individuals for a variety of work settings in the areas of health and engineering. Moreover, technology gradu-ates should have the opportunity to complete baccalaureate degrees built upon credits earned while working on their diplomas. So much importance is placed upon the need for diploma graduates, that the Roblin Report rec-ommended doubling the participation rate in diploma programs over the next five years.

On the subject of access to postsecondary education, the Roblin Report expressed concern over the problems encountered by aboriginal Manitobans, Métis, and various disadvantaged groups, while noting the colleges' attempts to address those problems. However, the report also commented upon the limited participation of high-school graduates in college programs and sug-gested that increasing the quantity and diversity of such programs would help to attract younger students. The report further recommended that the three Manitoba community colleges should each have a mission that is in accord with its geographic context. In particular, KCC should become a comprehensive education and training coordinator for those in the North. This mandate should include the offering of general university degree courses in conjunction with the university consortium.

The Roblin Report anticipates a new and much more extensive mandate for Manitoba's colleges. However, whether the recommendations will be implemented, and whether the resources necessary to ensure their success will be forthcoming, remains a matter of speculation. Nevertheless, on several counts it appears that Manitoba's colleges are about to enter a new era. There is every indication that they are poised to become equal partners in the postsecondary educational spectrum of the future.

Ontario

Background
From the time of its creation in the mid-1960s, the postsecondary education system of Ontario (now comprising twenty-three colleges mandated to serve the needs of every region) has been an influential factor in the educational and economic life of the province. A system as large as Ontario's ultimately garners both the advantages and the disadvantages of its size.

Few would deny that any discussion of Ontario's future as the most highly industrialized region of Canada must include a major segment on the role of its colleges; these institutions are major players in the life of the province. In fact, a survey conducted in 1992 revealed that 43 per cent of respondents had had some contact with a college. Thousands of their graduates, from many hundred diverse programs, hold positions at all levels of the workforce. Numerous stories appear in the media which either attest to the success of the colleges, to problems associated with funding, to abilities of students, to new technologies, or to the varying concerns of the instructional staff. For example, in 1992 the *Globe and Mail* published a series of articles attesting to the range of activities in which Ontario's colleges of applied arts and technology (CAATs) were involved and to their contribution to the economic life of the province. Reference was made to programs for women, retraining initiatives, new course developments, partnerships with industry, and even the problems of fundraising. By 1992, full-time student enrolments approximated 150,000, with another 600,000 engaged in part-time learning. The annual operating grant to the college system exceeded $700 million (of a total budget of $1.7 billion), while the number of full-time staff, including teaching, support, and administrative staff, was over 16,000.

Not only is Ontario's college system large, it is centralized. A structure such as this inevitably leads to the emergence of powerful stakeholder groups which, while seeking and exercising power, at the same time tend to provide an interesting set of checks and balances. The Ministry of Education and Training (formerly the Ministry of Colleges and Universities), which now has responsibility for education at all levels, comprises a complex bureaucracy whose major role is the allocation of the colleges' operating and capital budgets. The Council of Regents has, to this time, conducted the critically important task of collective bargaining with another powerful organization, the Ontario Public Service Employees Union, which represents support staff and teaching faculty. Yet another body which is representative of management, the Association of Colleges of Applied Arts and Technology of Ontario (ACAATO), maintains an advocacy and communications role and assumes responsibility for a range of professional development activities. Each of these organizations exercises an important influence upon the overall health and vitality of the system, while the twenty-three individual governing boards direct their energies to the needs of their respective regions through the development of new programs and activities. With such powerful agents at work, it is inevitable that system-wide confrontations will sometimes occur. Much of what follows are consequences of such incidents.

Another distinguishing feature of Ontario's college system has been its relative independence within the province's overall educational spectrum. Created as a clear alternative to the universities, the colleges have maintained a separate identity and, in so doing (unlike the case in several other provinces), have forged little in the way of a formal relationship with the universities. While it is true that many cooperative program ventures have been created, most involve one college and one university. Transfer of credit, for example, is not uncommon for many students, but the arrangement is on an individual, rather than on a system-wide, basis. Difficulties experienced by college graduates in attempting to earn degrees, for example, has led to new efforts to resolve the problem of the two educational solitudes. On the other hand, it should be noted that a wide variety of school-college linkage projects have been negotiated between individual colleges and school boards. These projects not only provide formal program articulation but also an excellent opportunity for high-school students to begin college-level training.

As described later in this chapter, the CAATs of Ontario have entered a new phase of development. It has become clear that the changing nature of Ontario's economy, together with the emergence of an older student clientele seeking more flexible and more accessible educational and training opportunities, will require the colleges to make radical changes if they are to maintain their reputation for being responsive to community needs. The CAATs of the 1970s and 1980s can no longer accomplish the task, and government seems prepared to offer incentives for change. The remainder of this section will describe some of the most significant events in Ontario's college system since 1986 and indicate what direction it might take in the future.

Introduction
Ontario's CAATs could be viewed as maintaining an interesting contradic-

tion in their governing structures and educational objectives. At the provincial level, the Ministry of Education and Training has responsibility for funding the system and is involved in program development and approval. The quasi-independent intermediary body, the Council of Regents, is concerned with collective bargaining and also with issues referred to it by the minister of education and training (e.g., prior learning assessment and program accreditation and standards). As noted earlier, labour relations (re instructors) have been conducted between this council and the Ontario Public Service Employees Union, which represents the permanent teaching faculty and the support staff. However, each college is also governed through its local board, the members of which are mostly lay community representatives appointed by the Council of Regents (the other members consist of the president and one elected representative from the faculty, the administration, the support staff, and the students, respectively). This format is designed to ensure that colleges remain sensitive to the interests of their communities, while recognizing the concerns of internal constituencies which are directly affected by policies determined at the board level. Hence, while many of the most significant operational decisions (e.g., which new programs will be approved or the day-to-day working conditions of staff) are made at the provincial level, colleges are still expected to remain responsive to community needs and regional diversities. In effect, the management of each college is required to administer a collective agreement which it did not, itself, negotiate.

Labour relations in Ontario's colleges have proven to be an intermittent source of disruption and have been influential in several of the initiatives taken in the college sector since 1986. A strike involving the support staff occurred in January 1979, and five years later the instructors took job action which, after eighteen days, resulted in a legislated back-to-work order. Strike activity by teaching staff occurred again in 1989 and, after twenty days, was eventually resolved through binding arbitration. These actions, largely driven by concerns over workload, salaries, and sick-leave provisions, caused a province-wide disruption of college services and strong public reactions, resulting in the commissioning of a number of significant reports.

A Study of Instructional Assignment: The Skolnik Report
Under the chairship of Michael Skolnik, and in the wake of the 1984 strike, a committee was established by the government of Ontario to investigate and report upon the problem of workload – the primary factor contributing to the dispute. His final report, *Survival or Excellence? A Study of Instructional Assignment in the Colleges of Applied Arts and Technology* (Skolnik 1986), also

known as the Skolnik Report, addressed a number of issues pertinent to the climate of labour relations in Ontario's CAATs. It became clear that the identity of these institutions (i.e., whether their emphasis was upon education or training, whether they were quasi-autonomous institutions or extensions of government departments, or whether they followed a consultative form of decisionmaking or an industrial form with line authority) required clarification. It was evident to Skolnik that working conditions, class sizes, and teaching loads were ongoing sources of frustration which had consequences for instructional quality, professional development of teaching faculty, and program delivery.

However, the overriding factors in the unsatisfactory labour climate of the colleges were lack of trust, the alienation of the instructional staff, and declining morale. Among its many recommendations, the Skolnik Report identified various ways to involve faculty in decisionmaking and to increase their sense of professionalism. The workload issue was to be addressed later through changes in the formula which, in quantifying what a teacher does, would be more acceptable to faculty. At the time, Skolnik recommended against a province-wide formula; but, ultimately, his advice was not accepted by the Council of Regents.

The Pitman Report

Following the publication of the Skolnik Report, the minister of colleges and universities appointed Walter Pitman to advise on the governing structures of Ontario's colleges. While continuing to expand upon the theme of faculty alienation, *The Report of the Advisor to the Minister of Colleges and Universities on the Governance of the Colleges of Applied Arts and Technology* (Pitman 1986), also known as the Pitman Report, noted the perception that colleges were following an industrial model, with an increasing emphasis upon bottom-line budgeting and bureaucratic management techniques. Pitman stressed the need for a revitalized educational role for the colleges, with emphasis upon the quality of teaching, decisionmaking, and work relationships. After wide consultation, he prepared a set of recommendations designed to encourage 'participation, team-building and collegiality' (Pitman 1986:4).

Pitman centred his report on a new college mandate which would allow them to respond to an emerging industrial marketplace – a marketplace consisting of workers with different skills and levels of adaptability. To succeed in this task, Pitman emphasized that the college sector must be organized in such a way that it emphasizes its educational role. Consistent with this kind of environment, Pitman recommended that each college have an academic council (constituted mostly of teaching faculty) which would address all matters of academic policy and planning. The Board of

Governors should also be reconstituted to include representatives from the external and internal communities, and the Council of Regents should be replaced by a citizens' council, which would advise the minister of colleges and universities of policy relating to the college system. He also recommended that the Ministry of Colleges and Universities better coordinate its federal training purchases. Finally, Pitman emphasized the need for increased personal communication between ministry personnel and the college community.

After due consideration of the Pitman Report, the governing structure of the colleges was amended. Changes were incorporated to allow for election, by their respective constituencies, of one faculty member, one support staff member, one administrator, and one student, whose names would be forwarded to the Council of Regents for appointment to the Board of Governors. At first, these were to be non-voting members of the board, but, subsequently, each of the institutional representatives became full voting participants. In addition to this, the creation of a college council ensured that faculty and student advice would reach the president. Ministry guidelines provide the structure, composition, and terms of reference for the council, together with the procedures for communication between this body and the Board of Governors.

The Colleges' Collective Bargaining Commission: The Gandz Report
Pursuant to the Skolnik and Pitman reports, in 1987 the Minister of Colleges and Universities appointed Dr Jeffrey Gandz of the University of Western Ontario to undertake a study of the colleges' collective bargaining process. The primary charge to Gandz, as sole commissioner, was to assess the situation and to recommend changes that would improve the effectiveness of the collective bargaining process. In particular, he was to determine whether the parties to negotiation might be changed and which restrictions, if any, should be placed upon the issues eligible for submission to the bargaining process. At the time of the study, the two parties involved in bargaining were the Council of Regents and the Ontario Public Service Employees Union (OPSEU) representing college teachers.

The Report of the Colleges' Collective Bargaining Commission (Gandz 1988), also known as the Gandz Report, provided a comprehensive and politically sensitive analysis of the history of the bargaining process; the views of a team of experts on different aspects of labour relations; extensive discussions with a range of individuals from the union, government, college personnel, and managerial staff; and possible alternatives to current practice. In all, Gandz produced thirty-eight separate recommendations with wide-reaching implications. Among these recommendations, some of the more significant included the creation of a College Employee Relations

Association (CERA) (an employer agency to be comprised of representatives from the then twenty-two corporate college boards), which would replace the Council of Regents as the agent for management; the suggestion that academic staff employed on a sessional and part-time basis should be included within the bargaining unit, as should part-time support staff; the suggestion that system-wide grievances should be processed at the CERA level; and the idea that college personnel should be trained in contract administration while human resource management should be upgraded.

Even though all of these, together with other, recommendations were designed to improve the labour relations climate in the college sector, they comprised only part of a potential resolution to the distrust and alienation felt by instructors and articulated in the Skolnik and Pitman reports. However, Gandz debated one particular issue which could have implications beyond the labour relations arena – the question of centralized versus decentralized bargaining.

Since the early 1970s, labour negotiations have been conducted at the provincial level, although the governance of each college was under the jurisdiction of its respective corporate board. In effect, while the collective agreement was provincial, administration of the agreement was local – each college being required to apply a set of working conditions which it played no part in negotiating. Other tensions associated with this arrangement had been identified in the Skolnik, Pitman, and Gandz reports. The question of local bargaining was widely debated in the Gandz Report. He noted, inter alia, that while OPSEU, the Council of Regents, and most of the colleges favoured the continuation of the present system, the vast majority of experts from outside the system, including both Skolnik and Pitman, suggested a change to the local bargaining system as a solution to the problems within the college system in general.

Ultimately, Gandz recommended a modest compromise – a continuation of provincial bargaining with, where appropriate, increased opportunities for additional negotiations at the local level. In effect, he proposed a form of two-tier bargaining. It could be argued that, consistent with the concept of community colleges in Ontario (i.e., institutions sensitive and responsive to regional needs), faculty working conditions, at least, should be broadly negotiable at the local level.

Following the acceptance of the Gandz Report, legislation was introduced by the provincial government in 1992 to amend the Colleges' Collective Bargaining Statute in order to allow for CERA to replace the Council of Regents as the bargaining agent and in order to extend bargaining rights to all part-time staff who worked on a regular and/or continuing basis. Due partly to the fiscal implications of the latter, the amended legislation has not yet been passed.

Vision 2000: Quality and Opportunity

In October 1988, the then minister of colleges and universities requested the Council of Regents to begin a review of Ontario's colleges and to develop a vision of the college system in the year 2000. The process which followed may be described as one of the most broadly based reviews of a postsecondary education sector conducted in Ontario. Under the direction of the council chair, Charles Pascal, the study involved a steering committee of thirty-three stakeholder representatives from education, labour, industry, and government; five study teams; numerous hearings and briefs; and the energetic involvement of many hundreds of individuals. It is estimated that over 2,000 individuals participated in the process at one level or another.

The primary areas of concern in *Vision 2000: Quality and Opportunity* (Council of Regents for CAATs 1990) included reform of the CAAT system and the relationships between the colleges and the provincial economy, the community-at-large, high schools and universities, and the private sector. Questions of access, articulation, funding, curricula, quality, governance, training, and service to the francophone community occupied the attention of the steering committee for two years. The result was a broad statement regarding future college mandates and forty recommendations which addressed a long list of reforms. Some of the most significant guides for future action included: an increase in the general education component of technical and vocational programs; system-wide standards based on graduate learning outcomes; accreditation through regular program reviews; a commitment to adult upgrading through policy and funding; programs to create advanced training opportunities; reform of the ministry's funding formula; an emphasis on human resource development; and a structure to allow for degree completion in selected areas of advanced training.

The blueprint which emerged from *Vision 2000* projected a revitalized college system equipped and managed in such a way as to accommodate the challenges of new learning demands, changing provincial economic realities, and strategies to handle problems of equity, access, and quality. A number of specific government actions were taken in the wake of the final report. Several of these actions will be developed more fully later in this chapter.

The number of CAATs in Ontario was increased from twenty-two to twenty-three with the establishment in 1990 of La Cité Collegial, a French language institution located in eastern Ontario. Previously, Algonquin College, one of very few bilingual postsecondary institutions in Canada, had accommodated both English- and French-speaking students in that area. This change had a major impact upon Algonquin, which lost more than 100 instructional staff but which continued on with a largely unaffected enrolment. Subsequently, the minister of colleges and universities announced the imminent creation of two more French-speaking colleges – one in Sudbury and another in Southwest Ontario.

The College Standards and Accreditation Council

One group of recommendations in *Vision 2000* was concerned with the need to improve the equivalence of learning outcomes from college programs, to set system-wide standards, to review programs as a prelude to accreditation, and to increase the general education component of all college programs. All of these recommendations revolved around a proposal to establish a College Standards and Accreditation Council (CSAC) which would be charged with implementing and maintaining appropriate action.

In consequence, the Ministry of Colleges and Universities created an advisory board to plan the policies upon which such a council would operate. After extensive hearings and numerous briefs, largely from the college community, a final report was published. It was clear that unanimous agreement on several of the *Vision 2000* recommendations was not obtained. In particular, the issue of general education was contentious. Some individuals seemed to feel that the vocational thrust of college education would be compromised; others argued that not only did students, and many employers, not seek general educational competency at the college level, but that the university or the high school was the appropriate place for a curriculum of this nature. Ultimately, the recommendation was to define general education in terms of learning outcomes rather than content. The percentage of such education in various programs should be increased gradually. Additional concerns were expressed regarding the costs of implementing this recommendation. It was also recommended that a system-wide set of program standards, defined in terms of both generic and program-specific skills, should be established. Furthermore, the council should oversee a program review process in which graduate performance would be assessed. If these periodic reviews were satisfactory, the program would be accredited and funding granted. Part of the accrediting process would be to examine the appropriateness of admission requirements and to assess student progress.

Representation was an important issue for CSAC. It seemed essential to reinforce the concept of internal control over CSAC's affairs. Members of the college community – governors, presidents, administrators, faculty unions, and students – were all to be represented. In addition, representatives from employer agencies, labour, professional associations, other educational levels (the K-12 system and the universities), and the community would also be voting members. Finally, non-voting representatives from the Council of Regents, the Ministry of Colleges and Universities, and other quasi-governmental bodies would also serve on CSAC.

All in all, it was evident that every effort had been made to allay concerns that CSAC would be overly bureaucratic, force high levels of conformity upon college curricula, and/or discourage institutional creativity in program planning and administration. At the same time, however, the intent of the recommendations in *Vision 2000* was recognized in that it was essential for college programs and graduates to be creditable in the view of employers, universities, and the public. The potential costs involved in implementing this initiative remained a problem, and, eventually, CSAC established four separate councils to deal with standards, general education, generic skills, and prior learning assessment (which has become increasingly important), respectively.

The Prior Learning Assessment Report
Yet another issue which emerged from *Vision 2000* was the topic of prior learning assessment (PLA) and how it might be implemented to encourage greater access to college programs for an increasingly diverse student clientele. In the summer of 1991, the minister of colleges and universities commissioned the Council of Regents to study the issue. The resulting report left little doubt as to the importance of PLA within the college community.

The concept of prior learning assessment flows from the recognition that many adults acquire a considerable amount of skill and knowledge through a wide range of formal and non-formal experiences. Full college recognition of such learning would not only broaden access and encourage further education for adult students, but it would also reduce the amount of training required to earn advanced credentials.

The document *Prior Learning Assessment: Enhancing the Access of Adult Learners to Ontario's Colleges* (Johnston 1992), also known as the PLA Report, not only endorsed the principle of PLA but also provided a rational basis for its implementation. Prior learning, for example, might be assessed through a policy of current course challenge, an evaluation of courses taken outside the college system, standardized test results, or the preparation of individual portfolios. Language proficiency and ethnic diversity were also recognized as important considerations in PLA. Having adopted the principle of prior learning assessment, the remainder of the PLA Report is devoted to ways of managing the concept. It was recommended, for example, that in the initial stage a student may earn up to 75 per cent of his or her college credential through PLA, but a minimum of 25 per cent of his or her program credits must be earned in college. In conclusion, the PLA Report noted: 'However, creating a comprehensive PLA system is just one step. Colleges must also work to ensure that flexible options are available to adult learners beyond PLA. We must provide a variety of entry points into the system, facilitate the transfer of credits among Ontario colleges and further develop the use of learning contracts and independent study' (p. 49).

The Ontario Training and Adjustment Board

In the late 1980s, an increasing awareness of the need to restructure and improve opportunities for employment training if Ontario was to remain competitive in the new global economy resulted in the publication of a number of reports. Foremost among these were two from the premier's council: *Competing in the New Global Economy* (Ontario 1988) and *People and Skills in the New Global Economy* (Ontario 1990b). After wide consultation with business, labour groups, community organizations, educators, and other concerned individuals regarding the substance of these reports, the provincial government proposed the creation of a new structure – the Ontario Training and Adjustment Board (OTAB).

OTAB is designed to be an independent, self-governing organization composed of representatives of key labour force partners, employer and union organizations, trainers and educators, women, people with disabilities, racial minorities, and aboriginal peoples. OTAB's mandate is comprehensive and challenging – it is to ensure that Ontario's economic objectives are met through well-designed programs; increased access, equity, and broader participation; and a higher level of private investment in training programs. The targets for increased training opportunities are to be new workplace entrants, displaced and dislocated workers, apprentices, and individuals seeking workplace re-entry. The primary thrust behind establishing OTAB is to shift the responsibility for employment training from the provincial government to a partnership comprised of those groups having a major stake in such training. Placed in the hands of the most affected groups, it is postulated that employment training programs will be more relevant, participatory, and productive.

In association with the OTAB proposal was the more recent federal initiative to create local boards, also widely representative, which would assess the need and type of training programs necessary to meet regional requirements. Local boards began as part of an attempt by the Canadian Labour Force Development Board to involve local leadership in constructing training programs and to reduce overlaps and duplication. The twenty-two proposed local boards will coordinate the disbursement of federal and provincial funds and incorporate the objectives of forty-eight different provincial programs and services concerned with labour force development in Ontario.

Not surprisingly, the colleges recognized that they held a large stake in this new training initiative. The Association of Colleges of Applied Arts and Technology (ACAATO) was quick to respond to the proposals and, in so doing, designated the colleges as the cornerstone of the training system. Citing several examples of entrepreneurship and partnership between colleges and various public- and private-sector agencies, ACAATO emphasized the importance of making colleges full partners in setting training policy. The ACAATO response noted the need for much greater standardization and, hence, portability of program credentials as well as a flexible system of prior learning assessment. In describing the role of the colleges, ACAATO noted that they bring 'a comprehensive, full-service mandate; each college functions as an educational institution, a training delivery agent, and a community player with extensive linkages with all major labour market partners including employers' (Association of Colleges of Applied Arts and Technology of Ontario 1992). Colleges' concern over OTAB, however, was heightened when their sole representative was replaced by someone from a university.

Restructuring the Postsecondary Education System
By mid-1992, a variety of reports at both the provincial and federal levels had identified numerous issues which Ontario colleges and universities would have to address if they were to meet the demand for their services in an uncertain fiscal environment. The pressures on the system stemmed from the rapidity of economic and social change, the numbers and mix of students seeking both new and traditional education and training programs, and the limited ability of government to provide sufficient resources to meet this demand. It was becoming increasingly clear that a fundamental restructuring of the public, tertiary education system was necessary if it was to accommodate the challenges of the future.

In response, the minister of colleges and universities announced the creation of two broadly representative committees which were to address the restructuring process for the college system and the university system, respectively. A third committee was charged with coordinating these activities. The mandate for the committees was to develop a prioritized agenda of issues, to identify potential options, and to recommend strategies which might accomplish the goal of restructuring. In particular, a major task was to bring greater coherence to the postsecondary sectors as well as to introduce a set of new initiatives into the colleges.

The committees were also provided with a number of government policy statements designed to stress the uncertain fiscal health of the province and the unlikelihood of the emergence of new resources; they also received a set of 'policy parameters' to guide their activities (including statements regarding the need for both diversifying and coordinating the system, maintaining maximum access for all segments of society, maintaining quality, preserving shared funding, and maximizing student mobility and lifelong learning opportunities). Hence, broadly instructed by a wealth of reports from Ontario and beyond, and with explicit government direction contained in background statements of fiscal, educational, and training policy, the restructuring committees have begun their task.

From the government's point of view, economic renewal is a clear priority. It is important to note that, in addition to the creation of these committees, the government had already taken a major initiative with respect to restructuring by allocating almost $40 million to the postsecondary system for specific projects. Part of this fund is for transition, and part is for economic renewal. Projects funded under this policy include the development of joint college-university programs, improvements in instructional technology (including distance learning, partnerships with business and industry, prior learning assessment, and programs designed to involve francophone and aboriginal communities). Additional areas of concern include self-directed learning, compressed and flexible program delivery, resource sharing, and student retention. Another important initiative was to be a re-examination of the funding formula under which colleges currently receive their operating grants.

Advanced Training
One issue which arose during the *Vision 2000* debate, and which was targeted for further attention, was the need for greater opportunities for advanced training for those graduates of the college system who wished to upgrade their skills and credentials. This issue contained within it the long-debated question of transfer of credits between the college and the university sectors. Advanced training was seen as a combination of practical, career-oriented training together with theory and analytical skills. In response to the recommendation in *Vision 2000,* a provincial task force, under the chairship of Walter Pitman, was established in order to identify the need for advanced training in the province and to recommend ways in which it might be implemented. The final report was entitled *No Dead Ends: Report of the Task Force on Advanced Training to the Minister of Education and Training* (Pitman 1993).

In reviewing the current status of advanced training, the report noted that, while an increasing number of college-university transfer arrangements had been put in place, there was neither a formal recognition of credentials nor coherent province-wide policies which could ensure equity of access to students seeking advanced learning. The need for expanded opportunities in these areas was clearly documented by each constituency the task force surveyed, including students, graduates, and employers. Several arguments in favour of advanced training were consistently repeated – arguments which cited changing demands in the workplace, particularly for upper and middle management; the impact of rapid technological changes; credential-based barriers to career advancement; and requirements for new skills in the knowledge-driven job market (e.g., decisionmaking, problem-solving, and planning).

Briefs presented to the task force from both individuals and corporations stressed the need for flexibility in the provision of advanced education, often making reference to on-the-job learning, part-time study, and co-operative programming between institutions and the private sector. In many instances, the baccalaureate degree was cited as the credential of choice. The task force concluded that, in comparison with other jurisdictions in Canada and elsewhere, Ontario had failed to develop policies which would create the 'seamless educational continuum which it sees as prerequisite to [the] long-term success' of advanced learning opportunities (Pitman 1993:7).

No Dead Ends noted several ways to improve the current situation in Ontario. Partnership among colleges, universities, and the private sector with respect to the planning and implementation of advanced learning was emphasized, as was the need for additional funding to stimulate new transfer arrangements. But the most controversial recommendation promoted the creation of an independent, provincial institute, the Ontario Institute of Advanced Training (OIAT) to 'initiate, negotiate, coordinate, promote, and allocate funds for advanced training programs at the first degree level' (p. 12). OIAT, with a widely representative governing board, would have designated degree-granting power. Furthermore, it would organize relevant programs with a practical-theoretical balance, subscribe to prior learning assessment, and engage in flexible course delivery.

OIAT is similar to the National Council on Academic Awards, which functioned until recently in the United Kingdom and which held the authority to award degrees through the polytechnic institutes. Given its uniqueness in Canada, however, credibility would not be immediately bestowed upon OIAT, and wide recognition of the credentials of its graduates will take time. However, given the long-standing lack of university cooperation with respect to creating a coherent transfer credit policy, OIAT appears to offer a viable alternative.

Concluding Comments

Although the foregoing catalogue of new initiatives undertaken by the Ontario college system is impressive, it is by no means exhaustive. Many other important, albeit often less dramatic, issues have been, and are being, addressed as the system adjusts and adapts to the challenges of a new era in college education. Large bureaucratic organizations do not normally change without massive disruption. Nevertheless, the wealth of activity aimed at reforming a provincial college system with deeply rooted values and an entrenched culture is quite remarkable.

In addition to those already described, Ontario's colleges have also embarked upon numerous other projects. Some of these include: a central application system for students; several multicultural development activities; an exploration of provincial needs for advanced training; implementation of an educational and training strategy for First Nations peoples; a study of the effectiveness of the policy of distribution of budgetary resources; studies of gender equity, harassment, discrimination, and race relations; and a review of student financial assistance programs. In April 1994, the Ministry of Education and Training announced a project to develop a college-university transfer guide under the joint sponsorship of the Council of Ontario Universities and ACAATO.

Nor is the litany of new ideas confined to the provincial level. An examination of the annual reports of each of the twenty-three individual institutions reveals an almost endless list of new program initiatives, analyses of student needs and program effectiveness, follow-up studies of graduates, and creative attempts to establish partnerships with other agencies. Colleges have also produced detailed strategic plans which contain references to mandates, missions, values, goals, and objectives.

It would be optimistic in the extreme to expect that all of these ventures will translate into the successful and productive reform of the college system. Inevitably, some new ideas fail to penetrate the defensive bureaucratic shell with which many organizations cover themselves. Creative instruments of change are too often discarded after protracted disputes over who is responsible for their implementation. Nevertheless, there seems to be a conviction in Ontario that the colleges must either confront the obstacles to reform or they will sink into a deep pit of irrelevance.

Several of the long-standing problems in the Ontario college system have not been alleviated. Labour relations issues remain largely unresolved. Also, the problem of governance arouses intense reaction. While faculty unions seek to gain a more formal voice (along with statutory power) in the management of colleges, some at the administrative level fear that the co-management of governance could lead to chaos. Meanwhile, the colleges face the problems created by ongoing underfunding and point to statistics which show a continuing decline in the real dollars allocated to their operating and capital budgets. Ontario's fiscal ill-health, coupled with its deep concern over an increasing provincial deficit, indicates that substantial additional resources will not be forthcoming in the near future. Hence, colleges are seeking ways, and being offered incentives, to increase operational efficiency. Not surprisingly, all of these activities have raised the stress level among college instructors, who envisage a potential threat to job security.

It appears, however, that in spite of these unresolved issues, public confidence in the college sector remains strong. A recent survey (Ontario Institute for Studies in Education 1992) assessed public attitudes to education in Ontario and came up with some interesting results. Over 80 per cent of respondents expressed satisfaction with the performance of the CAATs. A consistent majority also agreed that colleges prepared graduates adequately for job entry and that their career-oriented focus should be maintained. Furthermore, colleges were perceived to be the appropriate locus for community-based efforts to stimulate the economy through labour force development. Clearly, Ontario's colleges continue to enjoy the confidence of the public.

In conclusion, the evidence suggests that Ontario's CAATs are entering a new era in program delivery, community expectations, and economic uncertainty. While this is not an easy course to chart, it appears that commitment and energy are two ingredients which are widely distributed throughout the system. The next five years will undoubtedly tell an interesting story of change and redirection in one of Canada's largest and most complex community college systems.

Québec

The College Network
Born of the collective assertion that accompanied the Quiet Revolution of the 1960s, the Québec college network presents an impressive scoreboard. Its public, tuition-free colleges – commonly referred to as Cegeps (collèges d'enseignement général et professionnel) – numbered forty-seven in 1994. Five of these Cegeps assume responsibility for associated national schools which focus on such areas as fishing and aerotechnology, and another eighteen encompass specialized centres that undertake applied research and provide advanced technological assistance to small- and medium-sized enterprises which focus on such areas as robotics and pulp and paper. In 1991, these public colleges occupied nearly two and one-fifth million square metres of floor space in 460 buildings. Personnel records showed over 17,400 full-time employees, 56.2 per cent of whom were teachers (Québec 1993d; Corriveau 1991).

In addition to the Cegeps, there are eleven college-level institutions (under the mandate of various provincial ministries) that grant diplomas which are sanctioned by the Ministry of Education and Science (e.g., Institut de tourisme et d'hôtellerie and Conservatoire de musique de Chicoutimi). One also finds fifty-two recognized private colleges. Of these, twenty-four are non-profit institutions that are declared to be of public interest. Their diplomas are issued by the Ministry of Education and Science and they receive substantial government funding. Twenty-eight proprietary schools complete the picture; they operate under permit, issue attestations and certificates, and receive no government funding (Québec 1993d). So there is a grand total of 110 institutions providing college-level studies.

In Québec, there is an intermediary level of studies inserted between the traditional sectors of secondary and postsecondary education. College students choose between pre-university and technical/professional streams of study; the former proposes five general education programs (spread over a two-year period) that lead to university matriculation and a bachelor degree conferred after three additional years of study, and the latter offers over 130 programs (divided into five groupings) that provide advanced skills and know-how for direct entry into specialized job markets. With programs lasting for over three years, this technical/professional stream also provides a strong dose of general education subjects in the hope of generating a workforce capable of adapting to the requirements of a rapidly evolving postindustrial economy. A significant and growing number of technical/professional graduates go directly to university (Québec 1993d).

Achievement and Change

Greater accessibility, increased retention, democratization of structures, improvement of technical/professional studies – these constitute the primary objectives set forth in the *Report of the Royal Commission of Enquiry on Education in the Province of Quebec* (Québec 1964), hereafter referred to as the Parent Report, that prompted the major educational refashioning mentioned above. And it was the Parent Commission that saw the importance of creating a public, comprehensive, and postsecondary college sector to play a key role in orchestrating the process of change. The establishment of the Cegeps in 1967 permitted a break from the past and a bridge to the future without traumatizing existing traditions and cultures.

During the 1991-2 academic year, the regular college day programs included approximately 163,000 full-time registrants. Over 50 per cent of the province's seventeen- to twenty-one-year-olds made their way to postsecondary studies, as opposed to 16 per cent at the time of the Parent Report. Approximately 46 per cent of this college population was enrolled in technical/professional programs, and three out of four students from the total college population came from families in which the highest level of educational attainment was a high-school certificate. Moreover, the fact that the breadwinners in over half of these families belonged to the ranks of the unskilled or semi-skilled indicates, without question, a major social shift (Québec 1993d; Conseil des collèges 1991b).

To this picture one must add the 68,000 part-time and not-so-young students enrolled in continuing education diploma and certificate programs and the 32,000 following non-credit job-training programs (Conseil des collèges 1991b; Québec 1993d). A distance education initiative run from one of the Cegeps is also providing college-level learning opportunities to 12,000 students. And one must also take note of the thousands of people following evening and weekend self-financed popular education courses – from ballroom dancing to how to start a small business – that have become part of the response of the colleges to broad community needs.

This pattern of growth especially benefited francophones, women, and individuals living in rural areas – groups that had been underrepresented in the past (Conseil des collèges 1992). In recent years, the province's burgeoning immigrant population has added to this pattern. In part, this is attributable to the geographic development of the Cegeps, with at least one college situated in each administrative region of the province. It also has much to do with the ups and downs of the economy, the fact that regular Cegep day programs are tuition-free, and the growing recognition that a high-school certificate is no longer adequate. Growth is buttressed by an open-door policy that prompted the arrival of many students with poor academic backgrounds and/or with low academic aspirations who were to become enthusiastic about postsecondary studies. This warming-up process crossed age and gender categories, and it really began to take on importance in the early 1980s (Daignault 1992). Finally, the existence of a common curriculum for all colleges and a régime pédagogique established by the Ministry of Education and Science also contributed to improved retention rates. Switching programs and/or colleges could be accomplished with relative ease, and it is estimated that one in three students do so during their college careers (Lévesque and Pageau 1990).

Over 650,000 diplomas and certificates have been conferred since the inception of the college system. A recent study indicates that 72.3 per cent of those entering pre-university and 63.7 per cent of those entering technical/professional studies eventually complete their program requirements (Lévesque and Pageau 1990). The figures speak for themselves, and, considering that 87 per cent of those enrolled in college studies attend a Cegep, the crucial role of this institution in Québec's distinct educational paradigm becomes explicit.

Over the years, much has changed in the Cegeps. Originally conceived as institutions for high-school graduates enrolled in full-time day studies, now an ever-increasing number of students elect to work and study at the same time. A student must take a requisite number of courses in order to retain full-time status, but the time allotted for obtaining a diploma has been extended. By 1988-9 only one in three Cegep graduates completed the program in the projected two- or three-year time period. At the same time, there has been a noticeable increase in the over twenty-five age group in the Cegeps (Conseil des collèges 1992). By 1989, this group constituted 31 per cent of total college enrolment. All indicators suggest that these changes will continue at an accelerating rate – a situation which is only now starting to receive the attention that it merits.

To keep its college network going, the Québec government allocated $1.2 billion in operating funds in 1991-2. In addition to this, $64 million went into capital expenditures, and another $164 million found its way into debt servicing. Cost recovery, although on the increase, amounted, at best, to 7 per cent of the total annual outlay (Québec 1993d; Fédération des cégeps 1991). An impressive financial effort, yet one that is straining to keep up with the need and the economic-political demands of the day.

The Institutional Reality
The process of modernization that accompanied the Quiet Revolution fuelled the development of a greatly expanded and active civil service which, with time, took on the character of an independent technocracy. The emerging college sector, in this regard, provided fertile ground for this growth. From the early 1970s on, the Cegeps found themselves entrapped in regulations, procedures, and structures that grew exponentially to the detriment of the partnership role envisaged by the Parent Report. By 1991-2 the Directorate of College Education (DGEC), funded by an annual budget of over $10 million and with a full-time staff of 164 civil servants (and countless other consultants, whose presence is well disguised in annual government reports) had imposed its will on virtually all aspects of college life (LeBlanc 1992). In the eyes of a growing number of proponents, the college network has, de facto, turned into a collection of branch plants beholden to the agenda of a government agency that is never evaluated and that is not held accountable for its actions (Gingras 1989).

Hand in hand with the above came the massive growth of organized labour. By the mid-1970s, the Cegeps had essentially become closed shops affiliated to either the Centrale de l'enseignement du Québec (CEQ) or the Confédération des syndicats nationaux (CSN) – unions which wielded tremendous influence on the daily running of the colleges. Fielding their own bureaucratic apparatus, tempered by the Common Front struggles of the 1970s and early 1980s, and driven by an ideology of confrontation, the unions were able to – for better or for worse – change the face of the college scene. The climate of suspicion and *attentisme* that this created had a fossilizing effect on both perceptions and actions. It was inevitable that big government and big labour would come to blows.

The centralist, industrial management model that emerged produced a meltdown in the assumptions and values that accompanied the ideal of collegiality that traditionally nourished the higher education sector. Consequently, the type of participation that takes place in the colleges today is usually circumscribed within structures formalized by collective agreements, and independent action is more and more exceptional (Conseil supérieur de l'éducation 1992a, 1993). One simply does not see teachers and other personnel investing in their institutions as they did in the past – it's not part of the job description. The result of this is manifested in a bunker-like mentality at all levels: covering ass and not taking responsibility has become a consummate art, conformity and compliance continually stifle creativity and risk-taking, and calls for new leadership only serve as an excuse for not getting involved.

It should not come as a surprise to see this situation intertwined with reductions in public financing. Between 1978-9 and 1991-2, the college sector assimilated $112 million in budget cuts despite a 10 per cent increase in its full-time student population. Public financing of the Cegeps went from $4,908 per student to $4,257 per student, and comparative data show that the college sector was hit harder than were the other education sectors. Increased teacher workloads, reduction of support services, non-renewal of equipment, growing criticism of union strategies, waning public support of education, and so on would all take their toll on the morale of the troops and the vigour of the system. The bloom is definitely gone (LeBlanc 1992; Corriveau 1991).

The coherence that had accompanied the educational transformations of the 1960s and early 1970s also came under siege, and this situation was aggravated in 1985, when it was decided to split the Ministry of Education into two separate ministries: one for elementary-secondary education and another for higher education. In principle, this was not a bad idea, but the timing could not have been worse. In many regards, the different education sectors had already been drifting apart, as separate directorates developed their own inclusive visions of what was necessary and possible – visions that had been formulated by upwardly mobile technocrats with little input from major players in the education system. The ministerial reorganization permitted the technocracy to advance its proposals, many of which found champions in newly appointed ministers and deputy ministers seeking to leave their mark. Program and curriculum development were the casualties of this systemic fragmentation, and the college sector, functioning as a bridge between elementary-secondary education and higher education, was left in a very uncomfortable position (Conseil des collèges 1991c).

The Ontology of the Cegep Network

The originality of the Cegep network, in large measure, accounts for the chronic malaise that has accompanied its development since 1967. Where exactly is it situated in the educational structure? Is it a culmination of secondary studies or the initiation to university work? How does it compare to other networks in North America or, for that matter, in the world? What is the purpose of its distinctiveness? These and several other questions have seethed below the surface since the inception of the Cegep network, and they have provided the basis for a dozen major studies that have taken place under government auspices – four of them since 1986. The result of these enquiries exposed a variety of problems within the college system, and, over the years, they produced a lengthy list of suggested changes. Hindsight shows, and it is important to note, that the majority of the recommendations that came from these studies were shelved or were considerably watered down when finally implemented. Not until very recently did any of the studies call into question the Cegep network itself. It was as if the college system had a credibility all its own – as if its ambiguity served the interests of the various establishments and groups that constituted it.

This impression, however, has to be counterbalanced by acknowledging the high degree of approval and confidence that the public has bestowed upon the Cegep network over the years. For the average citizen and student, it would seem that the hair-splitting of educational purists is really not a pressing concern. Public opinion polls taken as recently as 1992 indicate that 82 per cent of the province's population believe that the arrival of the Cegep network on the educational scene was a good thing. When it comes to the calibre of education and services provided, 85 per cent of those polled report that they were satisfied or very satisfied with the education they received from Cegeps (Québec 1992). Even the province's employers have very positive things to say about the technical/professional graduates in their organizations. A study done in 1990 indicated that 94 per cent of employers were satisfied with Cegep graduates' productivity, 87 per cent were satisfied with their competence, and 86 per cent were satisfied with their adaptability (Québec 1993d). The passage of time has done its work; the Cegep network has become anchored in the culture. The major issue at hand is whether or not the Cegep system as it is presently fashioned is capable of doing the job in these trying and rapidly changing times.

Movement Towards Reform

Just as the college sector was about to celebrate its twenty-fifth anniversary, the newly appointed minister of higher education, Lucienne Robillard, dropped a bomb that has continued to echo to this day. With little advance warning, she publicly called for a parliamentary commission to look into the future of the Cegep system, and she made it quite clear that everything was to be put out in the open. Over 200 briefs poured in during the next five months. With the exception of one, all called for, in one degree or another, the implementation of significant reform in order to allow the Cegep to play a more decisive role.

Through her forthrightness, her willingness to poke sacred cows, Robillard tapped into an aquifer of concern that immediately gushed over. As the review process advanced, it became more and more apparent that Robillard was being offered a blank cheque to implement – rather than to negotiate – change. Crucial to this turn-around was the effective action of the Fédération des cégeps. In the past, this lobbying agency of the public colleges had generally hedged its options by seeking safe rather than radical surgery; but, in this instance, it jumped on a bandwagon that would undoubtedly both disrupt and energize it. Its plan of attack was simple: highlight what is done well, propose concrete solutions to what is not done well, and ensure that everyone understands that the Fédération's position is the bottom line of the public colleges (Fédération de cégeps 1993).

In April 1993, Robillard presented her plan for the renewal of college studies to the National Assembly (Québec 1993a). Two months later, after minor modifications, Bill 82 and Bill 83 were sanctioned by the lieutenant-governor (Québec 1993d). In essence, these laws and the accompanying consensus

- reaffirmed the crucial importance of the college network to the realization of the province's educational vision
- emphasized that college-level studies belong to higher education
- expanded the mission of the colleges to cover community outreach, regional economic development, international cooperation, applied research, and pedagogical research
- heralded the continuity of public financing by making tuition-free studies available to all full-time students in authorized Cegep programs.

With this came a series of concrete measures that would, when applied, bring about a significant re-engineering of the college reality. A primary focus of this process of change is quality of education, which is to be achieved by

- establishing a competency-based approach to learning throughout the college system
- formulating an enriched and coherent general education curriculum that is adapted to various student needs (objectives, standards, and learning activities to be determined by the ministry)
- granting the colleges, in collaboration with the universities, a greater role in the elaboration and revision of learning activities in all pre-university program courses (objectives and standards in these courses remain under the authority of the ministry)
- implementing a similar formula for the technical/professional streams with input from representatives of business, industry, and service sectors (objectives and standards in the courses to remain under the ministry)

- harmonizing the technical/professional program offerings of the colleges with the vocational offerings of the high schools
- rationalizing the number of technical/professional programs offered as well as their distribution within the college network
- increasing academic entrance requirements for college studies
- establishing an introductory pre-session for promising but inadequately prepared and/or unoriented students
- imposing financial penalties on full-time students who accumulate a certain number of course failures.

The second focus of re-engineering addressed the matter of accountability. At the level of the institution, each college has to:

- review its internal regulations on the evaluation of student learning in the light of the changes brought about by reform
- implement an exit assessment to validate the learning that took place in each student's program of study
- establish internal regulations covering the evaluation of its programs of study as well as of its personnel.

The government, for its part, is to establish a semi-independent three-person commission mandated to:

- evaluate the quality of programs of study
- evaluate the effectiveness of internal review regulations developed by the colleges
- prepare recommendations to the government and its ministries on the impact that their policies and regulations have on the academic administration of the colleges
- publicize the results of the evaluations that it undertakes.

No sooner was the reform legislation promulgated than it was announced that the government would bring about an internal reorganization that would consolidate all educational matters under a minister of education and science. Robillard, to no surprise, was given this portfolio. Before anyone could catch his or her breath, she announced a major review of what was and was not taking place in the elementary and secondary schools. She also made strategic moves towards regaining the upper hand vis-à-vis the technocracy. The appointment of a deputy minister who was given cross-sector responsibility for technical/professional and vocational education set the tone for ministerial reassertion. A return to a systemic educational vision was in the making.

The initial signs from this whirlwind of activity are quite favourable. The deadlines for the implementation of the renewal at the college level – August 1993 to August 1997 – are being adhered to, and all reports indicate a renewed sense of purposefulness and cooperation amongst stakeholders.

The basis for a true partnership is perhaps in the making. However, there is a sense that Robillard's timetable for change is too compressed. There are far too many compromises and loose ends, and there are a few black holes that may well come to haunt any attempts to apply proposed modifications. Moreover, the socioeconomic-cum-political climate of Québec is unstable and could throw the entire initiative off track.

The Opportunities, Shortcomings, and Risks of Reform

A recent document of the Conseil supérieur de l'éducation proposes a new set of accessibility benchmarks which call for: (1) 70 per cent of the under twenty age group to enrol in college studies; (2) 60 per cent of the under twenty-five age group to attain a diploma of college education; (3) a 50/50 split between pre-university and technical/professional program enrolment; and (4) a significant increase in the number of male students who graduate from college (Conseil supérieur de l'éducation 1993). Government spending on college education, however, is stagnant, and just to implement the proposed reforms it is projecting an increase of $52.6 million over the next five years. Calculations by the Fédération des cégeps propose the need for at least $19 million more! If this is not daunting enough, there is also the presence of Act 198, which calls for a major reduction in the provincial civil service (which has seen its numbers balloon by 9.7 per cent since 1986). The act calls for a 20 per cent reduction in management personnel by 1995, and a 12 per cent reduction in all other categories of personnel by 1998 (Québec 1993e). Although the colleges are not part of the civil service and, hence, are not held to this target, Robillard had to nevertheless present a five-year redressment plan, taking into account both fiscal realities and the spirit of Act 198. Something had to give.

Robillard pointed to the increasing number and variety of students enrolling at Cegeps and argued that expenditures for education are an investment in the future (unlike expenditures which consist in distributing money to persons for day-to-day needs). She kept her proposed reductions in direct student grassroot services as small as politically feasible and the silverware has been spared for the moment. Cuts, however, will be made in the colleges. Class size, which has remained reasonable in spite of roll-backs in the mid-1980s, will climb. Full-time personnel appointments will, under pressure, give way to further contracting-out and to the hiring of more part-time and occasional employees in all categories. A wholesale onslaught to reduce social and other fringe benefits will also characterize the movement to do more with less. Finally, the sacrosanct job-security provisions (acquired over the years by more than 60 per cent of college employees) will be considerably whittled down and refashioned. From another angle, cost recovery will take on greater importance as entrepreneurship receives its epaulette. Although Cegeps will remain tuition-free, a host of administrative and user-fees will appear, and their audacity will increase with each passing year.

What is troubling about this process of change is that it is taking place with little input from those who stand or sit in front of a class. Indeed, it is the quiescence of the teachers – and their unions – that gives cause for pause. Certainly they are on the defensive, as their fiefdoms come under attack from all fronts. Obviously, it has been difficult for them to adopt a single discourse, more so than ever now that a third organization, the Fédération autonome du collégial, speaks for them. But between the present and the not-so-distant past (when Cegep teachers constituted a major element in the militant vanguard of the public-sector union movement) there is too great a disparity. Either there will be one hell of a whiplash, or there will be a rendering of arms. Either situation gives cause for concern.

What takes place in the classroom, in the final analysis, is what the current movement of reform is all about. If the teachers do not find their place in the process, it is the students that will be shortchanged. Now more than ever, there is an opportunity to resurrect the principles and values of collegiality, and this must be seized. The danger that awaits the Québec college system is that, without the presence of a countervailing force, it is quite possible that the reform process will be hijacked by an unholy alliance between the bureaucracies of the Ministry of Education and Science and the public colleges, which will standardize administrative and educational practices. This has to be avoided, and a mixed system of institutional collegiality, checked and balanced by a healthy union presence and operating within the context of a two-tier bargaining model (with the strong involvement of college boards of directors) is the preferred arrangement. This may sound easy, but province-wide bargaining legislation that is currently on the books for the para-public Cegep service is a major obstacle to progress.

It is obvious that a major reorganization of the college curriculum is under way and the recent election of a Parti Québécois government will not significantly modify this. If this change is approached in a positive manner, if it receives support and understanding, it will stimulate the many teachers who have been doing the same thing for what must seem to them an eternity. Indeed, teacher complacency is something that the colleges must address as they convert reform proposals into classroom action. Failure to do so will short-circuit the entire operation.

Teacher complacency, however, pales in comparison to the crisis of staff non-renewal that will traumatize the college system in the coming decade, regardless of what occurs to current reform proposals. Between now and 2004, over 40 per cent of Cegep personnel will be pensionable. This underscores the lack of staff movement characteristic of the college network. Hiring of regular full-time employees has been a luxury since the late 1970s. The increase in student population from the 1980s on did not necessarily result in concomitant increases in staffing. Moreover, negotiated labour agreements focused on seniority rights with respect to job retention, which, in practice, led to the elimination of the last-hired (whom, as one would expect, were usually the youngest and most up-to-date). Promoters of the college system point to the wealth of experience that such agreements provide; others point to their shortsightedness (LeBlanc 1992; Corriveau 1991).

The crisis of staff non-renewal does not stop at the classroom; it also seriously affects the administrative ranks, where a countdown to retirement is under way. The overall issue was raised in the original position paper that the minister prepared before the parliamentary commission sat (Québec 1993a), but it slipped from view with the tabling of reform proposals. Was the intention to bring it forward at a later point? This remains to be seen. The reform agenda (supposedly in place at least until 1997) suggests that there is a good chance that appropriate planning will not take place; that the wealth of experience that presently exists will not be transmitted; that the erosion of collegiality will continue; and that a new generation of college teachers and administrators, without experience or training, will appear overnight. In other words, a personpower strategy for the colleges is sadly lacking, and this is most distressing.

It seems that little has been assimilated from the massive overhaul that took place when the college system came on-line in the late 1960s. Over the years, there has been much talk but little concrete action regarding the formal task of preparing new personnel to deal with college administrative and teaching assignments. To this day, those without experience and/or training are figuratively dropped into deep water without a life preserver. Professional support is shoddy at best, and meaningful evaluation and feedback is a rare experience. Advanced training programs in the universities of Québec simply do not measure up to the requirements of the college sector. Also, one must consider the competency-based approach to education that is coming on line. On paper it sounds great, but from where is the expertise to come? Assuredly, there is a link missing.

Concluding Comments

With a quarter of a century of experience under its belt, with a proven record of survival within a context of compromise and contradiction, and with a reaffirmation of its strategic importance to the development of the province of Québec cast in stone (until the next enquiry!), the Cegeps are resolutely set to confront the future. The challenge that awaits the college network is formidable, as is the spirit that has animated its short history. The coming half-decade will tell the tale.

New Brunswick

Introduction

Of all community college structures in Canada, New Brunswick's is closest to being a system, in the strict sense of the term. Consistent with its designation as Canada's only formally bilingual province, the nine campuses of the New Brunswick Community College (NBCC) are comprised of five anglophone (Saint John, Moncton, Miramichi, Woodstock, and St Andrews) and four francophone (Dieppe, Bathurst, Campbellton, and Edmundston) institutions, although all offer community education courses in both languages. Each campus operates under the direct aegis of the Department of Advanced Education and Labour (DAEL), an arrangement which places the latter's deputy minister as the de facto CEO responsible for setting an overall policy emphasizing cohesion and system-wide planning. DAEL also assumes responsibility for all other components of postsecondary education in the province, including five diploma-granting schools of nursing and the universities.

Although, by Canadian standards, a relatively small administrative unit for postsecondary education, DAEL involves itself in a variety of planning and management exercises. For example, each year the department conducts an environmental scan in three major areas, education, socio-demographics, and business-economics. The results guide policy changes which are sensitive to the fluctuating needs of the province. In addition, a number of performance indicators (e.g., applications, enrolments, human resources, labour market outcomes) are utilized systematically in order to evaluate DAEL's performance. DAEL's educational mandate is expressed as follows: '[It] is responsible for providing human resource development opportunities for New Brunswickers. This entails offering, coordinating and assigning to others all publicly funded education and training programs designed to serve the adults of New Brunswick' (New Brunswick 1991:1).

The nine campuses of NBCC form the delivery arm of the department's services and individually administer programs in pre-employment training with respect to trade, technical, and technology levels, along with literacy and upgrading courses as well as a variety of part-time, short-term credit and credit-free activities. The NBCC also has responsibility for provincial apprenticeship programs and, in partnership with other agencies (including the federal government), has implemented a number of job-training strategies. These include: Youth Strategy, a program for unemployed people between the ages of 15 and 24; NB Works, which provides training and work experience for unemployment insurance (UI) recipients; the Community Academic Services Programme, a community-based initiative to deliver literacy training (for which the college provides coordination and curriculum materials); and the Distance Education Network (now TéléEducation NB), which has over twenty distance education centres throughout the province.

Assessment of Performance

DAEL initiates a number of surveys designed to assess how effectively college programs meet the needs of their stakeholder groups. *The Community College Graduate Follow-Up Study Report* (New Brunswick 1992a) involved the interviewing of 1,737 graduates, which constituted 87 per cent of the graduate population. The results indicated that employment levels had dropped to 66 per cent, the lowest in the past five years (this was largely attributable to the economic recession). Females enjoyed higher employment rates than did males. Graduates were highly positive in their evaluation of program content (92 per cent favourable) and quality of instruction (87 per cent favourable). However, they were less complimentary with regard to counselling services (63 per cent favourable) and library services (65 per cent favourable). Similar results were obtained from part-time clients in a 1990 survey.

Another indicator of performance is the rate of student retention in regular programs. A series of studies since 1986 indicate that between 70 per cent and 75 per cent of students complete these programs successfully (although most of the unsuccessful candidates withdrew rather than failed). Yet another important source of NBCC assessment is the general public. In 1989, DAEL conducted a telephone poll to determine public opinion regarding the quality of education in the province (including accessibility to programs and future training needs). The results showed that community colleges received the highest ranking with respect to quality, were viewed as geographically accessible, and were perceived as well able to accommodate training needs (New Brunswick 1990).

Finally, another measure of accountability utilized in New Brunswick is a study of program performance conducted by the Labour Market Analysis Branch of DAEL (New Brunswick 1992b). Using five specific indicators (applications, enrolments, program completions, and two measures of graduate employment), this study examined program data over the previous five years and produced a list of programs having unsatisfactory performances.

To Live and Learn: The Challenge of Education and Training

Perhaps the most significant influence in determining the future of the NBCC will be the report of the Commission on Excellence in Education. The commission surveyed all levels of the educational and training structures in the province and recommended a number of important changes. Its second report, *To Live and Learn: The Challenge of Education and Training*

(New Brunswick 1993), was addressed primarily to the postsecondary sector, and the community colleges received a great deal of attention.

With respect to the colleges, *To Live and Learn* drew attention to the apparent contradiction of an organization, centrally controlled and administrated, attempting to function in an environment in which it was expected 'to mount temporary programs on short notice and to make decisions in shorter time-frames than characterize many of the management processes in the school and university sector' (p. 40). Furthermore, in spite of the use of 'community' in its title, New Brunswick's college provides little opportunity for local public input into its governance structures and, hence, suffers from the lack of lay leadership enjoyed by schools and universities. Even the campus administrators do not serve on the management team, which is mostly staffed by personnel from DAEL.

In reaction to these concerns, the commission recommended that the college operate as a Crown corporation. It believed that, in time, this would bring the NBCC certain advantages (such as facilitating broader representation of public interest in the management of a public enterprise), and which would remove centralized control (which limited innovation and timely decisionmaking). The corporation should be governed by a broadly representative board of directors from major stakeholder groups, including the general public. Each campus of the college would have an advisory board, and the principal would have responsibility for making decisions regarding course delivery, curriculum, and contract training.

A second major concern raised by the Commission on Excellence in Education was accessibility. Commenting upon enrolment statistics, *To Live and Learn* noted that, while enrolment as a percentage of the 18 to 24 age group had almost doubled in the university sector of the province since 1975, enrolment in colleges had stayed essentially the same. Furthermore, participation in the NBCC was considerably lower than it was in its counterparts in other provinces. Participation of high-school graduates was particularly low. It was apparent that the number of places provided in the college was well short of those needed, and that efforts were needed to increase capacity. Strategies suggested included the expansion of distance education, year-round operation, greater part-time student access to regular programs, and expansion of cooperative education.

In its extensive review of the college system, the commission also recommended action respecting the transfer of credit, tuition fee policy, improvement of plants and facilities, the apprenticeship system, and the literacy issue (noting that 115,000 people in New Brunswick had not completed Grade 9). In all, *To Live and Learn* provided a comprehensive analysis of the NBCC and offered a number of constructive, some might say even radical, recommendations.

Implementation

Within two months after the publication of *To Live and Learn,* the minister of advanced education and labour responded. Noting the importance of NBCC in the economic future of the province, the minister announced a number of initiatives. Four hundred additional places would be provided immediately (including 200 for high-school graduates); admission to all regular programs, except for those dealing with upgrading, would require a Grade 12 diploma or equivalent; the NBCC would be established as a special operating agency (rather than as a Crown corporation) within the Department of Advanced Education and Labour.

With respect to distance education, it was announced that action was imminent. The New Brunswick Distance Education Network will be established and allocated $10.5 million over five years. The network will include twelve distance education centres located throughout the province. Reference was also made to most of the other recommendations in the commission's report. For example, it was evident that the minister supported the commission's view that greater investment in training was to be expected from the private sector and that a separate private training industry development office was to be funded immediately in order to expedite activity in that area.

Concluding Comments

Given the uniquely centralized nature of the NBCC, there is little difficulty in initiating a lively debate as to its wisdom, effectiveness, and efficiency. In its original 1974 design, the college existed as a provincial corporate body with board members and a permanent chair. Furthermore, each of the five regions served sought advice from a lay advisory board. Since that time, the trend of organizational change has been towards a bureaucratic government structure with little or no provision for external advice.

There is no denying that the present model places a high priority upon clarification of mandate and functional efficiency. Core programs exist in each campus, and specialized programs are limited in order to avoid duplication and to lead to centres of excellence where there is an optimal use of faculty and resources. Moreover, the province has been most active in responding to the short-term training needs of its adult population, primarily through contract training. Community education, while responsive to local needs, is restricted by its budget. Central management leads to the effective use of resources, both human and material, and to the efficient application of the overall budget. New Brunswick is not blessed with large fiscal resources, and its budget must be carefully administered. Another factor which deserves to be recognized is New Brunswick's commitment to providing equitable services in both official languages. In the college sector, the current organization has contributed to the realization of that goal.

Having said all this, it is equally important to note that the classical concept of the community college emphasizes increased access (particularly for disadvantaged groups), flexibility and responsiveness vis-à-vis changing clienteles, sensitivity to regional and community needs, and a public image which evokes values such as relative autonomy and an orientation to the needs of students of all backgrounds. The NBCC does not appear to meet these criteria. Furthermore, as noted in *To Live and Learn*, the college has difficulty responding to a changing environment – an environment in which the essential ingredients for success include entrepreneurship, flexibility, and a decisionmaking process which involves those whom it will most affect.

As in all debates of this nature, evaluation, in the formal sense of weighing advantages and disadvantages, remains a challenging task. It would be as inappropriate, for example, to impose an Alberta college model upon New Brunswick as it would to do the reverse. New Brunswick's educational history, its linguistic duality, its population, and, above all, the economic character of its workforce all require a specific college structure. Whether the best possible model has been chosen remains a subject of debate.

With respect to the professional development of the faculty and administration, important initiatives have taken place in recent years. A comprehensive assessment of the career plans of all employees has been conducted (New Brunswick 1992b). Recent agreements between the Department of Advanced Education and Labour and the universities of Moncton and New Brunswick have provided the instructional staff with opportunities for advanced education in instructional skills, communications, and adult education. Nevertheless, constraints regarding the participation of personnel in out-of-province professional activities have limited their opportunities to share ideas with their counterparts in other jurisdictions.

It must be acknowledged that the attention given to accountability regarding the performance of the college system, the assessment of outcomes, and the gathering of input from graduates and the wider community is more sophisticated and comprehensive in New Brunswick than it is in many other provincial systems. Undoubtedly, the centralized departmental structure has contributed to this important activity.

In conclusion, the NBCC is about to enter a new phase of development. Its performance to this date has evoked mixed reviews. While its services are regarded highly, accessibility remains a problem, as does public image. Both the recent commission's critical analysis and the urgency of the official government response suggests that the community college is regarded as an essential component in the economic future of the province. The potential for reform is evident; the outcomes will be critical.

Nova Scotia

Introduction

Prior to 1988, Nova Scotia remained the only jurisdiction in Canada which had not instituted, in the formal sense of the term, a community college system. Notwithstanding this observation, however, it must be acknowledged that many of the programs, services, and functions which are normally associated with a community college have been available for some time in a variety of tertiary institutions in Nova Scotia. With regard to postsecondary education, Nova Scotians have long been well served. Before 1988, in addition to its thirteen degree-granting institutions, the non-university sector included thirteen regional vocational schools (which accommodated both high-school students and adults), two adult vocational training centres, an institute of technology, a nautical institute, and a college of geographic sciences. Even within the degree-granting sector (notably, the University College of Cape Breton), certain programs were offered which, in other provinces, would fall under the community college umbrella.

In light of Nova Scotia's historical commitment to education beyond the secondary level, it is not surprising that it did not follow other provinces in creating a community college system. However, in 1986, the Community College Study Committee was appointed by the minister of education. Cognizant of changes in both the workplace and in education brought about by technological advances and economic restructuring, the committee was charged with exploring the need for utilizing the community college model of education and training as a means of addressing the future needs of the people of Nova Scotia. More specifically, governmental expectations were summarized in the Throne Speech of that year. In considering the college idea, attention was to be given to

- making the system operational throughout the year
- making courses of study and training available on a modular basis
- enhancing cooperative work experience, education, and training opportunities
- developing a tiered approach to training so that the student may move from vocational to technical to university education.

The work of the committee entailed two years of consultation, debate, public hearings, briefs, and submissions. In the process, an issues paper and a Green Paper were circulated as a means of stimulating additional responses. Ultimately, *Foundation for the Future: A White Paper on a Community College System for Nova Scotians* (Nova Scotia 1988) was published in February 1988; it became the blueprint for the reorganization of non-university education in the province.

Foundation for the Future: A White Paper on a Community College System for Nova Scotians

The primary theme of this White Paper was the provision of adult learning to a broad spectrum of society. Through implementing a more flexible delivery system, all Nova Scotians beyond high-school age would have continuing access to various levels of education and training. Colleges would offer academic upgrading; technical, trades, and vocational training; applied arts; and community education. Furthermore, university credit courses would be available on college campuses under a brokered arrangement.

The proposed organizational plan for the college system involved converting the current non-university institutions into seven colleges, six of which would be regional and anglophone and one of which would be provincial and francophone. Each college was to have a governing board which was to include both community and institutional representatives. A province-wide advisory board was to advise the minister of education on policy relating to the college system. Other topics raised in the White Paper included a provision for setting uniform province-wide standards for comparable programs and a recommendation that distance education be explored and expanded as a form of course delivery. One other reference of note was to the implementation of a plan for the development of human resources (particularly vocational instructors, who would work in the new community college environment). The White Paper made special reference to the need to accommodate certain target groups in the community – groups for whom conventional educational services had been limited. These included persons with disabilities, those requiring occupational training in French, women in non-traditional trades, and programs for visible minorities and the Micmac.

The Nova Scotia Community College

While the educational plan may have been viewed as progressive, and while support may have been widespread, subsequent implementation of the proposals in the White Paper was exceedingly slow and, in several respects, unrealized. The Nova Scotia Community College was formally established in 1988, but not quite in the form outlined in the White Paper. In all, eighteen separate campuses were created, essentially by altering the original designation of the regional vocational schools, training centres, and specialized institutions. In addition, a provincially based open learning institution, the Collège de l'Acadie, was established for the francophone community. The latter, obtaining 50 per cent of its funding from federal sources, now operates out of six learning centres and utilizes a variety of educational technologies.

The White Paper proposal to establish six regional colleges with individual governing boards was not implemented. Policy determination and general management of the multicampus college became the responsibility of a CEO, who was to report directly to the Department of Education. In fact, the previous Department of Advanced Education and Job Training was merged with the Department of Education in 1992 to create a common bureaucratic structure which was to manage the education system from Halifax.

One immediate problem resulting from the conversion of regional vocational schools to community college campuses was the dislocation of high-school age students who had previously participated in programs at the former. The secondary schools were expected to absorb such students, even though the attendant space and cost pressures were disconcertingly obvious to the boards of school trustees. Conversely, it was anticipated that if the new college campuses were restricted to adult learners, then this would broaden their appeal for those seeking job-entry training, academic upgrading, and literacy training either under their own initiative or under the sponsorship of Employment and Immigration Canada (EIC), the Workers' Compensation Board (WCB), or Community Services. Various forms of curriculum reorganization were instituted in order to accommodate the new college mandate. For the first time, student tuition fees were introduced as a way of supplementing the college budget.

Another initiative undertaken by the community college was the development of customized programs to meet the needs of both public- and private-sector organizations. Apart from being revenue-generating, these programs establish strong links between colleges and their communities.

Assessment of Performance

Although Nova Scotia Community College (NSCC) did not formally exist until 1988, a series of studies designed to measure placement rates for graduates from all occupational programs had been going on for some years. In 1991, a report entitled *The Community College Graduate Follow-Up Study: A Five-Year Summary* (Nova Scotia 1991) revealed that, in the period between 1985 and 1989, overall graduate employment rates ranged from 75 per cent to 80 per cent (although this varied widely by program). Out of over 15,000 graduates, 72 per cent responded to the follow-up study. A similar report published in 1992 indicated that, among all graduates from 1991, 51.5 per cent were employed in fields related to their training and 18.6 per cent were employed in unrelated fields (Nova Scotia 1992a).

Of further interest are the deliberations of two separate task forces. The first, *Report of the Committee on Training in the Apprenticeable Trades in the*

Nova Scotia Community College (Nova Scotia 1990), looked at training in the apprenticeship trades and, among other issues, recommended major changes in student assessment, curriculum, modular delivery of courses, and program quality. The second, *Report of Nova Scotia Community College System: Visible Minority Access* (Nova Scotia 1992b), examined problems of access to the college by visible minorities and produced several recommendations. These included: a race relations policy for NSCC, initiatives at the college level to recruit and support minority students, training to enable counsellors and other personnel to be more sensitive to the special needs of minorities, and curricula reform to reflect cultural relevance.

Concluding Comments

The story of community college development in Nova Scotia over the past six years has been one of renewed energy, productive ideas, and high hopes – ending in disappointment. Inevitably, the timing of new initiatives in postsecondary education is critical; and, in the economic downturn of the early 1990s, the government is not usually enthusiastic about the expansion of social programs and what that implies for the provincial budget. Unlike the golden years of educational development in the 1970s, public policy issues such as health and social services tend to dominate the political agenda in 1993. While there is general recognition of the potential contribution of education and training to economic regeneration, the concept of quasi-autonomous institutions, with seemingly unlimited aspirations to expand their services, raises government concern, particularly for those having operating deficits. In large part, this has been the case in Nova Scotia.

Nevertheless, there has been action. The NSCC exists in both form and function. By 1993, the eighteen campuses enrolled 7,000 full-time and 8,600 part-time students. The appeal of college services is reflected in the growing demand for seats in programs. College campuses are becoming increasingly integrated with their communities (Nova Scotia Community College 1992), and programming is moving from basic vocational to higher technical levels in response to the perceived demand for advanced skills in the workplace.

Under the direction of the CEO, the committees of principals from the various campuses have initiated several projects which complement NSCC's long-range plan. A mission statement is being articulated, a program approval and review process is being developed, and a province-wide calendar is being produced. Distance education is also being expanded, with the installation of Network Nova Scotia outlets at each campus. Although credit transfer agreements with universities are currently limited, there are a number of bilateral arrangements, primarily in business programs, whereby college graduates may receive credit on transferring from a college to a university. Furthermore, through partnerships, the college maintains close links with business and industry, and this leads to cooperative education and work placement.

However, developing the community college concept of education requires more than simply changing the signs on buildings. The transition from a school to a college involves adopting a new set of management priorities. Professional development at both the administrative and instructional level becomes a primary goal. Action is essential to raising public image; harnessing community and regional input and support; liaising with schools, universities, and private-sector organizations; and documenting quality of services. Even the broader issue of labour relations must be addressed; college instructors are expected to become more closely involved in policymaking in areas consistent with their expertise. Such involvement is somewhat of a departure from the methods of the centralized teacher's union, under which vocational school instructors in Nova Scotia have been organized.

The newly constituted NSCC is not short of challenges, and, in an uncertain fiscal climate, these assume even greater importance. Nevertheless, there is also much more opportunity for entrepreneurship in the area of revenue generation under the NSCC than there was under the previous structure. A recent change in government from Conservative to Liberal has given a new impetus to the college. A program rationalization and assessment process, which began in 1993, will make the campuses more responsive to labour market needs. There is also an indication that the NSCC will soon become a more independent agency, and this will result in its achieving greater visibility and a status more comparable with that of the university sector. After a long period of uncertainty, the college seems about to enter a new era of development. Nova Scotia may have been the last province to enter the community college culture, but its future is nonetheless intriguing.

Prince Edward Island

In Prince Edward Island (PEI), Holland College is the only non-university institution. Consequently, the development of policy and administration in PEI's college sector remains the responsibility of the Board of Governors of this particular college. This arrangement is free from many of the complexities found in larger provinces. Nevertheless, Holland College strives to meet the educational and training needs of all of PEI's population. Through a comprehensive galaxy of programs, courses, and other activities, the college provides educational and training services at thirteen separate campuses across PEI.

By the early 1990s, Holland College enrolled over 9,000 students, of which approximately one-third were involved in credit-free continuing education activities. Unlike the case in other provinces, enrolment in programs sponsored through CJS has increased significantly during the past three years. In addition, over 700 students are sponsored by EIC.

Of the college's approximately $22 million operating budget, a significant proportion is recommended to PEI by the Maritime Provinces Higher Education Commission (MPHEC). Holland College is the only provincial community college which is a member of MPHEC, and this tends to reinforce the regional focus of many of its programs. Another substantial portion of its budget is provided by the PEI Department of Education for the adult and high-school programs which it delivers. As noted later, Holland College's responsibility for high-school programs will end in 1995. A substantial portion of its budget is also generated through self-supporting programs and enterprises.

Governance of Holland College is the responsibility of a sixteen-member board, the composition of which, in comparison to that of most other provinces, is unusual. It includes three members from the business and industrial sector, three members appointed from government departments (or members which are also teachers employed by a regional school board), and two faculty and two students, each of whom is elected by his/her respective peers. There are also four members-at-large nominated by the college. The presidents of both the college and the university are also voting members of the board. According to the Holland College Act, 1988, the college is 'to provide a broad range of educational opportunity particularly in the field of applied arts and technology, vocational training and adult education' (pp. 3-4).

While change in postsecondary education in PEI since 1986 has been less dramatic than has been the case in some other provinces, there are a number of events and policy initiatives which deserve comment. One area of particular interest is vocational education. From 1969 to 1975, Holland College's programs were largely confined to those which required Grade 12 graduation. In 1975, a major change occurred when an entire range of pre-postsecondary curricula, including high-school vocational, trades, apprenticeship, adult upgrading, and the programs which had been offered in two provincial training centres (Prince County Vocational Institute and the Provincial Vocational Institute), were removed from the Department of Education and placed under the aegis of Holland College. The reason for this policy change was both practical (the college had the necessary facilities to accommodate these programs) and administrative (the Department of Education wanted to be relieved of responsibility) (Glendenning and Hall 1988:33-4). The resulting clientele included a large number of students who would not have met the conventional definition of 'postsecondary.'

The Report on Vocational Education

In 1988, a report commissioned by the Department of Education, entitled *Some New Directions: Vocational Education on Prince Edward Island* (Glendenning and Hall 1988), offered a number of recommendations regarding both vocational and adult education in the province. The major thrust of the report was that vocational education must be revitalized, that it should be integrated with academic courses in high schools, and that all secondary students should take a career-exploration program. Furthermore, it was recommended that vocational education at the high-school level be returned to the schools, leaving Holland College to concentrate on more specialized postsecondary-level programs.

With regard to adult education, the same report emphasized that the concept of adult education, to be consistent with the idea of lifelong learning, should be interpreted to include skill-training, bridging programs, and programs designed for personal development. An important implication arising from this point of view was that the term 'postsecondary education' should be redefined to include all learners registered in courses or programs other than those at elementary or secondary schools. Clearly, the intent of the recommendation was that adult education be fully integrated into the concept of lifelong learning. To this end, the report directed responsibility for policy and delivery of adult education to the Ministry of Education – even to the extent of creating a separate Division of Advanced Education. Programs funded through EIC, and those offered by Holland College, were to be coordinated through this new authority. While no action was taken with respect to this recommendation, it reappeared in a slightly different form in *Education: A Shared Responsibility,* the 1992 report of the PEI Task Force on Education (Prince Edward Island Task Force on Education 1992).

Vision 2000: A Long Range Strategic Plan

In 1989, after two years in preparation, Holland College produced a long-range strategic plan, entitled *Vision 2000*, which documented a consensus among stakeholders as to what direction it should take in the future (Holland College 1989). The plan included a restatement of Holland College's commitment to serving the educational and training needs of all segments of the population, and its educational role is summarized in Figure 1.1. The plan enunciated each of the three elements of the college (i.e., educational excellence, program services, and support services) which would contribute to the realization of its mandate and, in every case, provided a set of ideals and goals by which to guide future decisionmaking.

Figure 1.1

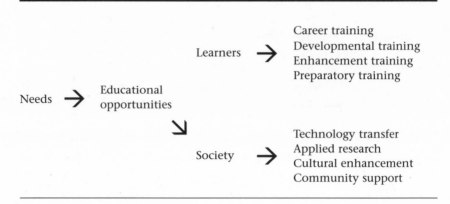

Vision 2000 was then followed by a detailed, three-year operational plan to cover the years between 1990 and 1993 (Holland College 1990c). This plan documented the activities to be carried out by each administrative and program unit in the college, together with a three-year timetable for implementation.

Concluding Comments

Among Canada's community colleges, Holland College continues to enjoy a number of unique advantages. As PEI's sole non-university institution of postsecondary education, it is able to plan and coordinate all the programs delivered through its multicampus organization. Leadership has been stable and sustained (it has had just three presidents in its twenty-four-year history). It also maintains strong links with government departments (both federal and provincial) and with industry.

The mission of Holland College is as follows: 'Dedicated to excellence in performance, Holland College stands committed to providing quality life-long learning opportunities to support learner, industry and community development' (Holland College 1990a). Another unique feature of the college is its competency-based curriculum development and instructional model (DACUM), which it has maintained since its inception. This technique has given the college an international reputation and has made it an object of study for numerous public- and private-sector agencies. Relevance of instruction is maintained through continuous interaction with industries, which hire its graduates.

With respect to programs, Holland College offers four major categories: (1) regional (Atlantic Police Academy, Culinary Institute), (2) provincial, (3) adult vocational and college preparation, and (4) customized training.

Constant efforts are made to develop appropriate new program options. The Electromechanical Department recently issued Canada's first training warranty – if the calibre of its graduates is not acceptable, they will be retrained at the college's expense.

One aspect of Holland College's performance which has not materialized is its association with the province's only university, the University of Prince Edward Island (UPEI). Although the presidents of each institution sit on each other's governing board, there appears to be little in the way of credit transfer or program articulation between them. Given that students need to upgrade their credentials and to pursue advanced training, it is surprising that opportunities in this regard are so limited in PEI.

Many of Holland College's future goals and objectives are dependent upon its obtaining adequate funding. As with other provinces, the fiscal health of PEI is doubtful, and the continuing extent of government support for higher education is uncertain. The college is pursuing an entrepreneurial approach to attracting new sources of funds. Contracts with public and private agencies (regional, national, and international) offer many excellent funding opportunities. Experience in other regions, however, suggests that an institution's priorities and activities need to be carefully monitored in order to ensure that the critical task of serving the needs of its immediate community is not undervalued. In addition to income-generation activities, program offerings are under review, with possible amalgamations of some areas and possible deletions of others, as the college attempts to reduce its budget.

There is every indication that Holland College will continue to evolve as new opportunities present themselves and as some established programs become less relevant or less central to its primary mission. For example, the discontinuation of the Canadian Armed Forces Base in Summerside has resulted in the availability of an excellent facility in which to develop new college programs. The college has moved its School of Justice to that site and is investigating other possibilities, such as an aerospace training centre. A gas turbine maintenance course also began on the former base in January 1994.

Since it was launched in 1984, the Holland College Foundation has accumulated more than $500,000 in its Scholarship and Bursary Fund and has acquired considerable equipment as gifts-in-kind. In 1992, the foundation launched Partners in Value, a capital campaign with a goal of $5 million. Holland College is also uniquely placed to expand its links with industry, to capitalize upon new federal government initiatives, and to become a regional centre for selected aspects of education and training in Atlantic Canada. In the words of its former president:

With our dedication to performance-based education, life-long learning, and excellence in education, the College will meet the challenges of the future. Although pressures for accountability will increase, new initiatives and management procedure will ensure the College has the necessary resources to continue to provide quality life-long training. (Holland College 1990a:1)

Newfoundland

Introduction

In 1986, Newfoundland's postsecondary system underwent a major re-organization. Up to that time, five institutions, Memorial University, two institutes of technology in St John's (the College of Fisheries and the College of Trades and Technology), Bay St George Community College in Stephenville, and the system of vocational schools comprised the full spectrum of postsecondary education. Given the difficulties created by a widely dispersed population and a fragile economy highly dependent upon natural resource exploitation, the level of participation in postsecondary education (at that time, approximately 20 per cent of the 18- to 24-year-old age group) fell well short of the Canadian average.

Fully cognizant of the need to invest in human capital, and recognizing that future economic vitality was heavily dependent upon a well-trained and well-educated workforce, the government of the time proposed an expanded and diversified tertiary education sector. The new system consisted of the addition of five multicampus community colleges (Labrador, Western Newfoundland, Central Newfoundland, Eastern Newfoundland, and Avalon Colleges of Applied Arts, Technology, and Continuing Studies) created from the former vocational schools and Bay St George Community College, an expanded campus of Memorial University in Corner Brook, and another technical institute (Fisher Institute of Trades and Technology) on the west coast. The College of Fisheries and the Newfoundland College of Trades and Technology in St John's were renamed the Institute of Fisheries and Marine Technology and the Cabot Institute, respectively.

Expansion of the college system was forged through policy provisions which clarified the mandates under which each institution would operate. The three institutes of technology, for example, were to offer two- and three-year diploma programs in appropriate areas and were to conduct applied research. The community college mandate was to be restricted to programs of one year or less, together with community-responsive short-term and part-time training opportunities.

By 1990, expansion of the college system had translated into considerable growth in both number of students and rate of participation. While the greatest increase occurred in the university, the colleges attracted a diverse student population. Many of these students were returning to formal education after a long absence. Part of the reason for the increase in university enrolment was a policy decision to offer first-year courses in the colleges. These students were then counted as part of Memorial's population.

Meanwhile, a change of government from Conservative to Liberal brought with it a new minister of education, Phillip Warren, a university professor with a long and extensive interest in postsecondary education. The separate Ministry of Career Development and Advanced Studies was incorporated with the Ministry of Education, although an Advanced Studies Branch was assigned responsibility for the tertiary sector. Under Warren's direction, a White Paper was prepared, which provided both an assessment of the performance of the college system and an agenda for its future.

The 1990 White Paper on Postsecondary Education
The White Paper acknowledged the growth which had occurred since reorganization but noted that limitations on space and funding had prevented the realization of some institutional mandates. Reference was also made to the challenges which continue to confront the system: 'A critical aspect of future educational strategies will be to respond to the under-education and illiteracy problems so that the labour force becomes retrainable and can adapt to the ever changing cycles of the economy' (Newfoundland 1990a:8).

The agenda for the future was contained within an overall policy framework which emphasized three major principles: (1) equality, (2) excellence, and (3) efficiency. Each of these principles was to be realized through specific strategies. Equality was to be achieved by increasing access to traditionally underrepresented groups, creating a wider geographic dispersal of educational opportunities, and creating greater flexibility in the delivery of instructional and student services. To this end, another campus of Memorial University was to be built in central Newfoundland; the university's campus in Corner Brook would be upgraded to a four-year institution, offering degrees in arts, sciences, and fine arts; non-university diploma programs were to be similar in their first year, thus allowing some transfer of credit to Memorial University (this initiative would provide opportunities for students to change programs without extensive loss of credit); specific community college campuses in Labrador, central, and eastern Newfoundland would continue to offer first-year university credits; the mandate distinction between institutes of applied arts and technology and colleges would be eliminated, allowing the latter to develop diploma programs where appropriate; and greater emphasis would be placed on part-time, ABE, and literacy programs.

The principle of excellence would be given major attention through high-quality teaching, leading-edge curricula, flexible delivery of courses, upgrading of the qualifications of teaching faculty, and ongoing assessments of the skills of graduates. Specific initiatives in this regard included placing a priority upon providing advisory and counselling services to students and upgrading or expanding the learning resources available throughout the college system. Finally, greater collaboration was encouraged between regional enterprise centres and public agencies in order to provide maximum development of human resources.

With respect to the principle of efficiency, the challenge was to extend access and to attain excellence in a cost-effective manner so that there would be a reduction in duplication of services and a maximal utilization of available resources – not an easy goal. Initiatives were based on the establishment of a two-tiered postsecondary system, consisting of Memorial University and five colleges of applied arts, technology, and continuing education. The Cabot Institute was amalgamated with the three campuses of Avalon Community College in order to produce a single, comprehensive, non-university institution for St John's; a formal affiliation was established between the Institute of Fisheries and Marine Technology and Memorial University; a single institution was created on the west coast, incorporating the Western Newfoundland Community College and the Fisher Institute of Trades and Technology; and the remaining campuses of the former Avalon Community College were combined with the Eastern Newfoundland Community College to form a single institution for eastern Newfoundland. Other measures of efficiency included the contribution of postsecondary education to the economy and evidence that a reasonable balance existed between the supply of, and the demand for, graduates in specific occupations.

The White Paper was widely distributed, and responses from the community were both requested and received. In particular, the idea of planning and implementing a province-wide system of credit transfer received wide approval. The general view was that virtually all new initiatives should proceed, with the exception of the construction of the proposed university campus in central Newfoundland (which was to be delayed due to the economic state of the province).

Shaping Our Future: A Five-Year Strategic Plan for the Postsecondary Education System in Newfoundland and Labrador

In June 1990, the Department of Education circulated a five-year strategic plan for the postsecondary education system (Newfoundland 1990c). Designed to cover the period between 1990 and 1995, the plan was comprehensive and detailed. It contained a mandate, a mission, an extensive analysis of the planning environment, a list of strategic priorities and issues in postsecondary education, and an account of funding. While making it clear that human resources development was the primary public policy issue, the report emphasized that the public sector must recognize its declining fiscal ability to provide the resources necessary to accomplish this goal, and that more must be done through the private sector.

The essence of the plan, entitled *Shaping Our Future: A Five-Year Strategic Plan for the Postsecondary Education System in Newfoundland and Labrador,* was reflected in the statement of its mission:

> It is the mission of the postsecondary education system to provide the high-est quality credit and non-credit life-long learning opportunities for the people of Newfoundland and Labrador through a commitment to the prin-ciples of equality, excellence and efficiency. Education and training efforts will respond to the needs of all sectors of society, will further the economic development strategy of the Province, and enable individuals to become productive and effective citizens. (Newfoundland 1990c:2)

The remainder of the plan was devoted to a detailed description of the part which each component of the public system would play in the provision of quality education and training, which was to be delivered in an accessible, flexible, and effective manner. While it was clear that each individual insti-tution, within its specific mandate, would be encouraged to plan programs in accord with community needs, this would be done in the context of the overall planning framework established by the Liberal government. The community colleges, under their new title of colleges of applied arts, tech-nology and continuing education, would have the flexibility to maintain programs appropriate to their respective locations and to the needs of their respective regions. For example, the first year of a degree program at Memo-rial University, or advanced two- and three-year technology programs, could become part of a college's offerings. All university programs throughout the province would remain under the aegis of Memorial University. Maximum transferability of credit would be ensured through common curriculum requirements.

Other initiatives which deserve recognition include references to coop-erative education, brokering of programs, and the role of the college sys-tem in labour force adjustment and economic development. In all, *Shap-ing Our Future* left little doubt as to the direction which Newfoundland's postsecondary institutions will be heading in the next five years. It also recognized the role of the private-training sector. The Department of Edu-cation, while acknowledging the growth in this sector, expressed its con-cern that quality programming and provincial standards be maintained.

To this end, private institutions in Newfoundland are regulated under the Private Training Institutions Act, 1988.

Concluding Comments

Together with the planning process, the government has conducted a major review of the legislation necessary to provide the legal authority for change. In addition to the Private Training Institutions Act, 1988, the legislature approved a new Department of Education Act, 1990, the Memorial University Act, 1990 (which was amended in 1991), and a revised Colleges Act, 1991. These acts indicate the intent and responsibility of implementing a coordinated system of postsecondary education specific to the needs of the province. For example, a unique feature of the governance structure of Newfoundland's colleges is that the president is appointed by the lieutenant-governor in council on the advice of the minister of education. All board members are similarly appointed, and they may include a representative from the Department of Education. The board also has one faculty and one student representative. The chairperson of the board is also named by the minister. The new legislation also makes it clear that the minister of education is responsible for reviewing, approving, and monitoring all courses offered by the colleges. The boards of governors, given corporate authority, set policy and evaluate the progress of their institutions.

Since 1986, policy and structural changes in Newfoundland's higher education sector have provided impressive evidence of government commitment to human resources development as a critical factor in economic recovery and labour force restructuring. As stated in Premier Wells's 1992 strategic economic plan:

> *Strategy Statement.* The Province will undertake initiatives to ensure that the education and training system is more responsive to changing labour market demands for a highly skilled, innovative and adaptable workforce. Special initiatives will be pursued which allow governments, business and labour to work together to improve the level and quality of education, training and re-training. (Newfoundland 1992:25)

Notwithstanding this optimistic assertion, there are certain caveats which the government has recognized and which merit comment. Newfoundland is a province of limited resources, both human and material. Many of the proposed reforms in the postsecondary sector carry considerable fiscal implications, and the ability of the province to provide the necessary resources will be critical. Furthermore, while comprehensive education and training programs have the capacity to produce a new cadre of well-prepared graduates, their futures will depend upon the ability of the economic sector to absorb them.

Finally, one new initiative which has potential for contributing to system-wide planning in Newfoundland is the Council on Higher Education (created in 1992). A joint venture of the Department of Education, Memorial University, and the colleges, the council is to become the locus for joint planning and coordination within the postsecondary sector and is to facilitate the transfer of credit between institutions. The council functions in an advisory capacity to the minister of education.

One of its first tasks was to establish a committee on transfer and admissions, modelled upon similar bodies in BC and Alberta. This committee has prepared an extensive set of principles and guidelines as the basis for a formal system-wide credit transfer policy. Articulation committees composed of representatives from business, engineering, applied arts, trades, health, and social sciences institutions will establish specific course and program equivalencies. While the council is just beginning its task, its formulation reflects a general concern in Canadian education for system-based arrangements which will allow students access to, and mobility among, all institutions as they pursue advanced credentials. This is one issue which continues to dominate discussions about the accountability and responsiveness of postsecondary education.

In comparison with other provinces, Newfoundland has made a remarkable commitment to the reform of postsecondary education. The government has adopted a proactive role with respect to planning and, through the Ministry of Education, has left little doubt as to how individual institutions are expected to respond. The system of postsecondary education in Newfoundland is designed to ensure maximum accessibility and responsiveness as well as the most efficient utilization of available resources. In so doing, it presents an arrangement falling somewhere between centralized authority and institutional autonomy. Thus, its organizational model differs somewhat from those being used in other provinces.

It is evident that, through the activities of a revitalized and reconstructed postsecondary education system, Newfoundland is determined to address the numerous problems created by illiteracy, economic instability, population dispersal, and a legacy of underdeveloped human resources. The next five years will reveal how successfully this system evolves.

Northwest Territories

The government of the Northwest Territories (NWT) faces the challenge of providing postsecondary education to a population of less than 50,000 people (over half of which are of First Nations descent), located in regions spanning over 3,000 miles, with an area equivalent to seven of the largest Canadian provinces. With a population embroiled in social, economic, and political change, the postsecondary system was required to be highly adaptable, innovative, and community-focused. The NWT consists of a mix of several small urban communities with an industrial and commercial economy (including a large public service) and widely scattered small settlements dependent on resource extraction, transportation, social services, and traditional economic activity.

The political aspirations of the Inuit of the Eastern Arctic and other aboriginal peoples resulted in the political division of the NWT. These divisions are expected to result in the creation of a second territory (known as Nunavut) in the Eastern Arctic by the year 2000. Each group and community was in need of adult education services, as a large proportion of the adult population had little secondary schooling. Much of the population could not participate in the economic changes, manage the effects of social dislocation, or effectively involve themselves in the political process. While a great deal of formal communication is transacted in several indigenous languages, written literacy and the command of English is a major concern.

The territorial government had been offering adult basic education and upgrading through Ministry of Education centres throughout the NWT prior to 1987. Arctic College (originally named Thebacha College) had been providing vocational, career/technical, and university transfer courses as well as contract training at the Fort Smith campus (or on an extension basis in other communities). Credit transfer arrangements with the University of Saskatchewan with respect to teacher education had also been established.

The decision, in the mid-1980s, to make Arctic College a fully comprehensive multicampus institution initiated a period of dramatic and continuous expansion of adult education services. The Arctic College Act, 1987, was among the most specific of any in Canada. It created a quasi-autonomous institution with a fourteen-member board consisting of regional, employee, and student representatives and with an ex officio seat held by the president. The senior administration officials (president and vice presidents) were appointed by the minister of education and are classified as public servants. The act is very specific in describing the board's responsibilities, including the nature of policies to be created. It designates where campuses should be located and how the student council should operate. The minister of education has authority over financial decisions in that he/she approves budgets and how they are disbursed. The college may seek other sources of revenue and enter into external contracts. Arctic College could be seen as a Crown corporation with a very broad mandate (which includes all adult education activities previously provided by other agencies).

Arctic College has seen explosive growth in the past six years. It now consists of six campuses, Thebacha (Fort Smith), Aurora (Inuvik), Keewatin (Rankin Inlet), Kitikmeot (Cambridge Bay), Nunatta (Iqaluit), and Yellowknife, together with over thirty-five community learning centres. The budget has doubled since 1986 to over $30 million in 1993. The college has over 200 full-time employees and an equal number of part-time/sessional faculty and staff serving 1,500 full-time students and 6,500 part-time students. The costs of delivering programs on a per-student basis in the North, especially under a decentralized model, are more than twice what they are in the South. At the present time, the costs per student on a full-time equivalent basis in Arctic College exceed $15,000.

Programs and Services of Arctic College
Since Arctic College assumed responsibility for ABE in 1987, it has become the largest program, accounting for over 40 per cent of the college's full-time students. Recently, the college completed a two-year initiative to develop an ABE curriculum and to provide a consistent, integrated approach to upgrading in the North. It is offered at all the community learning centres and is designed primarily to prepare students for further education. In 1992, the college won the Association of Canadian Community Colleges (ACCC) Partnership Award for its N'dilo, Literacy/Native Studies Programme. The college has also been recognized for its skill in forming business-education partnerships, winning the 1991 national award for business management training delivered in partnership with Inuit organizations. All of the programs are designed to address employment requirements specific to the North. In all cases, consideration of cultural and linguistic diversity is provided (e.g., teacher training programs which prepare teachers in their respective aboriginal languages and jewellery and art programs which reflect indigenous traditions). Programs focusing, for example, on how to operate heavy equipment, airport observer training, and renewable resources are designed to meet regional needs. The college has linked several of its diploma programs to universities in order to allow students to seek further education if they so wish. Arctic College provides over 40 per cent of its full- and part-time enrolments in off-campus locations, thereby providing access to a widely dispersed population. Use of distance delivery technology is in the early stages of implementation.

Arctic College has documented its program completions and job placement statistics. The completion average in 1992-3 was 68 per cent of those enrolled. Graduate job placements ranged from 70 per cent to 90 per cent, depending on the type of program. Arctic College is maturing in a rapidly expanding period of growth. Few colleges have had to accommodate a 30 per cent enrolment increase in each of the past three years. The importance of the college with respect to community and social development becomes evident when it is realized that it represents the only adult learning system in the NWT. With consistent, responsive funding support from the territorial government, and with increasing revenue from its contracting services, this institution enjoys reasonable fiscal support. In spite of the magnitude of the challenge created by environmental factors, there seems to be an abundance of the organizational energy and creativity so essential to its future success.

Further changes to the territorial college system are now being planned, and two significant initiatives are currently under way. The first is the amalgamation of Arctic College with the Science Institute of the Northwest Territories. This will expand the college's role to include increased responsibility for science- and technology-related activities across the North as well as functioning to improve links between northern educational offerings and southern-based researchers and research-related institutions. The second initiative will result in the division of Arctic College into two institutions. The creation of two colleges is a proactive initiative in preparation for territorial division.

The formal establishment of two separate colleges took place on 1 July 1994. As of that date, Eastern College began operating from its major campus in Iqaluit, while Western College opened in Fort Smith. Each college has three campuses and a number of community learning centres. Both are corporations directed by boards of governors, but provision has been made for students to transfer credits from one to the other. This coordination process is facilitated through the Colleges and Continuing Education Division of the Department of Education, Culture and Employment.

Yukon Territory

Although the formal establishment of Yukon College did not occur until 1988, it had been evolving as a postsecondary educational institution since its creation as the Whitehorse Vocational Training Centre in 1963. Its history has been a process of gradually meeting the needs of a unique territorial population. In reality, there are two populations: (1) the non-aboriginal (78 per cent), which is generally well educated, highly paid, urban, and mobile and (2) the aboriginal, which is poorly educated, unemployed, rural, and immobile (Statistics Canada, cited in Senkpiel 1993).

In March 1987, a consultant's report commissioned by the territorial government noted that Yukoners do not have the 'option to stay' in the territory, as lack of educational opportunities may force them to leave (Orlikow 1986). The report made several recommendations for the college, arguing strongly for its continuing development as an autonomous institution emphasizing community-based responsibilities and activities.

As a consequence, the College Act, 1988, reflects the particular character of the Yukon's geography, settlement patterns, and social and economic development issues. The act contains standard provisions for a board of governors, which would have powers similar to those of other colleges. But this act recognizes the Yukon's enormous need for higher education and community development. The twelve-member board is composed of at least three representatives of First Nations peoples, three representatives of community campus committees (groups advisory to rural college centres), an employee representative, a student representative, and the college president. The commissioner of the territory designates the board chairperson. Other features of the legislation which created Yukon College as a corporate entity include its mandated Program Advisory Council, community campus councils (responsible for establishing a system of local campuses), research functions, and its right to generate and retain surpluses and to create semi-autonomous enterprises.

Yukon College was carrying out most community college functions when it existed as a government-operated institution. The Ayamdigut campus in Whitehorse, a strikingly attractive complex featuring natural materials and indigenous decor, was opened in 1988. By that time, twelve local centres in widely dispersed communities were in operation. The curriculum was comprised of a variety of educational offerings, including literacy, career/technical, and vocational courses as well as university transfer and degree programs contracted through universities in the south.

The college reports to the Yukon Territorial Government (YTG) through the assistant deputy minister for advanced education. The YTG retains considerable discretionary power, including the approval of tuition-fee levels. The YTG provides several kinds of support, such as a free lease on the Whitehorse campus along with management computer services. While the majority (80 per cent) of the over $12 million operating budget comes in the form of base grants, there are also supplementary grants for specific activities, such as the Yukon teacher education program. Yukon College has the capacity to raise funds and to make contracts with the federal government and/or private agencies. In addition, the college has also built a small but growing endowment fund.

The responsibility of being the sole provider of all postsecondary services to the Yukon Territory's small (less than 30,000) and widely dispersed population, particularly at a time of both fiscal restraint and major social and economic changes, requires a broad mandate. Yukon College carries out functions which normally would be designated to other types of institutions, and it is the agent of substantial community social and economic development. It is also a centre for scholarship through self-initiated and sponsored research. While acting as the broker for university-degree level instruction, it is required to be a technical training agency and to provide distance education.

These multiple roles are defined by the college's statement of mission, values, and goals. Its values include 'respecting all people,' 'respecting the environment,' and 'utilizing the knowledge of First Nations' (Yukon College 1992:2-3). The college's goals resound with statements such as 'Incorporate First Nations' knowledge in our programs and services' and 'be sensitive to the environment and minimize our negative impact on the environment' (p. 2). Yukon College has also produced a set of strategic directions which are intended to assist in the implementation of unique courses, programs, and services. These directions are categorized under program headings such as 'Adult Basic Education' and 'Preparation for Employment and Further Education' and under service headings which refer to responsiveness, accessibility, relevance, and resources. The college's primary objectives are community involvement and high-quality services.

Accomplishments

Taken together, Yukon College's values, goals, and directions provide a framework for a complex and ambitious mandate. The institution has not yet achieved all its desires; but, even with a severely restrained operating and capital support grant, it is likely that its primary goals will be achieved within the planning cycle of 1992-7.

Programming activities, designed specifically for a northern resource-based economy, include renewable resource management, First Nations management, and northern studies. Attention to ABE/life skills goals and critical retention services have resulted in the improved performance of an increasingly large aboriginal student body. A strong commitment to regional diversity and community responsiveness has translated into generous program offerings at the fourteen campuses. Nevertheless, as Senkpiel notes, 'community development remains the *bête noir* of college administrators' (1993:30). While the needs are great, the communities are both small and diverse, and the costs of developing and delivering programs are excessive. The challenge is to find a balance between the extent and the cost-effectiveness of delivering services. The new Conservative government, elected in 1992, has strongly emphasized and promoted its commitment to fiscal responsibility. Ultimately, government pressures to reduce costs will have to be weighed against the college's commitment to extend its operations.

Meanwhile, creative use has been made of distance delivery methods and educational technology in the servicing of a vast geographic area containing small population pockets. Yukon College is a full partner in the Television Northern Canada project, and it has initiated some courses for broadcast. Teleconference linkage to small campuses is another effective tool of distance education. Applications of computer-assisted instruction and other interactive electronic technologies are employed at six different centres.

Partnership and contract programs for employees from public and private agencies have also been successful. The Community Adult Literacy Programme won the Association of Canadian Community Colleges Award in 1991, and the Northern Studies Programme captured the same award in 1992. Yukon College has collaborative and brokerage agreements with the University of British Columbia, Arctic College, and the Nechi Institute (a First Nations substance abuse and lifeskills and counselling agency in Alberta). The college's research, focused primarily on ways to develop greater access to college services, has been developed in sixteen projects and is centred at the Northern Research Institute at the Ayamdigut Campus.

In tight economic times, Yukon College has maintained its essential services and has encouraged the professional development of its faculty and staff. The college served 800 full-time and 2,000 part-time students (20 per cent of the adult population) in 1990-1. It has produced 3,000 graduates in its 28 years of operation. The present staff exceeds 160 employees. While the budget of over $12 million has seen virtually no growth in the past three years, the college's programs have been maintained through increased efficiency. Although the college has neither met its target for fundraising nor significantly improved its facilities, it continues to offer increased services to communities and has seen a steadily increasing enrolment. Yukon College, a fully comprehensive postsecondary educational institution with a difficult jurisdiction, is a good example of the classical model of the community college (i.e., it emphasizes operational flexibility and innovation).

Summary
While it is quite apparent that activities and themes respecting community college development vary considerably among the provinces and territories, there are also a number of observations which, to a greater or lesser degree, are applicable to all regions.

Studies and Reports
There have been a multitude of reports from committees, commissions, and task forces, usually initiated by provincial governments, which have been concerned either directly or indirectly with the mandate of the community college. Although many reports are carefully crafted, rational, and laudable in both intent and recommendations, it is difficult to discern many major changes which have ensued from them in either the short or the

long term. Even the language in some studies, particularly those dealing with disadvantaged learners, seems to convey desperation. It is evident that many of the most plausible recommendations would entail a large financial commitment, which appears to be most unlikely at this time. But it is also evident that there is confusion over which are the most appropriate directions/priorities.

Colleges, in their current role as social and educational organizations, appear to be at the crossroads in many regions of Canada. While acknowledging the inevitable conclusion that their present role cannot continue, they seem unclear as to which path to follow into the future. Government reports tend to portray colleges primarily as instruments to deliver training activities targeted at economic renewal. College-based studies, on the other hand, focus upon human resources development and concern for the individual learner. This ambiguity constrains any attempts to plan for the future with clarity or confidence. Some studies, such as New Brunswick's *To Live and Learn*, place the colleges firmly within a larger plan designed to reform the entire educational spectrum. Others, such as Newfoundland's *Change and Challenge* and British Columbia's *Premier's Summit on Skills Development and Training*, place them clearly within an economic development strategy.

With respect to their impact upon the college system, two reports stand out. In BC, the *Access* report has served as a catalyst for several important innovations, notably the creation of the university-colleges and new programs for First Nations learners. Ontario's *Vision 2000*, while taking longer to have its influence realized, has spawned a number of important new initiatives such as prior learning assessment, the Council on Standards and Accreditation, and *No Dead Ends* (the report on advanced training).

If there is a general theme which has emerged in the numerous studies of colleges in every region of the country, it is a call for a more responsive, more coordinated, and better articulated system of public postsecondary education – a system which is far more oriented towards economic goals. Just how this is to be accomplished, however, is not clear. In the Canadian tradition of higher education, governments are reluctant to intervene directly in the setting of new operational policies, and so the responsibility for change has rested with the institutions. In some cases, it appears that there is a reluctance to initiate more than incremental change, and governments appear to have reached a high level of frustration with the lack of movement in the postsecondary system.

The problem of generating effective reform is complicated even further by the strong message that increased spending upon public education is unlikely to occur in the foreseeable future. If additional financial support is to be garnered, it will have to come from the consumer (e.g., through higher tuition fees, through the privatization of programs, or through contracts with the private sector). This message is being delivered in all regions of Canada – only time will tell how well the colleges have listened.

Organization and Program Priorities

Consistent with the foregoing is the issue of how provincial and territorial systems of postsecondary education will be managed in the future. Given the emphasis placed upon institutional responsiveness and the pursuit of economic goals, the trend is towards more centralized control. In most provinces, intermediary advisory bodies have been abolished and their authority returned to government departments, legislation has been introduced to influence bargaining in the public sector, and funding formulae have become more program-specific. An interesting exception to this trend occurs in Manitoba, where the recent creation of college boards represents a move towards greater decentralization. A similar trend towards more decentralized control also appears to be imminent in Nova Scotia.

Directly related to the issue of management is the increasing use of two terms: 'restructuring' and 'accountability.' The notion of restructuring refers to attempts to bring greater coordination and articulation to the operation of the various sectors, community colleges, universities, technical institutes, and so on which comprise the postsecondary education system. It is apparent that governments are prepared to provide the necessary incentives to achieve these ends. Institutions are being challenged to engage in program coordination and credit transfer arrangements in ways which recognize students' demands for greater educational mobility and better opportunities for advanced training. Concepts such as 'rationalization,' 'credit banks,' and 'educational continuum' have also emerged in this context. Again, provincial governments seem willing to allow the institutions to assume responsibility for action and, to this time, no legislation comparable to Britain's Education Reform Act and Australia's imposed institutional amalgamation policies have emerged in any region of Canada.

The idea of accountability is widespread and has been exercised in a variety of formats. Colleges are increasingly aware of the need to document their performances if they are to compete successfully for public dollars. But the parameters of accountability depend to a large extent upon the source to which these institutions hold themselves accountable. In Ontario, for example, colleges have received a strong vote of confidence from a public opinion survey. On the other hand, college systems in New Brunswick, PEI, Manitoba, BC, and Nova Scotia all conduct formal performance assessment studies. Under the auspices of the Canadian Comprehensive Auditing

Foundation (CCAF), a framework for accountability (CCAF 1993) has been prepared and will be tested in BC. In the same province, a value-for-money audit of the Ministry of Advanced Education's role in funding and managing the college system (conducted by the Office of the Auditor General) was recently completed (British Columbia 1993d). Furthermore, at the national level, a study under the direction of Gilles Nadeau has resulted in the selection and validation of specific indicators of the quality of college and university performance (Nadeau 1993). This study has been funded by the Social Sciences and Humanities Research Council of Canada. All of the foregoing bear testimony to the current emphasis on accountability.

Yet another expression of concern about the survival of colleges in a difficult economic climate is reflected in the fact that organizations such as the Advanced Education Council of British Columbia and the Association of Colleges of Applied Arts and Technology of Ontario have been functioning as their advocates. In both BC and Ontario, public reports dealing with the roles of colleges, with the services they provide, and with the clienteles they serve (and are unable to serve) have been prepared by these professional organizations.

Responding to government priorities to provide expanded services to disadvantaged groups, colleges in virtually all regions have concentrated on access. In particular, First Nations peoples and other visible minorities, francophones in predominantly English-speaking provinces, adult learners (especially women), those unemployed as a result of economic restructuring, functionally illiterate individuals, and the physically and mentally challenged have all been the objects of numerous studies. It is apparent that, within the educational spectrum, colleges are the most appropriate (and in some cases the only) institutes to offer educational and training opportunities to disadvantaged adults. Furthermore, this is a role which has the support of both government and society at large.

Concluding Comments

While there are some obvious variations in the current thrusts of community college development across Canada, there are also (since 1985) a number of recurring themes. These provide a comprehensive profile of the current state of college education in Canada. There is little doubt that community colleges are entering a new and quite uncertain period of development. The environment of the 1990s is one of fiscal restraint, new clienteles, a workforce vulnerable to technological change and economic restructuring, and a clear government expectation that public institutions will emphasize greater productivity and efficiency.

According to the report of the British Columbia Human Resource Development Project (British Columbia 1992):

Education, training, and learning directed to future needs of individuals and society must by multi-dimensional. The social and cultural functions of learning must not be undervalued. Indeed, the interrelationships of economic, environmental, social, cultural, and intellectual dimensions of learning must be reinforced. Within this spectrum of needs, the importance of education and training in support of a sustainable economy merits particular attention. (p. 26)

The available evidence indicates that governments are well aware of the need for a multi-skilled workforce and of the role which colleges can play in its preparation. However, there is also much confusion as to how colleges may best achieve this goal. Many questions have been posed, but, as yet, they remain unanswered. These include:

- How may the needs of society and the expectations of individual learners be effectively balanced?
- Which institutional models are best able to accommodate First Nations peoples and other traditionally disadvantaged learners?
- What types of instructional formats can best ensure both quality and efficiency?
- Which new forms of leadership are needed in the changing social and economic environment?
- Which organizational arrangements will provide a more coordinated and articulated higher education system?
- How may the human resource needs of personnel be more effectively and efficiently met?
- In which ways can colleges gain the support and confidence of the private sector in the development of more relevant programs?
- What are the values which will influence and engender change in higher education policies?

The chapters which follow will propose answers to at least some of these questions. But predicting the future of Canada's community colleges has not proved to be an exact science in the past, and now even more variables seem certain to enter the debate.

Among the most important factors which will affect the performance of colleges is the role which will by played by the federal government. In the last few years, support for postsecondary education through Established Programs Financing (EPF) has declined to the extent that 'the demise of EPF is by now virtually certain' (Cameron 1992). In Cameron's view, any future federal contribution to the general support of postsecondary education will be confined to research support (which has little relevance to colleges) and to student loan programs. With respect to the other major role of the federal government, that is, its support of occupational training through Employment and Immigration Canada (now Human Resource Development Canada), the future is also unclear. Political pressure to place fiscal resources, such as those generated through the Unemployment Insurance Commission (UIC), under the authority of the provinces could result in quite new and different policies for the management and funding of training programs. One can only speculate upon the role which will be played by the provincial training and adjustment boards in the allocation of federal resources for employment training. It may well be that these boards, containing strong representation from business and labour, will determine how and under what conditions financial support to training and developmental programs will be administered. While CJS may have diverted large resources from public colleges to private-sector agencies, a more decentralized administration of federal training dollars may or may not prove beneficial to the colleges.

Another factor which will continue to affect the operation of public colleges is the consistent growth of private-sector training. The notable increase in the number and function of such institutions in the last few years duplicates, in part, the curriculum patterns in the public community colleges. Given the emphasis upon competition, coupled with declining fiscal resources, there is increasing pressure upon colleges to privatize many job-entry training programs. If, for example, students are required to either pay directly or be sponsored for the costs of training, the entire issue of access will become a major topic of debate. There are several competing views in the college sector regarding privatization – which shall prevail is a matter of conjecture.

Restructuring of the workplace continues to pose a major challenge to public postsecondary education. With the decline of the manufacturing and national resource exploitation sectors and the consistent increase in the service and advanced technology industry, both students and colleges are being required to rapidly adjustment their respective plans. The resulting instability will affect curricula, admissions, staffing, and resource allocation and will further cloud the long-term planning process.

Ongoing debate over national standards for education and training continues within Canadian political and educational circles. The mobility of the workforce, NAFTA, and interprovincial discussions respecting tariffs and other trade barriers will each have a bearing upon the future design and delivery of college education. The cumulative outcome of all of these factors will be college systems unsure of where to place priorities regarding the certification of graduates and the standardization of curricula. Follow-up studies show extensive and often dramatic variations in employment rates for graduates from many occupational programs – a revelation which concerns both the institutions and their students. Vocational and technical training has long suffered from a status problem, a problem often reinforced by the media. Efforts to raise the status and appeal of college training are not aided by the instability of employment opportunities for graduates.

Notwithstanding all of the foregoing, the most important resource in this nation is its people. Canada's most fruitful investment will continue to be educating and training its populace to its optimal level, along with eliminating illiteracy and removing the barriers which have for so long confronted the disadvantaged. What has become clear, however, is that in several regions there is a large gap between what colleges expect of themselves and what the government(s) and the wider community expect of them. It is quite apparent that colleges will be expected to make significant changes in how they deliver services, design curricula, and respond to economic restructuring. If Canada's colleges are unable or unwilling to adapt, governments will almost certainly turn to the private sector for pre-employment training and workforce upgrading, leaving academic and general education to the universities and the K-12 system. On the other hand, if colleges are willing and able to make the necessary changes, there is little doubt that they will continue to play a crucial role in the social, cultural, and economic life of this country.

References

ACAATO. See Association of Colleges of Applied Arts and Technology

Alberta. 1989-90. *Annual Reports.* Department of Advanced Education

–.1989. *Guidelines for System Development.* Edmonton: Department of Advanced Education

–.1990. *Responding to Existing and Emerging Demands for University Education: A Policy Framework.* Edmonton: Department of Advanced Education

–.1991a. *It's About Time: 1991-1993.* Edmonton: Department of Advanced Education

–.1991b. *Calgary into the 21st Century: A Strategy for Economic Development.* Calgary: Economic Development Authority

–.1991c. *Foundations for Adult Learning and Development Policy.* Edmonton: Department of Advanced Education

–.1991d. *Toward 2000 Together: A Discussion Paper on Alberta's Economic Options and Choices.* Edmonton: Queen's Printer

–.1994. *Adult Learning: Access Through Innovation.* Edmonton: Department of Advanced Education and Career Development

Andrews, M.D., E.A. Holdaway, and G.L. Mowat. 1992. 'Post-Secondary Education in Alberta since 1945.' Paper. Toronto: OISE Higher Education Group

Arctic College. 1990. 'Strategic Plan: A Summary of Directions, 1990-1995.' Yellowknife

Assiniboine Community College. 1992. '1992-1993 Operational Plan, Enrolment Statistics.' Brandon

Association of Colleges of Applied Arts and Technology of Ontario. 1992. *The Challenge: Training and Adjustment Renewal in Ontario.* Toronto: ACAATO

British Columbia. 1991a. *Forces of Change Influencing Education and Training.* Victoria: Ministry of Advanced Education

–.1991b. *Partners for the Future: Ministry Plan.* Victoria: Ministry of Advanced Education

–.1992a. *Access for Equity and Opportunity.* Vancouver: Advanced Education Council of British Columbia

–.1992b. *Client Survey Project.* Victoria: Ministry of Advanced Education

–.1993a. *1992 College Student Outcomes Report.* Victoria: Ministry of Advanced Education

–.1993b. *Premier's Summit on Skills Development and Training.* Victoria: Government Printer

–.1993c. *Survey of Adult Basic Education and English as a Second Language Students.* Victoria: Ministry of Advanced Education

–.1993d. *Value-for-Money Audits: Ministry of Advanced Education, Training and Technology.* Victoria: Office of the Auditor General

–.1994a. Bill 22: The College and Institute Amendment Act

–.1994b. *Skills Now: Real Skills for the Real World.* Victoria: Government Printer

British Columbia Human Resource Development Project. 1992. *Report of the Steering Committee.* Vancouver: HRDP

Cameron, D. 1992. 'Federation and Higher Education: Is There Life After EPF?' Speech to the Annual Conference of the Canadian Society for the Study of Higher Education. Charlottetown, PEI

Canadian Comprehensive Auditing Foundation. 1993. *Reporting on Effectiveness in Colleges and Institutes.* Ottawa: CCAF

Conseil des collèges. 1991a. *L'Education des adultes dans les cégeps.* Québec: Government of Québec

–.1991b. *L'enseignement collégial: Des priorités pour un renouveau de la formation.* Québec: Government of Québec

–.1991c. *Harmoniser les formations professionnelles secondaires et collégial: Un atout pour leur développement.* Québec: Government of Québec

–.1992. *Les Nouvelles populations étudiantes des collèges et des universités.* Québec: Government of Québec

Conseil supérieur de l'éducation. 1992a. *En formation professionnelle: L'heure d'un développement intégré.* Québec: Government of Québec

–.1992b. *The Teaching Profession: For A Renewal of The Social Contract.* Québec: Government of Québec

–.1993. *La Gestion de l'éducation: Nécessité d'une autremodèle.* Québec: Government of Québec

Corriveau, Louise. 1991. *Les Cégeps: Question d'avenir.* Québec: Institut québécois

Council of Regents for Colleges of Applied Arts and Technology of Ontario (CAATs). 1990. *Vision 2000: Quality and Opportunity.* Toronto: Ministry of Colleges and Universities

Cumming, Alister. 1991. *Identification of Current Needs and Issues Related to the Delivery of Adult ESL Instruction in British Columbia.* Victoria: Ministry of Provincial Secretary

Daignault, Louise. 1992. 'Le processus de warming up.' Québec: thèse de Ph.D., Université Laval

Day, Bill (Chair). 1992. *Continuing Education in British Columbia's Colleges and Institutes*. Vancouver: UBC Centre for Policy Studies

Dennison, J.D. 1986. 'A Commentary upon Survival or Excellence? A Study of Instructional Assignment in Ontario Colleges of Applied Arts and Technology.' *Canadian Journal of Higher Education* 26 (2):1-7

Dennison, J.D., and P. Gallagher. 1986. *Canada's Community Colleges: A Critical Analysis*. Vancouver: UBC Press

Dupré, J. Stefan. 1987. *Postsecondary Operating Grants in Alberta: An Equity Study*. Edmonton: Alberta Advanced Education

Faris, Ron. 1992. *Lifelong Learning for the 21st Century*. Victoria: Ministry of Education

Fédération des cégeps. 1991. *Mémoire de la fédération des cégeps au conseil des collèges sur les priorités de développement de l'enseignement collégial vers l'an 2000*. Montréal

–.1993. *L'enseignement collégial, un investissement essentiel pour la société Québécoise*. Montréal: Fédération des Cégeps

Gandz, J. (Commissioner). 1988. *The Report of the Colleges' Collective Bargaining Commission*. Toronto: Colleges Collective Bargaining Commission

Gingras, Paul-Emile. 1989. 'Le Conseil supérieur de l'éducation relit le Rapport Parent.' *Pedagogie collégial* 3 (1):4-7

Glendenning, D., and T. Hall. 1988. *Some New Directions: Vocational Education on Prince Edward Island*. Charlottetown: Department of Education

Gogo, John. 1992. *Letter to Chairman of Colleges and Provincial Institutes*. Edmonton: Ministry of Advanced Education

Gregor, Alexander D. 1990. 'Higher Education in Manitoba.' Winnipeg

Holland College. 1987-90. *Annual Reports*

–.1989. *Vision 2000: A Long Range Strategic Plan*. Charlottetown: Holland College

–.1990a. *Statement of Mission and Beliefs*. Charlottetown: Holland College

–.1990b. *Annual Report*. Charlottetown: Holland College

–.1990c. *Three-Year Operational Plan, 1990-1993*. Charlottetown: Holland College

Johnston, R. (Chair). 1992. *Prior Learning Assessment: Enhancing the Access of Adult Learners to Ontario's Colleges*. Toronto: Ontario Council of Regents

Johnston, R., and B. Shapiro (Co-Chairs). 1992. 'The College Standards and Accreditation Council.' Toronto

Jothen, Kerry. 1989. *An Analysis of Career, Technical, Vocational and Basic Training Needs in British Columbia, 1989-93*. Vancouver: Open Learning Agency

Kirkland, L. 1991. *College Talk*. A publication of North West Regional College, North Battleford. Vol. 1, no. 2

LeBlanc, André E. 1992. 'The Cegep – An Essential Institution at a Crossroad,' Brief submitted to Québec parliamentary commission. St-Lambert

Lévesque, Mireille, and Daniel Pageau. 1990. *La Persévrance aux études. La Conquête de la toison d'or ou l'appel des sirénes*. Québec: Ministère de l'enseignement supérieur et de la science

Local Board Secretariat. 1992. *Community Discussions: Training and Local Boards.* Toronto: University of Toronto Press

Manitoba. 1988. *Student Allowance Policy Manual.* Winnipeg: Queen's Printer

–.1991. Bill 49: The Colleges and Consquential Amendments Act

–.1993. The Colleges Act. Appendix: College Governance Initiative

Mitchell, A. 1986. 'Administrators' Perceptions of the Outcomes of Implementing Three Provincial Policies on Community Colleges in British Columbia.' Ph.D. thesis, Department of Administration, Adult and Higher Education, University of British Columbia

Mount Royal College. 1991. 'Institutional Development Plan 1991- 2000.' Calgary

–.1992. *Trends and Issues.* Calgary: Office of Institutional Analysis and Planning

–.1993. *Investment in People, Mount Royal College's Response Regarding the Restructuring of Alberta's Post-Secondary System.* Calgary: Mount Royal College

Nadeau, Gilles. 1993. 'Criteria and Indicators of Quality and Excellence in Canadian Colleges and Universities.' Paper distributed at Annual Conference of Canadian Society for the Study of Higher Education, Ottawa, June 1993

New Brunswick. 1990. *Students of New Brunswick Community Colleges.* Fredericton: Ministry of Advanced Education and Training

–.1991. *Manitoba Briefing Notes.* Fredericton: Ministry of Advanced Education and Training

–.1992a. *Community College Graduate Follow-Up Survey Report.* Fredericton: Department of Advanced Training and Labour

–.1992b. *Professional Development Framework.* Fredericton: Department of Advanced Education and Labour

–.1993. *To Live and Learn: The Challenge of Education and Training.* Fredericton: Commission on Excellence in Education

Newfoundland. 1990a. *White Paper on Postsecondary Education: Equality, Excellence and Efficiency: A Postsecondary Educational Agenda for the Future.* St John's: Department of Education

–.1990b. *Response to Public Submissions on the White Paper on Postsecondary Education.* St John's: Department of Education

–.1990c. *Shaping Our Future: A Five-Year Strategic Plan for the Postsecondary Education System in Newfoundland and Labrador.* St John's: Department of Education

–.1992. *Change and Challenge: A Strategic Plan for Newfoundland and Labrador.* St John's: Queen's Printer

Northern Alberta Institute of Technology. 1991. *Development Plan.* Edmonton: Northern Alberta Institute of Technology

Northwest Territories. 1987. Arctic College Act, Chapter A7

Nova Scotia. 1988. *Foundation for the Future: A White Paper on a Community College System for Nova Scotians.* Halifax: Province of Nova Scotia

–.1990. *Report of the Committee on Training in the Apprenticeable Trades in the Nova Scotia Community College.* Halifax

–.1991. *The Community College Graduate Follow-Up Study: A Five-Year Summary.* Halifax: Department of Advanced Education and Job Training

–.1992a. *The Community College Graduate Follow-Up Study Report.* Halifax: Department of Advanced Education and Job Training

–.1992b. *Report of Nova Scotia Community College System: Visible Minority Access.* Halifax: Department of Education

Nova Scotia Community College. 1992. *Annual Report 1991-92.* Halifax: Ministry of Education

–.1994. *Annual Report 1992-1993.* Halifax: Ministry of Education

Ontario. 1988. *Competing in the New Global Economy.* Premier's Council. Toronto: Queen's Printer

–.1990a. *Higher Education in Ontario: Some Vital Statistics.* Toronto: Communications Branch

–.1990b. *People and Skills in the New Global Economy.* Premier's Council. Toronto: Queen's Printer

–.1991. *Skills to Meet the Challenge: A Training Partnership for Ontario.* Toronto: Queen's Printer

Ontario Institute for Studies in Education. 1992. *OISE Public Attitudes Survey Towards Education.* Toronto: OISE

Orlikow, L. 1986. *The Option to Stay: An Education Strategy for the Yukon.* Whitehorse: Government Printer

Pitman. W. 1986. *The Report of the Advisor to the Minister of Colleges and Universities on the Governance of the Colleges of Applied Arts and Technology.* Toronto

–.1993. *No Dead Ends: Report of the Task Force on Advanced Training to the Minister of Education and Training.* Toronto: Ministry of Education and Training

Price Waterhouse. 1990. *A Funding System for the Arctic College.* Yellowknife: Price Waterhouse

Prince Edward Island Task Force on Education. 1992. *Education: A Shared Responsibility.* Charlottetown, PEI

Provincial Access Committee. 1988. *Access to Advanced Education and Job Training in British Columbia.* Victoria: Ministry of Advanced Education and Job Training

Québec. 1964. *Rapport Parent.* Tome 2. Québec City: Imprimeur de la Reine

–.1992. *Une 'cure de jeunesse' pour l'enseignement collégial.* Québec: Conseil permanent de la Jeunesse

–.1993a. *Des Collèges pour le Québec du XXIe siècle.* Québec: Ministère de l'Enseignement supérieur et de la Science

–.1993b. *Loi 82 – loi modifiant la loi sur les collèges d'enseignement général et professionnel et d'autres dispositions législatives.* Québec: Editeur officiel du Québec

–.1993c. *Loi 83 – loi sur la commission d'évaluation de l'enseignement collégial.* Québec: Editeur officiel du Québec

–.1993d. *Regard sur l'enseignement collégial. Indicateurs de l'évolution du système 1993.* Québec: Ministère de l'Enseignement supérieur et de la Science

–.1993e. *Loi 98 – loi sur la réduction du personnel dans les organismes publics et l'imputabilité des sous-ministres et des dirigeants d'organismes publics.* Québec: Editeur officiel du Québec

Regional Colleges Committee of Review. 1992. *Report.* Regina: Ministry of Education

Roblin, Duff (Chair). 1993. *Doing Things Differently: Report of the University Education Review Commission.* Winnipeg: University Education Review Commission

Saskatchewan. 1987a. *Annual Report*. Saskatoon: Ministry of Advanced Education and Manpower

–.1987b. *Preparing for The Year 2000*. Regina: Ministry of Education

–.1987c. *A Summary of the History of the Post-Secondary Education System in Saskatchewan*. Saskatoon: Ministry of Advanced Education and Manpower

–.1988a. Bill 46: An Act Respecting the Saskatchewan Institute of Applied Science and Technology

–.1988b. Bill 47: An Act Respecting Regional Colleges

Saskatchewan Community College Trustees Association. 1986. 'A Better Tomorrow.' Saskatoon

–.1988. *Manual of Regional Colleges*. Saskatoon: Ministry of Advanced Education and Manpower

Saskatchewan Institute of Applied Science and Technology. 1987-9. *Annual Reports*

Saskatchewan Institute of Applied Science and Technology Committee of Review. 1992. 'Final Report.' Regina

Seethram, S. 1991. *Yukon College: A Profile*. Whitehorse: Yukon College

–.1992a. *Summary Review: 1991-92 and Future Plans*. Whitehorse: Yukon College

–.1992b. *Understanding College Finances*. Whitehorse: Yukon College

Senkpiel, A. 1993. 'Higher Education in Canada: The Yukon Experience.' Unpublished Paper, Yukon College

Skolnik, M.L. (Chair). 1986. *Survival or Excellence? A Study of Instructional Assignment in the Colleges of Applied Arts and Technology*. Toronto: Ministry of Colleges and Universities

–.1988. 'The Evolution of Relations Between Management and Faculty in Ontario Colleges of Applied Arts and Technology.' *Canadian Journal of Higher Education* 28 (3):83-111

Southern Alberta Institute of Technology. 1991. *Development Plan*. Calgary: Southern Alberta Institute of Technology

Yukon College. 1991. *Annual Report, 1990-1991*. Whitehorse: Yukon College

–.1992. *Development Strategy, 1992-1997*. Whitehorse: Yukon College

Yukon Territory. 1988. *College Act, Chapter 3*. Whitehorse: Government Printer

2
The Challenge of Leadership
John Levin

The community colleges of Canada, as characterized by Dennison and Gallagher (1986), have a history of being directed and managed through a hierarchical system of authority. This system works its way down from legislators, college boards, and presidents, to senior administrators, mid-level and junior managers, and, finally, to faculty and other staff. The moral authority of this system rests, at least in theory, with its keeping faith with the principles underlying the community college. These principles include institutional responsiveness to community needs, the maintenance of a comprehensive curriculum, institutional emphasis upon teaching and providing services to students, and the articulation, if not necessarily the application, of democratic values in institutional governance (Levin and Dennison 1989).

For the 1960s, 1970s, and perhaps even the 1980s, the principles underlying community college development may have accurately reflected normative actions and behaviours. But given the advanced organizational development of community colleges and the social, political, and economic environment of the 1990s, neither a hierarchical structure nor guiding developmental principles will sustain these institutions. While it may be extreme to suggest that the community college is in crisis, it is clear that dramatic changes are in the offing. There is a clear recognition in business and industry, as well as a growing awareness within the public sector, that the postindustrial legacy means, among other things, that traditional approaches to organizational transactions have become obsolete or are at best only marginally useful. From government-supported health services to the harvesting of forests or oceans, the old order is passing before our eyes. The difference between the present and the past is that the former requires flexibility and responsiveness in order to adapt to a rapidly changing environment. This social, economic, and political change has arguably transformed societies worldwide.

A number of efforts to alter business practices, from Japanese-style management (Ouchi 1981) to Strategic Planning (Bryson 1991) to Total Quality Management (Deming 1986), have changed how we view organizations. The efforts of business, industry, and public-sector organizations to adjust to external forces have altered how we see their accomplishments and how they function to meet their goals and compete globally. The hierarchical structure has not disappeared, but it is no longer accorded its former preeminence. Parallel to the loss of military and political authority in Eastern Europe, the type of hierarchical management practised in the West over the past one hundred years (and even the system of rational management itself is in disrepute; Quinn 1988). The assumptions and achievements of Western management, with its hierarchical structure and its emphasis upon product, are being called into question. The structures and processes of leadership have also been challenged.

In recent decades, discussions about postsecondary education (and, in particular, about the management of institutions) have suggested that leadership in the late twentieth century connotes action, decisiveness, vision, and flexibility in an environment of restructuring, diversity, and equity (e.g., Roueche, Baker, and Rose 1989; Beckhard and Pritchard 1992). Such connotations suggest that leaders are powerful figures, capable of overcoming resistance and achieving lofty goals. Technological change and the increased pace that is a result of this change have also challenged organizations that are managed hierarchically. According to Mintzberg (1989), these organizations are ineffective in adapting to their environments because hierarchically managed organizations suffer from superficiality and are rooted in the drive for control. Thus, the qualities attributed to formal leaders are likely embellishments and do not accurately represent actual behaviour. The conception of leadership in postsecondary education is surrounded by mythology. In the 1980s in the US, appeals for improved leadership in higher education paralleled a general decline in institutional autonomy and in the quality of graduating students (Bensimon, Neumann, and Birnbaum 1989). The cure to such ills, it appeared, was to be found in robust, assertive, saviour figures (Keller 1983; Fisher 1984; Kerr 1984; Roueche, Baker, and Rose 1989). Leadership in community colleges, four-year colleges, and universities became synonymous with the presidency. The language describing leaders as transformational, visionary, and inspirational hid the reality of human behaviour.

It is probable that managerial characteristics of superficiality and the emphasis on control have obfuscated the required qualities of leadership (Mintzberg 1989): the ability to say 'no' in the face of pressures to conform; the ability to infuse an organization with human spirit, vitality, and purpose (Mintzberg 1989); the tolerance of ambiguity; and the power to create liberating, as opposed to constraining, structures (Torbert 1991). The challenge for the community college is to abandon the old conception of leadership (and its obsession with control) and to embrace a more vital and nourishing concept of leadership for the decades ahead.

Community colleges, although politically inspired and the formal creations of provincial governments, have provided postsecondary education to millions of Canadians. They allowed for dramatic social development by expanding opportunities for adult education and training (Dennison and Gallagher 1986). They also assisted in the creation of a democratic society through expanding the dissemination of information. From the classrooms of teachers of philosophy and literature to the shop floors of automechanics, information and knowledge passed from instructor to student. But not all efforts to sustain and expand the democratizing outcomes of the community college yielded positive results. A critical analysis of US community colleges notes that their managers and administrators may be bound by the power of major corporations or the state (Brint and Karabel 1989). The expansion of the community college mission is judged by some US observers and scholars to be detrimental to student achievement. The actions of community college administrators, government officials, and even external observers (such as university scholars and community college association officials) are held responsible for both student performance and a lack of social mobility (Richardson, Fisk, and Okun 1983; Brint and Karabel 1989; Dougherty 1988; Cohen 1990; Raisman 1990; McGrath and Spear 1991). An analysis of power and influence in the community colleges of BC suggests that they are controlled by organized forces which encompass government officials and college leaders including governing boards (Levin 1994). It is thus possible to argue that the work of college administrators, board members, government officials, and members of the community may have inhibited, frustrated, or even blocked the drive for social improvement through community college education. In spite of this accusation, community colleges succeeded in educating and training thousands of Canadians. As noted elsewhere in this volume, teaching is the community college's preeminent characteristic (see Conclusion).

For postsecondary institutions, the recognition of organizational culture (see Morgan 1986; Bensimon, Neumann, and Birnbaum 1989; Bergquist 1992) and the phenomenon of organizational change offer yet another interpretation of the concept of leadership. As has been mentioned, the heroic image of a leader was pervasive and was usually applied to community college presidents. However, experience and disillusionment of practitioners helped to redefine the presidency. Indeed, personal experience of organizational life, especially in academic institutions, changed the perceptions of college participants. Faculty and administrators experienced labour disputes and employment terminations; they watched proposals go awry and program funding diminish, even vanish; and they saw each other grow old. As the community colleges of Canada developed, so too did the personal lives of their employees. Both changing societal values and personal experience modified the concept of leadership as it pertained to the community college.

Higher education institutions possess organizational characteristics which affect the management and leadership of these institutions. Among these attributes, loose-coupling (Weick 1976), multiple technologies (Baldridge et al. 1977), ambiguity of goals (March and Cohen 1986), and a negotiating culture (Bergquist 1992), are most prominent. Recent attention to the culture of these institutions (Chaffee and Tierney 1988; Tierney 1988; Bergquist 1992) has further reinforced the proposition that they, including community colleges (see Chapter 4), are complex organizations. This complexity has led scholars to re-evaluate concepts of leadership (Bensimon 1988, 1989; Birnbaum 1989). The college is now viewed as a social construction which is constantly being interpreted and created by its members (Chaffee and Tierney 1988). Such interpretations and creations are part of a complex arrangement of relationships, and they influence 'how things happen' in an academic institution (Tierney 1988:20).

In discussions of postsecondary organizations, there is a schism between how to manage, direct, and control them and how to understand, conceptualize, and live with and within them. This division has often marked the distinction between practice and theory, but the gap is narrowing. Practitioners are beginning to adopt the contentions of those who argue that, in order to manage it, to act purposefully within it, and to change it, leaders must know how the community college works.

Four Quadrants of Leadership

By integrating theory with practice, one may conceive four conceptual categories of community college organizational behaviours. Each category is a quadrant, representing a specific way or frame of understanding and conceptualizing organizational behaviours. An accurate concept of leadership will have to incorporate components from all four quadrants. But at this point, each separate quadrant can be examined individually. These four quadrants are referred to as (1) developmental/analytical, (2) institutional, (3) hierarchical, and (4) managerial.

Developmental/Analytical Quadrant

One way of seeing and conceiving of behaviours within community colleges assumes that they are part of a developmental process and that they are connected to external social and cultural forces. This critical perspective describes and analyzes organizational behaviours within their historical, social, and cultural context. In the US, Kempner (1991) describes community colleges as marginalized, while Brint and Karabel (1989) describe them as reflective of larger social forces, where institutional participants, especially students, are engaged in playing out a societal conflict between upward social mobility and the status quo. The role of government in the development and operation of Canadian community colleges suggests that the community focus has been replaced with a provincial focus (Dennison and Levin 1989). Economic forces affecting both federal and provincial governments have led to alterations in financing postsecondary education, and educational policy is driven by political issues. A critical perspective would indicate that organizational behaviours in, for example, the colleges of Ontario are influenced by the general conflict between labour and capital. In other words, the historical relationship between management and labour, between the administration and the faculty, is in large part the product of an industrial model of management imposed upon the colleges in their formative years and left unaltered during the following decades (Skolnik 1988).

This quadrant encompasses recent critically-oriented scholarship on higher education, including postmodern criticism, neo-Marxism, and feminist scholarship. It questions assumptions, traditions, and accepted authority. Highly analytical, this perspective challenges the accepted accomplishments and directions of community colleges. These challenges can be seen in accounts of the erosion of curriculum quality (Richardson et al. 1983), of the decrease in educational attainment by students (Richardson and Bender 1987), and of the dominance of a practitioners' culture over an intellectual or academic culture (McGrath and Spear 1991).

Institutional Quadrant
This quadrant reflects the idealism which accompanied the development of the community college: community colleges are social organizations affecting both their students and society in general. For both practitioners and scholars, it is assumed that progress towards improvement is possible, whether in the area of university transfer rates, retention of students, social equity, or quality of learning (Cohen and Brawer 1982; Astin 1985; Dennison and Gallagher 1986; Tinto 1987; Nora, Attinasi, and Matonak 1990). The community college possesses the characteristics of a human service organization (Hasenfeld 1983): people are its focus, and the institution has a mandate to protect and promote their well-being.

This quadrant encompasses those who assess an institution's performance by its ability to improve the performance of students. Studies of the community college, viewing it as part of a larger social system, show that it is affected by both internal and external conditions. The relevance of organizational behaviours is dependant upon the interaction between the institution and its environment. This would explain why one year the energies of a college may be directed towards issues of equity or affirmative action, while in another year they may be directed towards making connections with other schools and universities through partnerships, credit transfer arrangements, and collaborative curriculum projects. An emphasis upon service to students and upon the college as an open system, where there is an exchange between internal and external activities (Morgan 1986), suggests that the community college is both responsive to societal needs and to the personal development and aspirations of its students (Cohen and Brawer 1982; Dennison and Gallagher 1986).

Hierarchical Quadrant

The missionary zeal which sustained the development of the community colleges in the US in the 1950s and 1960s, and in Canada in the late 1960s and early 1970s (Cohen and Brawer 1982; Dennison and Gallagher 1986), accompanied a certain set of values. The belief that the community college offered a pathway not only to personal fulfilment but also to social transformation underlay the 'messianic fervor' (McGrath and Spear 1991) that stimulated its development and growth. These values are reflected in the drive for improved performance both for students (Richardson 1984; Astin 1985) and for the organization itself (Roueche, Baker, and Rose 1989). It is also apparent in definitions of leadership (Chaffee and Tierney 1988; Roueche, Baker, and Rose 1989; Fryer and Lovas 1991). While the community college is supported by a philosophy that advances the cause of democratic principles (Dennison and Gallagher 1986; Levin and Dennison 1989), the concept of leadership is hierarchical and is seen to be embodied in a single individual (i.e., the college president) who possesses particular traits and who behaves according to certain expectations. In this quadrant, mission, vision, and values underscore the hierarchical and moral structure of community colleges. But the perspective from this quadrant also incorporates the more formal and bureaucratic structures and processes of organizational life.

Based upon the organizational principles of the clan or collective (Morgan 1986; Levin and Dennison 1989), organizational behaviours are bound to each other through a central value system. The philosophy and the resulting mission of community college, normally established at its founding, are embodied in a single, powerful figure (Dennison and Gallagher 1986). As an institution develops, the values become more diverse and its organizational behaviours become less bonded.

Managerial Quadrant

In the 1980s, community colleges, four-year colleges, and universities were characterized by their emphasis upon two distinct resources — financial and human. Higher education was as vulnerable to economic and social forces as were business and industry. In fact, it was suggested that post-secondary institutions cope with the external environment by using the same approaches as do business and industry (Kotler and Murphy 1981; Keller 1983). Strategic Planning as well as Total Quality Management were among these approaches. Strategic Planning with its emphasis upon institutional positioning in the marketplace based upon product specialization, is predominantly a decision-making process. Total Quality Management, with its emphasis upon continuous improvements of both product and service, is a management philosophy designed to connect institutional outcomes with market expectations. The path to survival, if not excellence, was to be found in a more entrepreneurial and business-like way of conducting organizational activities.

With its connection to the community, and as a consequence of its training focus, the community college is suitably disposed to adopt the practices and even the values of business and industry. While university values *have* influenced the community college (Dennison and Gallagher 1986), its focus on vocational and career programs, especially in those jurisdictions which exclude or downplay the transfer function, gives the community college a style that is more consistent with corporate/business operational styles. Faculty and administrators drawn from the private sector further the emphasis placed upon the managerial approach to administering a college. The many publications on managerial improvements in business and industry have meant that those in management positions in community colleges could find ready solutions to organizational problems.

Characterized by competence (Bergquist 1992) as well as by efficiency, the managerial quadrant is unlikely to be compatible with a collegial environment (Baldridge et al. 1977; Cohen 1990; Raisman 1990), or even with an environment that stresses service rather than products or profits (Hasenfeld 1983). Organizationally, community colleges began to resemble corporations and businesses, emphasizing efficiency, praising innovation, and addressing employee relations.

Summary

While each of the four quadrants identified above represent particular emphases in the organization and functioning of community colleges, no college falls solely within one quadrant. In all community colleges history, values, social conscience, and control (i.e., legal authority) play important roles. Each institution places particular emphasis upon one or more of the characteristics in each quadrant. While leaders should be able to address all four quadrants, the prevalent concept of leadership has been unidimensional, stressing one quadrant at a time. For decades, the hierarchical quadrant has been predominant; but, recently, community colleges have shifted towards the managerial quadrant.

The Concept of Leadership in Institutions of Higher Education

Leadership in the community college continues to be conceived of and spoken about as largely residing in the office of the individual who is referred to as the chief executive officer (CEO). Organizational structure influences perceptions of power (Birnbaum 1992), and it accords the CEO (or president) a position at the pinnacle of the college hierarchy. 'Our culture,' notes Birnbaum in referring to US higher education (1992), 'has led people to ascribe leadership to persons in formally designated leadership roles, such as presidents' (p. 105).

Historically, the topic and concept of leadership in higher education assume a hierarchical model of organization – both in structure and function. Perhaps as a result of a perceived crisis in higher education in the early 1980s, re-examinations of both presidential leadership (e.g., Kerr 1984) and the management and functioning of postsecondary institutions (e.g., Keller 1983) reflected a major trend, which may have undermined the traditional concept of leadership. Social and economic forces (including greater institutional attention to issues of cultural diversity and equity as well as increased pressures for changes to methods of financing) no doubt challenged how colleges and universities were managed. The leadership role of the president was also called into question (Birnbaum 1989, 1992).

While continuing to identify presidents as leaders and leaders as presidents, observers of community colleges signalled a need for change in the mid-1980s (Deegan, Tillery, and Melone 1985; Dennison and Gallagher 1986). These were largely appeals for community colleges to cope with and adapt to forces of change which were sensed rather than clearly identified. By the end of the decade, however, these forces were clear; they included government policies, local community employer and employee needs, administrative workloads, governing boards' calls for greater accountability, labour relations within the colleges, and changing profiles of student populations (Dennison and Levin 1989) as well as economic and political conditions (Levin 1994). These forces resulted in a decline of staff morale, administrative and faculty burnout, and hostile faculty-administrative behaviours (Deegan 1992). It is likely that the values, cultures, missions, and governance structures of community colleges, which were connected to a hierarchical concept of leadership (Richardson 1984; Cross

1985; Dennison and Gallagher 1986; Vaughan 1986), were eroding in the 1980s.

The first act of recovery was a shift from a hierarchical to a managerial leadership model, indicating that community colleges were businesses and would behave in a business-like fashion. Thus there was a rise in innovative business practices at the community college, from the Roueche, Baker, and Rose (1989) adaptation of Peters and Waterman (1982), to Total Quality Management, to the concept of integration (Senge 1990). The act of faith was that executives could inspire, provide vision, and empower followers so that organizations could transform and become both profitable businesses and effective community colleges.

It remains to be seen if the managerial approach will do the job. Such an approach contradicts accepted beliefs about how postsecondary institutions actually work (Weick 1976; Hasenfeld 1983; Cohen and March 1986; Birnbaum 1988; Fryer and Lovas 1991; Bergquist 1992). However, it has been suggested that community colleges may be more susceptible to managerial approaches than are universities or four-year colleges (Bergquist 1992; Levin 1993). This is because of the community college's lack of traditions (Cohen and Brawer 1982), its ambiguous educational identity (Brint and Karabel 1989; Kempner 1991), and its system of governance (with power vested in administrators or else negotiated through collective bargaining). Underpinning the conception of a managerial culture (Bergquist 1992) are the assumptions that community colleges can be directed (Deegan, Tillary, and Melone 1985), that change can be managed (Levin and Dennison 1989), and that management can be rational (Quinn 1988).

The shifting community college environment does make a managerial approach inviting and its attendant conception of leadership comforting. Management teams, executive leadership, quality circles, and other similar terms reflect an environment in which technical and administrative experts may work together. Thus, one noticeable difference between hierarchical and managerial concepts of leadership is that the former focuses upon a single authority figure whereas the latter focuses upon a group of authority figures. Both conceptions, however, cling fast to the view that leadership is for the select few and that leaders occupy formal positions at the apex of the authority structure. A team, for example, is thought of as the president's team (Bensimon and Neumann 1993).

Leadership for the Future

Since the early 1980s, the recognition of a changed and changing external environment has been a central feature of organizational studies. The application of this perception clearly fits the condition of the academic institution (Keller 1983). The traditions, multiple technologies (Baldridge et al. 1977), highly interpretive approach to action (Chaffee and Tierney 1988), and loose-coupling qualities (Weick 1976) of colleges and universities help to stabilize these institutions, making them resistant to external forces (Birnbaum 1992). Nevertheless, in the 1980s and 1990s, there is ample evidence to suggest that dramatic changes have taken place, and economic forces among others have received prominent attention as the precipitators of these changes (see *Journal of Higher Education* 1993).

The changing external environment is of even greater relevance to the community college than it is to the university. Colleges are the academic institutions which have defined themselves as adaptable and flexible, as responsive to community needs (Levin and Dennison 1989). They embrace missions (Cross 1985; Deegan, Tillery, and Melone 1985) which identify them as capable of adapting to change. Thus, future leadership is required both to respond to external forces of change and to confront and solve internal problems. The case of Ontario's colleges of applied arts and technology (CAATs) has exemplified how a relationship between the faculty union and management affects institutional life (Skolnik 1988). This relationship, notes Skolnik, is 'the greatest barrier to the academic development and functioning of Ontario's twenty-two Colleges' (p. 83). The road to change, he suggests, is through the development of trust – through acts which involve risks and conditions that make the risk-taker vulnerable 'if the trust is abused' (p. 109). Effective leadership will be that which leads Canada's colleges into an environment of trust.

While there are recipes for leadership (Vaughan 1986; Roueche, Baker, and Rose 1989; Fryer and Lovas 1991; Birnbaum 1992), given the repetition of behaviours which have led to organizational problems or dysfunction, it appears that they are not useful. Fryer and Lovas (1991) appeal for greater sensitivity to the complexity of leadership. Birnbaum (1988) and Bensimon, Neumann, and Birnbaum (1989) advise that leaders make use of cognitive complexity (i.e., that they avail themselves of multiple perspectives and behaviours). Birnbaum (1992) also advises presidents to know when to resign, as the presidency is not supposed to be a career. Notwithstanding such advice, leadership, as it now exists, is not appropriate for today's community colleges. Empirical studies suggest that improvements in college leadership may require more than a magic pill. Cooper and Kempner (1991) document presidential failure to understand the culture of a community college, and the price of that failure is institutional disintegration. Similarly, Owen (1992) provides an account of presidential misjudgment resulting in organizational dysfunction.

Educational leadership is not simply based on objective behaviour, theoretical constructs, or even situation (Bensimon, Neumann, and Birnbaum 1989). Furthermore, while symbolic theory (Smircich and Morgan 1982) offers an attractive way to conceive of leadership, it categorizes groups and organizations into polarities – the ruler and the ruled, the leader and the led. That leaders define the reality of others should give us pause (Smircich and Morgan 1982). Even social exchange/transactional theories which 'downplay the charismatic and directive role of leaders' (Bensimon et al. 1989) may place limits on the president's control over institutional functioning. In these theories, as in contingency theories (Bensimon et al. 1989), while dominance is rationalized, the hierarchical structure of the leader/follower relationship is implicit. Leadership theories drawn from sources outside of education – from politics, for example (Burns 1978) – may have little relevance to community colleges given the character sites of these institutions and their human service qualities (Hasenfeld 1983). The democratic and communal character of the community college suggests that hierarchically based leadership is inappropriate.

A democratic and communal approach to leadership can be found in cultural theory. From this perspective, leaders are conceived of as anthropologists researching and clarifying organizational culture (Chaffee and Tierney 1988; Tierney 1988). And it is through understanding institutions that leadership may become a shared or community activity. This perspective insists that leaders should act as protectors and communicators of both institutional values and history (Chaffee and Tierney 1988). Presidents of small, private US colleges who acted in this way were viewed as more effective than were those who did not (Chaffee 1984). Such an approach may be applicable to other academic institutions as well. It is certainly accurate to say that this approach to leadership diminishes the dominance of single leaders. Perhaps because such a leadership model does not entail the attractive image of decisive, powerful figures, there are, in practice, few examples of it. 'Practitioners have not embraced the [cultural approach] ... The image of the leader with which we are presented is of someone in control of the campus, setting goals and priorities, making decisions, and providing direction and a vision of the future' (Bensimon et al. 1989:76).

Another promising approach to leadership is articulated by Torbert (1991). Effective leaders, he asserts, create liberating structures wherein there is a shared purpose, increasing self-direction, and the generation of quality of work. Structures (e.g., roles, communication and decisionmaking processes, even power) are simply vehicles for action, and action reflects purpose (Mintzberg 1983). Purpose which is shared is reflected and supported by process, which is liberating. Action is change, and where there are liberating structures, action can be transformational (Torbert 1991). Actions (i.e. the work and achievement of organizational members) constitute productivity; and legitimacy may be thought of as the recognized worth of those actions. Organizational success – perhaps, ultimately, organizational survival – depends upon increasing productivity and legitimacy, empowering members, and coping with and adjusting to the external environment (Torbert 1991).

How does this apply to the community college? Struggling on a number of fronts, community colleges continue to question their identity, their mission (Cross 1985), their purpose (Dennison and Gallagher 1986), their social role (Brint and Karabel 1989), and their theoretical foundations (Kempner 1991). They are, according to recent studies (Dennison and Levin 1989; Cooper and Kempner 1991; Levin 1993), vulnerable to dysfunction and to unplanned change (e.g., to being taken over by external stakeholders, by internal interest groups, or by a single, autocratic president). As Mintzberg (1989) notes in his discussion of management, a source of organizational dysfunction resides in how managers attempt to control their organizations. Instead of managers being obsessive over control Mintzberg (1989) appeals for them to create a more spontaneous environment – one which calls for belief in and commitment to organizational values. 'Only when it is infused with human spirit – with energy, ideology, culture ... does the organization come alive. And that energy cannot reside exclusively at the top of a formal hierarchy' (Mintzberg 1989:364).

The empirical evidence regarding community college functioning and dysfunctioning is limited. However, two recent studies, one American and the other Canadian, attempt to address this issue. The US study notes that chaos 'ensues when leaders are insensitive to local culture' (Cooper and Kempner 1991:21). Respect for local culture is essential to the effective functioning of any college. The Canadian study notes that shared meanings and definitions enable the community college to function by allowing it to address and resolve its problems and conflicts (Owen 1993). 'A common way of making sense of their [organizational members'] experience seems to persist' (Owen 1993:25), and this corresponds to the 'open and participatory way of interacting that characterizes the college's past and present' (p. 24).

Community college leadership is not the sole domain of CEOs or of any single authority figure. Leadership can and should be a shared process. It should involve many college members in the joint development of a mission and goals, in the tolerance of dissent and criticism, in the sharing of governance as well as of work, and in the creation of an institution that is viewed as a leader rather than as a follower. These are some of the characteristics of a community college made up of a community of leaders – a college where those in positions of responsibility aid others to practise leadership in meeting rooms and/or class rooms.

In practice, leadership requires the delegation of authority throughout the institution as well as greater decentralization of power. This should permit greater participation by organizational members, not only in decisionmaking but also in the daily work of the institution. Participatory institutional cultures arguably result in the most effective postsecondary organizations (Cameron and Ettington 1988).

Leadership, then, is moving in the direction of providing the encouragement as well as the means for sharing in managing the community college. As Mintzberg (1989) says, this comes about through managers, especially those at the apex of the institution, relinquishing their control. Leadership as a collective form of action, as an interactive process, is seen to be consistent with women's experiences and perspectives (Astin and Leland 1991; Bensimon and Neumann 1993). Organizational structures are at odds with these perspectives and appear to inhibit or resist collective leadership (Mintzberg 1989; Bensimon and Neumann 1993). Organizational theory tends to regard leadership as singular (Torbert 1991). Ideologies and structures in educational administration support not only images of masculinity (Blackmore 1993) but also images of singularity. Perhaps the community college, with its potential for innovation and its disposition towards organizational change, will live up to its reputation of being untraditional (Cohen and Brawer 1982) and modify its structures and processes to embrace a collective form of leadership.

References

Astin, Alexander. 1985. *Achieving Educational Excellence.* San Francisco: Jossey-Bass Publishers

Astin, Helen, and Carol Leland. 1991. *Women of Influence: Women of Vision.* San Francisco: Jossey-Bass Publishers

Baldridge, Victor, David Curtis, George Ecker, and Gary Riley. 1977. 'Alternative Models of Governance in Higher Education.' In *Governing Academic Organizations,* edited by Gary Riley and Victor Baldridge, pp. 2-25. Berkeley: McCutchan Publishing Corporation

Beckhard, Richard, and Wendy Pritchard. 1992. *Changing the Essence: The Art of Creating and Leading Fundamental Change in Organizations.* San Francisco: Jossey-Bass Publishers

Bensimon, Estela. 1988. 'Viewing the Presidency: Perceptual Congruence between Presidents and Leaders on their Campuses.' Paper presented at annual meeting of American Educational Research Association, New Orleans

–.1989. 'The Meaning of "Good Presidential Leadership": A Frame Analysis.' *Review of Higher Education* 12:107-23

Bensimon, Estela, and Anna Neumann. 1993. *Redesigning Collegiate Leadership: Teams and Teamwork in Higher Education.* Baltimore: Johns Hopkins University Press

Bensimon, Estela, Anna Neumann, and Robert Birnbaum. 1989. *Making Sense of Administrative Leadership.* Washington, DC: George Washington University

Bergquist, William. 1992. *The Four Cultures of the Academy.* San Francisco: Jossey-Bass Publishers

Birnbaum, Robert. 1988. *How Colleges Work: The Cybernetics of Academic Organization and Leadership.* San Francisco: Jossey-Bass Publishers

–.1989. 'Presidential Succession and Institutional Functioning in Higher Education.' *Journal of Higher Education* 60 (2):123-35

–.1992. *How Academic Leadership Works.* San Francisco: Jossey-Bass Publishers

Blackmore, Jill. 1993. 'In the Shadow of Men: The Historical Construction of Educational Administration as a "Masculinist" Enterprise.' In *Gender Matters in Educational Administration and Policy: A Feminist Introduction,* edited by Jill Blackmore and Jane Kenway, pp. 27-48. London: Falmer Press

Brint, Steven, and Jerome Karabel. 1989. *The Diverted Dream: Community Colleges and the Promise of Educational Opportunity in America, 1900-1985.* New York: Oxford University Press

Bryson, John. 1991. *Strategic Planning for Public and Nonprofit Organizations.* San Francisco: Jossey-Bass Publishers

Burns, James. 1978. *Leadership.* New York: Harper Collins

Cameron, Kim, and Deborah Ettington. 1988. 'The Conceptual Foundations of Organizational Culture.' In *Higher Education: Handbook of Theory and Research,* edited by John Smart. New York: Agathon Press

Chaffee, Ellen. 1984. 'Successful Strategic Management in Small Private Colleges.' *Journal of Higher Education* 55 (2):212-41

Chaffee, Ellen, and William Tierney. 1988. *Collegiate Culture and Leadership Strategies.* New York: American Council on Education and Macmillan Publishing Company

Cohen, Arthur. 1990. 'The Case for the Community College.' *American Journal of Education* (August):426-42

Cohen, Arthur, and Florence Brawer. 1982. *The American Community College.* San Francisco: Jossey-Bass Publishers

Cohen, Michael, and James March. 1986. *Leadership and Ambiguity.* New York: McGraw-Hill

Cooper, Joanne, and Ken Kempner. 1991. 'Lord of the Flies Community College.' Paper presented at the annual meeting of Association for the Study of Higher Education, Boston

Cross, K. Patricia. 1985. 'Determining Missions and Priorities for the Fifth Generation.' In *Renewing the American Community College,* edited by William Deegan, Dale Tillery, and associates, pp. 34-50. San Francisco: Jossey-Bass Publishers

Deegan, William. 1992. 'Proven Techniques: The Use and Impact of Major Management Concepts in Community Colleges.' *American Association of Community and Junior Colleges Journal* (April-May):26-30

Deegan, William, Dale Tillery, and Rudy Melone. 1985. 'The Process of Renewal: An Agenda for Action.' In *Renewing the American Community College,* edited by William Deegan, Dale Tillery, and associates, pp. 303-24. San Francisco: Jossey-Bass Publishers

Deming, W. Edward. 1986. *Out of the Crisis.* Cambridge, MA: MIT Press

Dennison, John, and Paul Gallagher. 1986. *Canada's Community Colleges: A Critical Analysis*. Vancouver: UBC Press

Dennison, John, and John Levin. 1989. *Canada's Community Colleges in the Nineteen-Eighties*. Toronto: Association of Canadian Community Colleges

Dougherty, Kevin. 1988. 'The Politics of Community College Expansion: Beyond the Functionalist and Class Reproduction Explanations.' *American Journal of Education* (May):351-93

Fisher, James. 1984. *Power of The Presidency*. New York: Macmillan Publishing Company

Fryer Jr., Thomas, and John Lovas. 1991. *Leadership in Governance*. San Francisco: Jossey-Bass Publishers

Hasenfeld, Yeheskel. 1983. *Human Service Organizations*. Englewood Cliffs, NJ: Prentice-Hall

Journal of Higher Education. 1993. Special issue on retrenchment. Vol. 6, no. 3

Keller, George. 1983. *Academic Strategy: The Management Revolution in Higher Education*. Baltimore: Johns Hopkins University Press

Kempner, Ken. 1991. 'The Community College as a Marginalized Institution.' Paper presented at annual meeting of Association for the Study of Higher Education, Boston

Kerr, Clark. 1984. *Commission on Strengthening Presidential Leadership: Presidents Make a Difference*. Washington, DC: Association of Governing Boards of Universities and Colleges

Kotler, Philip, and Patrick Murphy. 1981. 'Strategic Planning for Higher Education.' *Journal of Higher Education* 52 (5):470-89

Levin, John. 1993. 'Success Community College: An Examination of Organizational Change.' Paper presented at the Canadian Society for Studies in Higher Education, Learned Societies Conference, University of Ottawa, Ottawa

–.1994. 'Power in the British Columbia Community College.' *BC Studies*, forthcoming

Levin, John, and John Dennison. 1989. 'Responsiveness and Renewal in Canada's Community Colleges: A Study of Organizations.' *Canadian Journal of Higher Education* 19 (2):41-57

March, J., and M. Cohen. 1986. *Leadership and Ambiguity: The American College President*. Boston: Harvard Business School Press

McGrath, Dennis, and Martin Spear. 1991. *The Academic Crisis of the Community College*. Albany: State University of New York Press

Mintzberg, Henry. 1983. *Power in and around Organizations*. Englewood Cliffs, NJ: Prentice-Hall

–.1989. *Mintzberg on Management: Inside Our Strange World of Organizations*. New York: The Free Press

Morgan, Gareth. 1986. *Images of Organizations*. New York: Sage Publishers

Nora, Amaury, L. Attinasi Jr., and Andrew Matonak. 1990. 'Testing Qualitative Indicators of Precollege Factors in Tinto's Attrition Model: A Community College Student Population.' *Review of Higher Education* 13 (3):337-56

Ouchi, William. 1981. *Theory Z: How American Business Can Meet the Japanese Challenge*. Reading, MA: Addison-Wesley

Owen, Starr. 1992. 'An Interpretive Approach to Leadership: Developing a Theme from a Case Study.' In *Educational Leadership: Challenge and Change,* edited by E. Miklos and E. Ratsoy, pp. 259-84. Edmonton: Department of Educational Administration, University of Alberta

–.1993. 'College in Transition: A Case Study in Progress.' Paper presented at the Canadian Society for Studies in Higher Education, Learned Societies Conference, University of Ottawa, Ottawa

Peters, Tom, and Robert Waterman. 1982. *In Search of Excellence: Lessons from America's Best-Run Campuses.* New York: Warner Books

Quinn, Robert. 1988. *Beyond Rational Management.* San Francisco: Jossey-Bass Publishers

Raisman, Neal. 1990. 'Moving into the Fifth Generation.' *Community College Review* 18 (3):15-22

Richardson Jr., Richard. 1984. 'Responsible Leadership: Tipping the Balance Toward Institutional Achievement.' In *Community College Leadership for the '80s,* edited by John Roueche and George Baker III. Washington, DC: American Association of Community and Junior Colleges

Richardson Jr., Richard, and Louis Bender. 1987. *Fostering Minority Access and Achievement in Higher Education.* San Francisco: Jossey-Bass Publishers

Richardson Jr., Richard, Elizabeth Fisk, and Morris Okun. 1983. *Literacy in the Open Access College.* San Francisco: Jossey-Bass Publishers

Roueche, John, George Baker III, and Robert Rose. 1989. *Shared Vision.* Washington, DC: Community College Press

Senge, Peter. 1990. *The Fifth Discipline.* Toronto: Doubleday

Skolnik, Michael. 1988. 'The Evolution of Relations Between Management and Faculty in Ontario Colleges of Applied Arts and Technology.' *Canadian Journal of Higher Education* 28 (3):83-111

Smircich, Linda, and Gareth Morgan. 1982. 'Leadership: The Management of Meaning.' *Journal of Applied Behavioral Science* 18 (3):257-73

Tierney, William. 1988. *The Web of Leadership.* Greenwich, CT: JAI Press

Tinto, Vincent. 1987. *Leaving College: Rethinking the Causes and Cures of Student Attrition.* Chicago: University of Chicago Press

Torbert, William. 1991. *The Power of Balance: Transforming Self, Society, and Scientific Inquiry.* Newbury Park: Sage Publications

Vaughan, George. 1986. *The Community College President.* New York: American Council on Education and Macmillan Publishing Company

Weick, Karl. 1976. 'Educational Organizations as Loosely Coupled Systems.' *Administrative Science Quarterly* 21:1-19

3
Organization and Function in Postsecondary Education
John D. Dennison

Introduction

Although the term 'system' is used freely in government publications and in the higher education literature to designate the postsecondary education sector, there are no actual provincial 'systems' in Canada.[1] Among the twelve provincial/territorial jurisdictions there are a variety of structures in which universities, community colleges, technical institutes, and similar institutions articulate and coordinate their activities, either through voluntary agreements or through more formal arrangements (in which governmental authority usually plays a role). The situation is further complicated by a lack of coherence between the public and private sectors and by the existence of specialized institutions, such as First Nations colleges. In the most restricted sense of the term, a true system of higher education would operate as an integrated organizational unit with a single governing body, which would assign specific responsibility for aspects of education and training to each component part of the organization. While systems of this kind do exist in other jurisdictions (e.g., Hawaii), no such arrangement is found in Canada. [2]

What *does* exist in this country, however, are twelve provincial and territorial 'quasi-systems,' which have few universally comparable features but which have a number of independent arrangements for dealing with such matters as curriculum, accessibility, student mobility, and planning. (Sheffield et al. 1978; Dennison and Gallagher 1986; Skolnik 1986; Skolnik and Jones 1993). There are many reasons for this Canadian phenomenon, which may be described as one of the most diversified postsecondary systems in any developed nation. Constitutionally, education at all levels is under provincial authority. As a result, community colleges (which have tended to sustain a closer relationship with government than have universities) have developed features which reflect the particular historical, sociocultural, and economic characters of their respective provinces and territories (Dennison and Gallagher 1986; Gallagher 1990; Campbell 1971). This chapter provides an analysis of the organization of postsecondary education at the provincial/territorial level, and focuses specifically upon the management of access, coordination of curriculum, and student mobility.

Organizational Structures

Institutions of postsecondary education exist in Canada under a variety of titles, mandates, and functions, modes of governance, and legislated arrangements. In the public sector, universities operate on a continuum from those which emphasize research to those which emphasize undergraduate teaching. Notwithstanding their primary role, however, universities which emphasize undergraduate teaching also maintain a research orientation and a culture in which teaching faculty are rewarded for scholarly activity, teaching, and service. It is important to note that no public university in Canada presents itself purely as a teaching institution. Universities in the private sector (which are small in number and church-related) are accurately described as offering a four-year liberal studies program. It is also important to note that institutions called universities normally only accept those who have attained at least high school graduation or its equivalent. As will be described later, there are some exceptions to this (which contributes to role-confusion in some colleges and universities).

While the title 'community colleges' is used freely, missions, curricula mix, and student profiles vary widely. All, however, claim a commitment to high-quality teaching and student services. Instructional services may range from basic literacy to baccalaureate degrees. Privately controlled community colleges, the majority of which are in Québec, tend to offer a much more specialized academic curriculum than do publicly controlled community colleges.

Under the designation of private training colleges, literally hundreds of institutions offer a highly selective assortment of education and training opportunities, ranging from hairstyling and fashion design to language training and computer programming. Among others, these institutions include institutes of technology, agricultural colleges, adult vocational schools, colleges of art and design, schools of nursing, vocational centres, conservatories of music, and First Nations institutions. Curriculum patterns and student characteristics vary according to function, and many programs do not require a high-school diploma as a basis for admission.

In most provinces, the various institutions described above were developed independently in response to government initiatives or as part of political agendas, often influenced by the availability of federal dollars during the 1960s (when both capital and operating grants were available). Between 1960 and 1975, when the postsecondary sector massively expanded, many established universities were converted from private to public control, new public universities were established, adult vocational and technical schools became component parts of community colleges, and programs such as nursing and law enforcement were placed under the college umbrella. During that period, the horizon of higher education was redefined.

However, notwithstanding this period of expansion, policies to create formal relationships among the components of the postsecondary educational galaxy were not often entertained – an omission which was to attract the attention of several critics and which has generated extensive debate ever since. However, in some regions within-system relationships were given early attention. The community colleges in both BC and Alberta were created largely to overcome barriers to access (be they geographic, financial, or academic) to university degree programs. Given this mandate, the problem of student transfer from college to university, with full recognition of appropriate academic credits, became a priority. In both of these provinces, formal transfer agreements were negotiated, with varying levels of cooperation from the university sector and with varying degrees of difficulty.

The other notable exception to this lack of coordinated planning is to be found in Québec. The collèges d'enseignement général et professionnel (Cegeps) constitute a mandatory level of education between secondary school and university, in which articulation with, and transfer between, all levels are prescribed. However, it should not be forgotten that the Cegeps offer essentially academic and technical curricula, while many other post-school programs, such as vocational training and adult upgrading, are provided largely outside the college sector.

In the remaining provinces, postsecondary education is provided through independent sectors (i.e., universities, colleges, and a variety of other institutions, both public and private). Coordination, even at an informal level, has been spasmodic at best and, in some regions, virtually non-existent. Historical factors, limitations upon mandates and missions, and political agendas all contributed to this situation at a time when the idea of a coordinated system was either ignored or not viewed as a priority.

In recent years, however, a considerable amount of attention has been devoted to what has become recognized as a deficiency in the organization of higher education. The escalating demand for access to further education at all levels; a recognition of the need for greater mobility by students seeking advanced credentials; concerns about lack of recognition of previous learning; artificial barriers to transfer from one institution to another; increasing costs of maintaining a large number of institutions; and the realization in political circles that higher education is not being used to its greatest effect have all contributed to a new emphasis upon the need for reform

(British Columbia 1988; Council of Regents 1992; New Brunswick Commission on Excellence in Education 1993; Newfoundland 1990b). One result of this reassessment has been the extensive use of the term 'restructuring' as it is applied to the postsecondary system. Initiatives taken by ministries responsible for postsecondary education in Alberta, Saskatchewan, Ontario, New Brunswick, and Newfoundland between 1991 and 1993 have led to a plethora of conferences, studies, and reports – all of which are concerned with finding ways of improving coordination among postsecondary institutions. As Skolnik and Jones (1993) note in their study of coordination between universities and colleges, general agreement exists in all provinces that cooperation is important, inter alia, for better 'system planning, funding, and rationalization of resources and facilities' (p. 70). Reflective of the past lack of coordination between the university and the college is an observation made recently by Lorna Marsden, president of Wilfrid Laurier University: 'It became clear years ago that our students saw university and college serving different but equally important roles in their lives and plans. But as an ordinary professor, or even an academic administrator, I had no contact with the colleges unless I sought it personally. Very strange; very Canadian; peculiarly Ontarian' (quoted in Vale 1994).

The question which remains is, how may improved coordination with respect to policy, planning, budgeting, and course delivery be accomplished most efficiently and effectively, given the context of Canadian higher education? In addressing this question, it is important to recognize that certain predetermined caveats exist. Canadian universities enjoy a privileged measure of autonomy seldom equalled by comparable institutions in other highly developed nations. Autonomy in this context refers to independent control over admissions policies, curricula, requirements for degrees, and so on, and it is often seen as a necessary condition for the establishment of a high-quality institution (Macdonald 1963). It follows, in the culture of the Canadian university, that any government intrusion would be viewed as antithetical to tradition. If arrangements were to be formalized to provide for coordinated policy with respect to student transfers, for example, such arrangements would have to be voluntary and would have to involve the full cooperation of the participating institutions.

While this caveat must be recognized, there are actions which government might take to encourage greater coordination. For example, quasi-governmental agencies have been created in Alberta and BC to serve as forums in which to discuss transfer and articulation issues among postsecondary institutions as well as to develop guidelines, policies, and procedures which facilitate student mobility from one institution to another. These councils on admissions and transfer involve representatives from both public and private institutions, all of whom attempt to develop and improve methods of coordination. For instance, one of their major contributions has been the preparation and production of transfer guides, which list all courses and programs which have been negotiated as 'credit equivalent.' Students are given assurance, through reference to the transfer guide, that they will receive credit for all relevant courses completed if they qualify for admission to a university or college. In each province, the role of these councils is to bring various institutions together, to articulate problems, and to encourage the negotiation of resolutions. The outcomes of negotiation, in the form of courses or programs, are then documented formally in the transfer guide and serve as a contract between and among these institutions.

Forms of Coordination

The single arrangement leading to system coordination which is most frequently referenced in the higher education literature is the Master Plan of the State of California (California Postsecondary Education Commission 1960). As Rothblatt (1992) notes, it was the master plan which initiated the creation of a new coordinating body, the California Postsecondary Education Commission. In turn, the commission assigned formal roles and functions to each sector of the state's postsecondary system. Intersegmental cooperation became the principle which guided both articulation and transfer, practices which allowed for the free movement of students within the system (provided they satisfied predetermined academic criteria).

No comparable master plan has yet been developed in Canada, although Québec incorporated many of the criteria of the California model during the establishment of the Cegep system in the 1960s. However, it is now appropriate to turn to a discussion of some of the less formal arrangements which may be made within a provincial postsecondary system in order to better serve the interests of students. It should be noted that the arrangements which will be described vary in complexity and formality. Some are essentially ad hoc, while others involve major structural changes in how education and training are provided.

Brokering of Courses and Programs

Originally a distinguishing characteristic of Saskatchewan's postsecondary system, program brokering has been adopted in various forms in several other regions. This arrangement involves the offering of courses by one institution, using a regular face-to-face instructional format, on the campus of another institution. For example, both Saskatchewan universities and the Institute of Science and Technology offer credit courses on college campuses. These courses constitute part of degree or diploma programs. In Alberta, degree programs, such as nursing and business, are made accessible to students in selected colleges. Normally, these students have accumulated college credits up to the diploma level but cannot complete the degree under the current college mandate.

A brokering arrangement does not require interinstitutional agreements about credit equivalences and/or transfer credits, as they are offered by the same institution which is responsible for granting them. Students are able to continue their education under a conventional format without moving from their communities, an arrangement which ensures a more convenient form of access. Further to this, more extended and efficient use is made of the college's facilities and equipment. Nevertheless, there are potential problems in the brokering approach. As courses are offered some distance away from the major campuses of the delivering institutions, problems of securing fully qualified instructors inevitably arise. These faculty often hold sessional or part-time appointments, and, while they may be highly competent teachers, they are excluded from the mainstream of their institution and are usually not involved in scholarly activity (broadly defined). The long-term priority which an institution assigns to the offering of brokered courses is critical to their continuity and quality; and in difficult financial times, pressures to protect 'essential' programs are inevitable. Relatively minor issues, such as allocation of organizational responsibilities, distribution of costs and student fees, and selective admission of students to courses or programs may also arise.

Bilateral Agreements

In the province of Ontario, where the college and university sectors are functionally independent, two institutions may negotiate informal agreements whereby university X will recognize and assign advanced program credits for designated courses completed successfully at college Y. Usually such agreements are made between institutions which are located close to each other and where students find it geographically advantageous to continue their education. There are many such arrangements in the province, restricted to the particular institutions involved. As noted in a recent report from Ontario (Pitman 1993), the number of such arrangements is growing and they have led to improved transfer opportunities. In 1988, there were nineteen arrangements between colleges and universities: four years later that number rose to seventy. One notable example of such an arrangement is the new University of Waterloo/Conestoga College print journalism course that was offered in 1994. Students will graduate with a Waterloo degree and a Conestoga diploma in four years. Lakehead University offers degree programs designed specifically for community college transfers in business, engineering, medical laboratory sciences, physics, and nursing. Interestingly, although a cooperative program in art history between University of Toronto's Erindale College and Sheridan College was begun as early as 1969, it was not until 1991 that these institutions organized other programs, such as early childhood education. The overriding principle behind such models is mutual respect and a 'different but equal partnership' between two institutions (Vale 1994).

While there are obvious benefits to this approach, there are equally obvious disadvantages. Much of the initiative for planning comes from committed individuals with administrative authority. However, one potential problem which is always present has been articulated by Richardson (1993) as follows:

> A familiar scenario repeats itself in never-ending cycles. Two committed and academic administrators establish an effective collaborative relationship in Gotham City. Articulation blossoms. After two years, one leaves. Within six months, every trace of progress has been erased. (p. 42)

Bilateral agreements are course- or program-specific. Only those students involved in the designated programs in the selected institutions can benefit from them. There are few, if any, provisions for extending these agreements. Certainly it is better than nothing, but with regard to establishing an articulation policy which is province-wide, it accomplishes little.

Credit Transfer
The principle of transfer is primarily a North American phenomenon, although in recent years it is becoming better understood in higher education circles in Europe. The French have a credit system, 'unites de valeur' (Organization for Economic Cooperation and Development 1990), and Scotland has long allowed for student interchange between its universities (Rothblatt 1992). Although these are exceptions, with the emergence of the European Community, educational programs have been established (e.g., ERASMUS and LINGUA) which operate on the principle of interinstitutional transfer. In the US and Canada, where transfer policy is well established in virtually all constituencies, the key to its workability is the widely practised modular system of instruction, by which all institutions award academic credits for successful completion of term, semester, or quarter-long sets of instructional units called 'courses.' Such credits then become a common currency which may be cashed by the student throughout the postsecondary system, provided an acceptable level of performance has been attained.

But even this last principle rests upon an assumption which is effectively untestable; that is, that the academic standards which are maintained in these courses are comparable. As Rothblatt also notes, it is impossible to standardize an education system which is itself divided into independent units. The wide diversity of mandates, roles, and functions among many different institutions militates against any uniformity of standards. Nevertheless, because North American postsecondary education is largely consumer-oriented, assumptions regarding comparability of academic standards are rarely debated. To do so would invite debate of a political nature and so complicate the practice of transfer as to make it unworkable.

Notwithstanding the foregoing, the principle of credit transfer has been recognized, at varying levels of formality, in several regions of Canada. Where practised, a province-wide policy, which involves the formal recognition of credits transferred on a course-by-course basis, requires a complex set of conditions. The fundamental values which underscore such a policy are equity and fair treatment of students (re the awarding of appropriate advanced credits) when they elect to transfer from one institution to another. Policies and procedures are based upon principles and guidelines, which are themselves developed through a process of consultation involving all affected institutions. As it is crucial that the integrity of each institution be protected, any agreement is both delicate and deliberate.

An abbreviated set of principles, extracted from those utilized in Alberta and BC, reads as follows:

- Accessibility and mobility to and among postsecondary institutions are primary goals.
- Course or program credits for transfer should be based upon equivalency of academic achievement and of knowledge and skills acquired.
- Eligibility for transfer will be based upon student performance after his/her initial entry into postsecondary education rather than upon secondary school achievement.
- While minimum conditions for transfer may have been met, admission may be limited by availability of resources.
- Students will be provided with information on course equivalences, prerequisites, and required levels of performance before beginning their programs – and published agreements will be honoured by all participating institutions.

In translating policy into practice, there are innumerable details which require attention. Matters such as levels of credit (e.g., classification of individual courses as being either for specific credit or for unassigned credit by department, program, or faculty) must be determined. The current credit transfer policy is applicable to all postsecondary institutions (both public and private) where appropriate and, hence, applies to all students in all regions of the province. In order for this to be the case, a provincial agency must coordinate and monitor all agreements. For reasons noted earlier, a government body is not the best choice for this task; rather, the best choice would be an agency at arm's length from the provincial government and with the power not to institute policies but to encourage their participatory development and approval. The authority of such an agency would flow from the credibility of its membership and its perceived objectivity.

The locus of negotiation of course transfer equivalencies is not the administration of the participating institutions but their relevant academic departments. The latter's authority with respect to academic governance is another important characteristic of Canadian universities. Given this, the key agents in working out course equivalencies are articulation committees, which are composed, for example, of representatives from history, physics, or business departments from all institutions. These committees meet at least once a year, exchange information, and maintain contact among the disciplines. Debates in articulation committees are not without problems. Power, if it can be defined as such, largely resides in the receiving institutions, usually the universities. Trust, goodwill, and 'parity of esteem' constitute the ingredients of a productive relationship. Collective institutional egos do exist, autonomy may be misinterpreted or abused, and traditions may be too deeply ingrained. When these factors are present, the essential catalyst in the negotiation of satisfactory agreements is a sensitive and objective provincial agency.

It is important to recognize that student mobility takes several paths, although much of the attention has been given to the college-to-university route. While there is a body of Canadian literature on this topic (Vaala 1991, 1993; Dennison, Forrester, and Jones 1982; Dennison and Jones 1970; Dennison 1978), there is relatively little on transfer patterns from university to college, college to college, university to technical institute, and so on. If articulation is really to be province-wide, published course credit equivalencies should reflect the variety of transfer paths available to students. Too often, colleges or technical institutes are openly critical of a university's transfer policies while neglecting to acknowledge their own failings with respect to those students moving from one college to another.

A provincial transfer credit policy is not easily negotiated, particularly in a system which is composed of historically different institutions with independent admission policies, curriculum patterns, and mandates. However, the current reality of student expectations and the concerns raised by the primary funding sources (i.e., the provincial governments) suggest that new thinking regarding this issue is well overdue.

Associate Degrees
Another component in the facilitation of a more coordinated system of postsecondary education is the concept of the associate degree. Although well established in many US states, the Associate in Arts (AA) degree, as it is

usually called, was unknown in Canada until 1992, when it was legislated into practice in BC.

Students may qualify for the AA degree by undertaking a relatively stand-ardized curriculum covering the equivalent of two years of full-time study. Students are normally required to complete a minimum number of credits in specific disciplines (e.g., English, social sciences, physical sciences, etc.) and achieve a pre-established grade-point average to qualify for the creden-tial. The associate degree may be offered in both the college and the univer-sity sectors.

In practice, associate degrees with full transfer credits are usually con-fined to either the arts or the sciences – a limitation which immediately invites controversy. Most community colleges (and equivalent institutions) in Canada offer two- or three-year diplomas in business, health sciences, engineering, social services, and other areas. Often referred to as career or technical programs, these are designed to lead to employment and, in ef-fect, become 'terminal' programs. Rarely do career programs allow for transfer with substantial credit to baccalaureate degree programs (with the notable exceptions of nursing and, in some regions, dental hygiene and medical laboratory technology). In the eyes of many college educators, this practice is unfair and discriminatory. Furthermore, the title of 'degree,' when con-fined to academic areas, connotes a status which is not ignored by those involved in diploma programs. Hence, while attention has often been paid to the issue of transfer credit with respect to career programs, such interest tends to increase when associate in arts and associate in science degree pro-grams are put into place.

One major matter of debate surrounding associate degrees in the arts and the sciences is what particular status degree-holders will attain on seeking transfer to university. One argument is that, rather than submitting them to the more conventional course-by-course method of credit approval, full recognition for two years of study should be granted to associate degree-holders. Many universities in Canada would be wary of this line of argu-ment, largely due to their insistence upon independent control over credit courses. A less radical approach would be for universities to agree to give preferential access to AA degree-holders, on the assumption that such gradu-ates would have completed a disciplined and demanding academic exer-cise. At a time in which seats for transfer students are increasingly limited by available resources, a preferential policy of admission for associate de-gree-holders would be well received.

There is yet another related aspect to the associate degree concept. This involves the notion of 'two-and-two' program planning, in which students would take the initial two years of postsecondary study to earn a diploma and then have the option of pursuing an additional two years at university in order to complete the baccalaureate degree. Degree fields such as journalism, business, hotel management, dental hygiene, and criminal justice are all appropriate examples. The initial college years might have a practical orientation, followed by the option of field experience and eventually culminating in the theory-oriented university years. In a certain sense, the two-and-two principle of program planning is similar to the associate-degree principle of program planning in that it provides a coherent two-year curriculum at the college level, followed by two more years at university, culminating in the award of an undergraduate degree. Again, however, it is necessary to emphasize the need for a quasi-independent agency to take the initiative in setting guidelines if the two-and-two degree is to be successfully implemented on a provincial basis.

Open Learning

A provincial open learning authority represents a medium of education delivery as well as an organizational option, and, as such, it deserves comment. An agency committed to open access to advanced learning can become a mechanism by which programs and courses offered by conventional institutions may be articulated to the benefit of students. An open learning institution is designed to offer programs which allow students to earn various credentials through a range of instructional formats.[3] Course delivery may utilize numerous technologies in addition to more conventional correspondence packages. The intent of open learning is to provide optimal access, which will accommodate a student's geographic isolation, lifestyle, or preference for instruction (Sweet 1989).

Part of the optimization of access provided by an open learning institution is to recognize, where appropriate, a student's previous learning. One example of this approach is to create a credit bank for each applicant. In practice, a student seeking to enrol in a program will submit all credits which he or she has accumulated from previous educational institutions. These credits will be assessed for their relevance and legitimacy and, subsequently, will be accepted as advanced credit in the program in which he or she enrols. This form of advanced credit assessment translates into the creation of the credit bank. Academic credits previously earned from recognized institutions, either in the public or private sector, qualify for inclusion in the credit bank. Due to its design, an open learning agency has sufficient flexibility to overcome some of the traditional barriers which more conventional institutions come up against in assessing credits earned by students from other colleges and universities.

A policy such as this places a priority upon the learner and his or her individual accomplishments, goals, and needs rather than upon the conditions imposed by educational institutions. While the system itself may not be articulated, a mechanism can be created by an external agency which, de facto, allows a student to accumulate course credits from many individual institutions.

Prior Learning Assessment

The idea of prior learning assessment (PLA) is, itself, another part of a strategy to make postsecondary education more accessible and efficient. PLA is predicated on the argument that, throughout their lives, adults acquire skills and competencies through a variety of formal and non-formal learning experiences. The latter may include work, volunteer and community activities, involvement in organizations, or self-study. Hence, when a student enrols in a formal program of study in an institution of non-compulsory education, it is simply a continuation of his or her lifelong learning. There are several ways in which PLA may be implemented, including challenge examinations, standardized testing, and, more commonly, assessment of previous learning. Before beginning a program, a student would submit a portfolio which documents evidence of his or her previous learning activities. This record is then assessed by the institution with a view to giving the student advanced credit or standing for previous learning activities relevant to his or her chosen program of study (Council of Regents 1992).

A system of prior learning assessment encourages advanced study by recognizing and rewarding an individual's learning experiences. In this regard, it is student-focused rather than institution-focused. PLA also discourages unnecessary duplication of activities and is thus cost-effective. Again, access is enhanced and postsecondary education is seen as both flexible and responsive to student needs.

There are, of necessity, a number of principles and standards which guide the PLA process. The following are examples of those established in BC after extensive consultation with institutional representatives.

- PLA should occur within the broader context of education-, career-, or life-planning.
- Learning assessed for postsecondary credit should be (1) defined in terms of what was learned and what the person can do as a result rather than in terms of the amount of time spent; (2) transferable to contexts other than the one in which it was learned; (3) current, and (4) at a level of achievement equivalent to that of other students engaged in that program/subject area.
- Credit should be awarded only for demonstrated learning, not for experience per se.
- Credit should be awarded only for learning which is appropriate to the content of the course or program to which it is being applied.

- Credit should be awarded only for learning which has that balance between theory and practical application which is appropriate to the subject or course.
- The determination of competence levels and of credit awards would be made by academic/career technical specialists in consultation, as appropriate, with representatives from industry and the community.
- Credits awarded as a result of PLA should be so identified on the student's transcript.
- PLA should be developed first for those programs where the market demand (i.e., client need) is the greatest, and where institutional readiness and capacity are evident.
- PLA should be considered as a vehicle for enhancing access to appropriate education. Where possible, orientation or portfolio development courses should be offered on industry sites (BC Council on Admissions and Transfer 1994).

There are, however, a number of problems in putting PLA into action. The process of preparing and assessing an individual's learning portfolio is often complex, time-consuming, and expensive. In general, it requires considerable training, as well as resources, to provide counselling to prospective students and to evaluate their records. But the greatest potential problem is that managers of different institutions, and those involved in directing specific programs, will have different attitudes to PLA and different ways of assessing previous student achievement. Ultimately, formal acceptance of PLA lies at the program level.

Universities, in particular, are reluctant to recognize prior learning unless it is represented by formal courses completed in more or less conventional institutions. While challenge-for-credit opportunities are available in many universities, the idea of assigning advanced credit for job experience or for learning in non-formal settings is usually approached with caution, if at all. In the same vein, those who manage distinctive programs, such as in the applied sciences and health technologies, will be sceptical of the notion that volunteering or field experience compensate adequately for the courses which they consider essential to the attainment of specific credentials.

By 1994, three provinces, Ontario, BC, and Québec, had made PLA a priority and had established formal procedures its for implementation. As is the case with many new ideas, such as transfer credit or program articulation, implementation of PLA will succeed or fail on the performance of those who are first given the opportunity to take advantage of it. Successful implementation of PLA, certainly as a provincial policy, will depend upon how well students perform in their programs of choice. In the tradition of postsecondary education in Canada, implementation will rest with individual institutions which carefully guard their own admission and pro-motion policies. Government and quasi-government agencies can only encourage the study of PLA, set appropriate standards, and stimulate de-bate over its efficiency. While numerous incentives are possible, with re-spect to radical change in postsecondary educational policy, preservation of the academic integrity of each institution is paramount.

Restructuring the System

In 1993, the term most associated with reform of the postsecondary educa-tion system at the provincial level was 'restructuring.' Ministers of advanced education from Newfoundland to BC have established committees or initi-ated formal discussions to examine what possibilities exist for restructuring arrangements in various institutions regarding (1) better service to students and (2) better utilization of available resources.

There appears, however, to be some uncertainty, even confusion, as to what restructuring entails, who should manage it, and what determines its dimensions. In Ontario, three restructuring committees were asked to ad-dress issues such as autonomy and diversity, assurance of quality, the role of governance, the preservation of shared (government and student) funding of the system, and the maximization of student mobility and lifelong learn-ing. Furthermore, while several innovative and cooperative projects have been funded, these fall far short of fundamentally realigning institutional roles and practices.

The history of institutional development in most provinces and regions of Canada does not indicate that any basic changes are attainable, at least without major controversy. Many observers have long agreed, for example, that there are too many degree-granting institutions in Nova Scotia; others have questioned the role of the Cegeps in Québec; and still others have argued against the two solitudes of universities and colleges in Ontario. Universities in every province have always resisted any potential encroach-ments upon their autonomy. Certainly, the fiscal pressures of the 1990s cannot be ignored, but whether or not real restructuring will occur may depend upon one's definition and interpretation of the term.

The University-College Idea

Notwithstanding the reservations expressed in the last paragraph of the preceding section, it must be acknowledged that one major experiment in the modelling of postsecondary education has occurred in BC. This is the creation of the university-college. While this structure is not entirely new (the University-College of Cape Breton takes precedence, although its cur-riculum pattern is not fully comparable), it is undeniably innovative (Dennison 1992).

The primary motivation behind the university-college idea was, initially, to increase access to programs leading to degrees, specifically for those living outside Vancouver and Victoria. A report initiated by the provincial government (British Columbia 1988) had drawn attention to the discrepancy between degrees awarded in BC (3.07/1,000 of population) and degrees granted in Canada as a whole (4.5/1,000). In particular, access to degree programs was most restricted for those living in rural regions and for a variety of disadvantaged groups, including First Nations peoples. As part of a plan to create an additional 15,000 places in degree programs in the province, one specific recommendation led to the development an entirely new structure – the university-college.

The report recommended that a select number of community colleges, located in relatively large, non-urban population centres, should be given degree-granting status. This suggestion was quickly adopted, and three colleges (a fourth was added later) were designated as university-colleges. Initially, degrees were to be awarded under the aegis of one of the three established universities in the province, but, ultimately, the colleges were to grant degrees on their own.

The university-college model brought under one operational roof many of the cultural characteristics of two postsecondary institutions with two quite different mandates. On the one hand, those from the university tradition emphasized research and scholarly activity; practised bicameral governance, in which faculty members exercised considerable influence over academic affairs; placed a strong emphasis upon theory; and emphasized orientation towards one's discipline rather than institutional loyalty. On the other hand, those from the college tradition emphasized teaching; allowed for only an advisory role for faculty with respect to academic governance; were accustomed to a broadly comprehensive curriculum incorporating a wide range of academic levels and placing a strong emphasis on practice; and identified with a community-responsive college environment (Johnston 1991). Thus, the university-college was formed within the confluence of two different cultural streams, and it was enjoined to produce a new postsecondary cultural identity.

The point of the foregoing discussion is not to debate the university-college idea but to emphasize the complexity of restructuring a system of postsecondary education in which the components have long forged distinctive mandates, missions, and values. The university-college undoubtedly opens access to new programs for a particular segment of students. It holds the potential for developing new kinds of degrees which will respond to contemporary changes in the technology-driven workplaces of the next millennium. The university-college can inculcate new values in instructor performance by merging teaching and scholarly activity. These new institutions can provide unlimited opportunities for students to progress along various channels to advanced credentials. If the commonly stated objectives of government and educational planners (i.e., to encourage more responsive, flexible, and efficient postsecondary institutions) are to be realized in a practical sense, the university-college concept represents a noble attempt at accomplishing just that.

All of this is largely speculative. The university-college will go through an extensive and challenging period of adjustment before it defines its unique culture. It may well establish criteria which embody both the university and the community college concept and, in so doing, create an entirely new kind of institution.

A Unitary System of Postsecondary Education

Perhaps the most radical approach to reorganizing the system of higher education comes in the form of an idea rather than in the form of a plan. It is the idea that a student, having enrolled in any public postsecondary institution, regardless of program or course, becomes a student of the system as a whole. While the idea itself is not complex, its implications are immense.

As a student of the system, rather than of an individual institution, the progress an individual makes would be based upon equitable treatment. In other words, relevant criteria (e.g., courses completed, grade-point averages, work experience, etc.) would apply to all students seeking advancement – regardless of the institution they are attending. In pursuing transfer from college to university, for example, a student would be in competition with all applicants, including those already progressing through the university. A similar principle would apply to students transferring from college to college or from university to technical institute – the only relevant criteria would be the level of previous accomplishment and the appropriateness of preparation.

It must be recognized that, to put this idea into practice, colleges and universities would collectively offer a multidimensional array of courses, programs, credentials, and so on, each of which would be assigned to an institution consistent with its purpose. Students who seek mobility within the system could have access to whatever position they needed, provided they had achieved the appropriate preparation. It cannot be denied that one consequence of this approach would be greater standardization of curricula, certainly with respect to equivalent programs. Some observers would also argue that differentiation among and between institutions would probably be eroded, thus diluting quality and discouraging innovation. It may, on the other hand, be possible to reach a middle position which would preserve the crucial student-centred component of the idea while still allowing for institutional differentiation. One possible approach might be to agree upon a common first and second year for arts and science programs in both colleges and universities, while allowing for specialization in the third and fourth years.

The concept which is being promoted here requires acceptance of the idea of a 'student of the system.' Building upon this idea, the task then becomes how, through organizational adjustments, to put policies in place in order to accommodate it. If nothing else, the process would require individual institutions to examine and to assess current policies on admission and curriculum design, both in their own and in other constituencies.

Conclusion

This chapter began with the thesis that no real system of higher education, in the most literal sense of the term, has been developed in any of the differentiated structures found in Canada. Nevertheless, quasi-systems, ranging from Québec's two-tiered model to Ontario's two solitudes, have grown in response to the historic, economic, and sociocultural realities of each region. In general, these structures have met the needs of a population seeking different forms of advanced education for different reasons and in different times.

However, as the third millennium approaches, postsecondary systems are experiencing new pressures to change. The forces are many and complex. They include government concerns over being asked to sustain, and in some respects expand, expensive components of the public sector while being under sever spending constraints. Another factor is a fast-emerging economic reality which roots national competitiveness in human resources development and the acquisition of advanced skills and knowledge (Newfoundland 1990a, 1992; New Brunswick Commission on Excellence in Education 1993; Council of Regents 1990, 1992; British Columbia Human Resource Development Project 1992). Still another form of pressure stems from students demanding a flexible and responsive education and training system which allows for more convenient access, more extensive recognition of previous learning, and better preparation for technological change. Overall, there is recognition that postsecondary education should become a cooperative endeavour in which government, business, labour, and the private-training sector play more deliberate and explicit roles.

One other issue which is frequently ignored in discussions on this topic is the low status usually assigned to technical and vocational education, particularly with regard to apprenticeship training. These areas have received very little recognition from traditional educators, in spite of their importance to the economy. Greater recognition of these aspects of postsecondary education is long overdue in any debate about the future of provincial systems.

All of this points to the need for fundamental change in the organization and management of higher education. Whether the operative word be restructuring, coordination, articulation, or cooperative planning, the ultimate challenge is for institutions to find ways to respond, while still ensuring the preservation of their integrity and quality. Given the current character of provincial systems, the magnitude of the task seems to be immense.

This chapter has described some of the options for organizational change. Some of these may be called modest, tentative, or even cosmetic; others might be seen as bold, adventurous, or even radical. Either way, there will be some risk-taking. There is no denying that any changes should be monitored and evaluated, in part to determine whether any new design may be an improvement upon the original. Many writers have commented upon the inflexibility of postsecondary educational institutions, and such comments are by no means confined to conventional universities. Organizations with long-held values are, by their nature, resistant to change, and colleges, technical institutes, and universities are no exception. Nevertheless, their independence, and even their survival, may well rest upon their willingness to reform.

Notes

1 It should be noted that the term system is not being used in a technical sense (e.g., as in 'open systems'). Rather, it is used as a general term to designate the galaxy of postsecondary educational institutions within a given jurisdiction.
2 In the remainder of this chapter, the term 'system' will be used to describe the current sets of arrangements.
3 Open learning institutions are often referred to as distance education agencies.

References

Alberta. 1991. 'Toward 2000 Together: A Discussion Paper on Alberta's Economic Options and Choices.' Edmonton

British Columbia. 1988. *Access to Advanced Education and Job Training in British Columbia: Report of the Provincial Access Committee.* Victoria: Ministry of Advanced Education

–.1991. *Forces of Change Influencing Education and Training.* Victoria: Ministry of Advanced Education

British Columbia Council on Admissions and Transfer. 1994. *Prior Learning Assessment.* Victoria: BC Council on Admissions and Transfer

British Columbia Human Resource Development Project. 1992. *Human Resource Development Project: Report of the Steering Committee.* Vancouver: BC Human Resources Development Project

California Postsecondary Education Commission. 1960. *A Master Plan for Higher Education*. Sacramento: California Postsecondary Education Commission

Campbell, G. 1971. *Community Colleges in Canada*. Toronto: Ryerson, McGraw Hill

Council of Regents for Colleges of Applied Arts and Technology of Ontario. 1990. *Vision 2000: Quality and Opportunity*. Toronto: Ministry of Colleges and Universities

–.1992. *Prior Learning Assessment: Enhancing the Access of Adult Learners to Ontario's Colleges*. Toronto: Council of Regents

Dennison, J.D. 1978. 'University Transfer Program in the Community College.' *Canadian Journal of Higher Education* 8 (2):27-38

–.1989. 'College to University: An Analysis of Transfer Credit Policy and Practice.' Paper prepared for Vision 2000. Toronto: Ontario Council of Regents of Applied Arts and Technology

–.1992. 'The University College Idea: A Critical Analysis.' *Canadian Journal of Higher Education* 22 (1):109-24

Dennison, J.D., and P. Gallagher. 1986. *Canada's Community Colleges: A Critical Analysis*. Vancouver: UBC Press

Dennison, J.D., and G. Jones. 1970. 'How BC students Fared in College-University Hurdles.' *Canadian University and College* 40:16

Dennison, J.D., G. Forrester, and G. Jones. 1982. 'A Study of Students from Academic Programs in British Columbia's Community Colleges.' *Canadian Journal of Higher Education* 12 (1):29-36

Gallagher, P. 1990. *Community Colleges in Canada: A Profile*. Vancouver: Vancouver Community College Press

Gregor, A.D., and G. Jasmin. 1992. *Higher Education in Canada*. Ottawa: Minister of Supply and Services

Johnston, I.C. 1991. 'Myth Conceptions of Academic Work.' *Canadian Journal of Higher Education* 21 (2):108-16

Macdonald, J.B. 1963. *Higher Education in British Columbia and a Plan for the Future*. Vancouver: University of British Columbia Press

New Brunswick Commission on Excellence in Education. 1993. *To Live and Learn: The Challenge of Education and Training*. Fredericton: Policy Secretariat

Newfoundland. 1990a. *White Paper on Postsecondary Education: Equality, Excellence and Efficiency: A Postsecondary Educational Agenda for the Future*. St. John's: Department of Education

–.1990b. *Shaping Our Future: A Five-Year Strategic Plan for the Postsecondary Education System in Newfoundland and Labrador*. St John's: Department of Education

–.1992. *Change and Challenge: A Strategic Plan for Newfoundland and Labrador*. St. John's: Queen's Printer

Ontario. 1991. *Skills to Meet the Challenge: A Training Partnership for Ontario*. Toronto: Queen's Printer

Ontario Premier's Council. 1990. *People and Skills in the New Global Economy*. Toronto: Queen's Printer

Organization for Economic Cooperation and Development (OECD). 1990. *Reviews of National Policies for Education: Higher Education in California*. Paris: OECD

Pitman, W. (Chair). 1993. *No Dead Ends: Report of the Task Force on Advanced Training to the Minister of Education and Training.* Toronto: Ministry of Education and Training

Richardson Jr., R.C. 1993. 'Faculty in the Transfer and Articulation Process: Silent Partners or Missing Link?' *Community College Review* 21 (1):41-7

Rothblatt, S. 1992. *Introduction to the OECD, the Master Plan and the California Dream: A Berkeley Conversation.* Berkeley: Center for Studies in Higher Education

Sheffield, E., D.D. Campbell, J. Holmes, B.B. Kymlicka, and J.H. Whitelaw. 1978. *Systems of Higher Education: Canada.* New York: International Council for Educational Development

Skolnik, M.L. 1986. 'Diversity in Higher Education: The Canadian Case.' *Higher Education in Europe* 11 (2):19-32

Skolnik M.L., and G.A. Jones. 1993. 'Arrangements for Coordination between University and College Sectors in Canadian Provinces.' *Canadian Journal of Higher Education* 23 (1):56-73

Stokes P. 1989. 'College Transfer Revisited: A Working Paper.' Paper prepared for Vision 2000. Toronto: Ontario Council of Regents

Sweet R. 1989. *Postsecondary Distance Education in Canada: Policies, Practices and Priorities.* Athabasca: Athabasca University Press

Vaala, L. 1991. 'Attending Two-Year College after Attending a Four-Year University in Alberta, Canada.' *Community College Review* 18(4):13-20

–.1993. 'Student Persistence: An Update on Student Mobility from Four-Year to Two-Year Institutions in Alberta, Canada.' *Community College Review* 20 (5):37-49

Vale, N. 1994. 'The Thaw Begins.' *University Affairs*, Association of Universities and Colleges of Canada 35(6):6-7

4
Organizational Culture and Community Colleges
Starr L. Owen

Community colleges are, among other things, workplaces. They are settings in which practitioners (e.g., staff, instructors, and administrators) practise their professions. They are also settings in which policymakers (e.g., board members and government officials) monitor the implementation of their plans. As workplaces, colleges are lively, complex, and often difficult to understand. Even insiders may be unclear as to how to make sense of certain information, processes, or events. For example, a plan may be carefully developed but never implemented, and a senior administrator who was seen as successful in one college may prove a dismal failure in another. The perspective taken in this chapter is that some difference in the cultures of any two colleges is likely to explain why the administrator may fail in one but succeed in another. I argue that understanding organizational culture is essential to understanding what happens in community colleges.

At first glance, culture is a commonsense idea, perhaps even an intuitive experience. People recognize, for example, that different organizations usually 'feel' different from one another and often have distinctive ways of doing things. Culture is often thought of as 'the way we do things here.' Culture is, in many ways, a familiar idea. It is most familiar, perhaps, as a popular perspective presented in the business press. For example, Peters and Waterman's (1982) bestseller, *In Search of Excellence: Lessons from America's Best-Run Campuses,* associates corporate success with a strong culture. In this view, a strong culture is unified and cohesive, created and managed by leaders, and rooted in consensual (i.e., widely shared) values. Culture is also, in some ways, an elusive idea; the literature reveals that there is no consensus on how to define it. The intent of this chapter is to provide some new ways of thinking about culture and to show that an awareness of both familiar and less familiar definitions of culture may permit a richer understanding of colleges.

Five recent studies are cited to support the argument that a knowledge of culture is useful when attempting to understand community colleges. The authors of these studies are experienced college instructors and/or administrators as well as researchers. The first one focuses on a small Alberta college with an agricultural mandate. Hall (1989) did not intend to study organizational culture when he began this work; his purpose was to explain how the college gained equilibrium with its environment and, more specifically, to identify the strategies with which the leadership accomplished this goal. He came to realize that he could not understand what was happening without looking at the college's culture. The values expressed, the action taken on the basis of those values, and how college members interpreted both were critical in determining how the college adapted to its environment. The new president, for example, modeled as well as encouraged openness and extensive consultation. The emphasis on those values allowed the establishment of a climate of trust and commitment within a college that, under the previous administration, had existed within a climate of mistrust. It also allowed the re-establishment of a connection with the surrounding rural community. These changes made possible the major organizational changes, supported by both college and community members, which transformed that institution (Hall 1989).

In each of the four other studies, the author begins with an awareness of the significance of culture. These studies concern four different Canadian community colleges, each of which is given a pseudonym. Success College is an urban college, in which the new president's arrival follows a period of low morale and coincides with a period of institutional expansion (Levin 1993); Multisite College, an established community college, is making the difficult transition to becoming a university college (Owen 1993); Brookview College, once a small collegial institution, has become larger and more complex in the last two decades, with tumultuous upheavals in its culture, structure, and leadership (Gawreluck 1993); and Eastside College is highly politicized – events there result in a public hearing in which some faculty and community members call for an inquiry into its management (Owen 1992).

Each of the five studies demonstrates that an awareness of its culture offers a way to understand what is happening in a particular college. The next section begins by looking at how all community colleges share a culture and then moves on to consider how each college also has a culture unique to itself. Two related purposes are intertwined throughout this chapter: one is to develop the idea of culture; the other is to show how it can be used to understand colleges – both individually and collectively.

Colleges and Organizational Culture

Community Colleges Share a Culture

To some extent, all Canadian community colleges share a common founding culture. They developed in the same period (the postsecondary expansion from the 1960s to the 1970s) and 'were founded upon ideals of democratization of opportunity, accessibility, adaptability, and comprehensiveness' (Levin and Dennison 1989:41). Among the characteristics associated with these ideals are a comprehensive curriculum with both educational and training components, a commitment to teaching and student service, and an orientation to the community (p. 43). These ideals continue to be seen as central values by many in the college community. Recognizing this is helpful in understanding what is happening at Brookview and Multisite.

Gawreluck (1993) identifies a focus on students and teaching as a critical value for the faculty and staff at Brookview. Brookview's administrators have a vision of their institution attaining degree-granting status; faculty and staff interpret this as a shift from an emphasis on students to an emphasis on programs. The administrators fail to recognize the depth of faculty and staff concern. This insensitivity has two results: one is that faculty and staff see the issue of degree-granting status with an increased sense of threat; the other is that it contributes to the increasing isolation and mistrust between administrators and other members of the college (Gawreluck 1993).

Another founding principle is to provide 'increased access to educational opportunity for a broad cross-section of people in the region' (Levin and Dennison 1989:43). Actions perceived as threatening access often trigger strong responses in colleges. During the study at Multisite (Owen 1993), for example, management prepares and presents a proposed plan on how to deal with a budget shortfall. The plan recommends, among other things, that the funding for a two-year career program be reduced so that it is offered on a part-time basis only. Students in the program speak during the public session of the board meeting. They describe what the impact on their careers and lives would be if the program were not available to them on a full-time basis. One of the students says to the board, 'Let me remind you: leadership is not doing things right; it is doing the right thing' (Owen 1993) – meaning that the board ought to sustain the principle of access. The plan that is eventually approved by the board is essentially the original proposal. One of the few substantive changes is that the reduction to the career program is less than originally recommended, allowing it to remain a full-time program, as the students requested.

To some extent, the culture of community colleges reflects the traditions and values of broader categories of organizations. For example, colleges are a subcategory of institutions of higher education (i.e., postsecondary institutions). There is a strong tradition in higher education of the 'dual authority' structure; that is, of there being two decisionmaking structures (administrative and faculty) within an institution. The authority of the faculty structure is rooted in professional values, norms, and expertise (e.g., Chaffee and Tierney 1988:26; Dill 1982). Professional norms are likely to take priority over bureaucratic rules, especially on academic issues. The American literature sees this tradition of faculty authority (on academic matters) as a distinctive characteristic of all postsecondary institutions.

In Canada, the dual authority structure is well established in universities, which have a bicameral system of governance, allowing the senate and the board to share decisionmaking. However, 'no colleges in Canada *formally* practice the principle of bicameral governance with respect to decision making on academic matters' (Dennison 1994:4, emphasis in original). In some provinces (i.e., Alberta and Québec), the responsibilities of academic councils (in Québec these are referred to as senates) are clearly defined; they are limited to providing advice. They lack the statutory decisionmaking power of university senates. In other provinces, (i.e., Ontario and British Columbia), colleges have the authority to establish advisory bodies, but the terms of references are vague. In British Columbia, for example, the legislation requires that colleges establish an advisory committee that includes professional employees and students; however, no information is provided on the role or purpose of this committee. 'Hence, practice is informal and varies dramatically among institutions, depending to a large extent upon the initiative of the chief executive officer' (Dennison 1994:3).

In a formal sense, then, the tradition of faculty authority has no status in Canadian community colleges. In a cultural sense, an expectation of substantive input from faculty on instructional matters seems (at least to this author) to be both pervasive and influential. This tradition has always been highly valued in at least some community colleges. As Dennison and Gallagher (1986) note, a collegial model, more or less in the style of universities, was one of the early models of college management and one that many college people found to be 'the most hospitable climate' (p. 198). Some colleges continue to enact this tradition, despite its lack of formal status. Multisite, which prides itself on its collegial and participatory style, has an approach to decisionmaking which involves both faculty and other organizational members (Owen 1993). Other colleges have found that ignoring the faculty's expectation of influence with respect to educational decisionmaking is risky. Eastside, with its open confrontation between faculty and administrators, appears to be an example of what can happen when this occurs (Owen 1992). The issue of the role of faculty in decisionmaking remains a source of tension in many colleges.

Colleges also belong to the broad category of educational organizations described as 'value rational.' This means that (professional) 'members have [an] absolute belief in the values of the organization for their own sake, independent of the values' prospects for success' (Dill 1982, citing Satow 1975). In particular, all educational organizations have a primary foundational value which is so basic it is easily overlooked. Educational organizations are rooted in and built around a belief in the value of education and the education process itself. Educational organizations are value-infused and value-driven. 'A culture is established around the production of something valued by its members ... The culture of academic organizations must thus be understood within the context of the educational purposes of collegiate institutions' (Bergquist 1992:3).

Community Colleges Differ from Other Organizations

One way to understand culture in colleges is by recognizing how they differ from other types of educational organizations. Institutes of technology, for example, are a part of the college (i.e., college, institute, and university-college) sector. These institutes share with colleges the ideals of institutional adaptability and high-quality instruction. Both types of institution are responsive to the demands of employers and to government priorities. Institutes of technology, however, are highly specialized. Their mandate is to prepare graduates for jobs well beyond the entry level; they offer technical programs that combine academic and applied studies (Dennison and Gallagher 1986:69). Colleges are non-specialized institutions by design; their mandate is to offer a comprehensive curriculum and to serve a wide range of community needs.

Universities have neither accessibility nor comprehensiveness as ideals. They admit students selectively, based on previous academic performance, and their curriculum is academic and theoretical. They evaluate faculty performance in terms of its contribution to knowledge (this includes research and service as well as teaching). They are not oriented to community needs in general; they respond primarily to development in research areas and to the demand for highly skilled graduates in selected programs (Dennison 1992).

The cultures of the conventional university and the comprehensive community college have been described as fundamentally different from one another (Dennison 1992:121). The contrast between college and university values is an important issue in many colleges. In BC, for example, four established community colleges are becoming university colleges. Structurally, this means that, initially, they offer degrees in cooperation with established universities; later, they will do so independently. (Academically, this means that they are adding the third- and fourth-year programs of the baccalaureate degree to the first- and second-year university transfer courses that have long been a part of their curriculum.) Other colleges and institutes in BC will offer degrees in the near future: some will do so by affiliating with another institution; others may attempt to gain university-college status. Brookview College, in Alberta, is also seeking degree-granting status.

Faculty and staff at Brookview fear that the traditional academic emphasis on the subject area will displace their historic focus on students and teaching (Gawreluck 1993). Some faculty at Multisite have this same fear; it is closely related to their concern that comprehensiveness may be threatened (Owen 1993). There is a pervasive belief among college practitioners in general that when an institution becomes more academic, the non-academic side suffers. This concern is well founded at least in terms of some precedents. For example, institutions in the United Kingdom, Australia, and Canada eliminated or reduced non-degree programs once degree programs were developed (Dennison 1992:118). However, there may be other ways of doing things. For example, at Multisite, the budget proposal was modified and this modification sustained the college value of accessibility. So far, there seems to be no apparent loss of comprehensiveness, although people remain watchful (Owen 1993). To have university and college programs coexist in one cohesive institution may pose major and ongoing challenges. It may be some institutions will meet those challenges successfully (Owen 1994a).

Colleges are different from other educational organizations in that they are institutions of an explicitly public nature. Their role is to serve citizens and society – they are publicly supported and publicly accountable institutions. Universities, in contrast, on the basis of their historic role as social critics, remain separate from the larger society. The public can choose to use colleges or not; the school system, in contrast, has a captive market. Colleges need to convince the public, over and over again, of the value of the services they offer. This is no small matter, especially in periods of restraint, when colleges are vulnerable because they serve a relatively small sector of the total population (Dennison and Gallagher 1986:144-5).

Each College Has a Unique Culture

Every college is unique by virtue of its geography, history, and internal dynamics. Externally, each college has its own communities and region, each region has its historic and changing demands, and each college has a history of responding to those demands. Internally, each college has its own institutional constituencies, with their histories and their ongoing interactions. The past and present attitudes and actions of students, staff, faculty, administrators, and board members, for example, will all be part of the internal context. How people interpret what is happening is context-specific; the same event or issue may be interpreted differently in different colleges. For example, the length of the appointment of department heads is an issue at both Eastside College and Multisite College, where some heads have held their positions for many years.[1]

Multisite College has a history of relatively harmonious relations. Differences in perspectives are recognized; individuals in particular roles tend to see those in other roles as collaborating in the pursuit of collective goals. Three main interpretations of the department-head issue are expressed. First, senior administrators prefer long-term service. They say that rotating the position among (all or most) department members can mean less efficient management, because individuals with little administrative skill may get the position. Second, some faculty, primarily those in non-academic (i.e., career) programs, also prefer continuing tenure. Their view is that longer service can mean better networks, especially with respect to groups of employers and relevant industries. These networks benefit both students (by helping them to obtain jobs) and programs (by keeping them in tune with the changing requirements of the workplace). Third, many faculty, primarily among those in academic programs and including many who are heads themselves, want the position of head to rotate among faculty. They say that senior administrators 'have a different view; they just don't understand [this preference for rotating].' These faculty say that those who remain as heads for extended periods 'change, they forget, they get to think like managers' (Owen 1994b). They see being a representative of faculty as distinctly different from being a manager, and they want heads to represent them.

At Multisite College, 'doing our job' seems to be the central concern, and most interactions are characterized by openness. Different interpretations seem to arise from differences in the dominant values that underlie a particular individual's perspective. For example, senior administrators value efficient administration, faculty in career programs value effective community connections, and academic faculty value a collegial style of managing departments. Different opinions are interpreted straightforwardly: people have different perspectives and sometimes do not understand the perspectives of others. All three positions can be seen as different interpretations of how best to attain collective goals.

Eastside College is highly politicized. There is increasing conflict between two groups, senior administrators and faculty with administrative responsibility (i.e., department heads and others). Three main interpretations of the department-head issue are expressed. First, the senior administrators say that, because the world is changing, they will implement a policy that limits the number of terms one individual can serve. Second, some faculty, primarily those without administrative experience, support this change in policy. The new policy will allow more people to gain administrative experience, and those who support it say that, as things are now, many faculty will never have the opportunity to do this. Third, some faculty, including many of those with administrative responsibility, are against the policy. Some say it is another power grab on the part of the administrators – an attempt to reduce the influence of a group of middle managers who tend to become more influential the longer they hold their positions.

At Eastside College, power seems a central concern, and mistrust underlies many interactions. Different interpretations seem linked to how the individual sees her/himself in terms of the chain of power struggles. Differences in perspective tend to be interpreted negatively. At the least, others are seen to be motivated primarily by self-interest; at the worst, they are seen to be driven by a sinister plan. The department-head issue does not appear to be considered in terms of the attainment of collective goals.

These examples illustrate that what is most important about any organizational event, process, or issue is not what happens but how it is interpreted. Events can have different meanings for different people. Many events, issues, and processes are ambiguous or uncertain: it is often difficult to know what happened, why it happened, or what will happen next (Bolman and Deal 1991:244). Interpretations are subjective and contextual. People interpret on the basis of their personal and organizational values, beliefs, recent experiences, and histories. They interpret within the context of a unique college culture, the deeper levels of which include the general community college culture and its common principles. Always influential, although neglected in this account, is the culture of the dominant society within which each organization is situated.

Meanings and Organizational Culture

Meanings
Culture is generally defined in terms of basic assumptions, values, or sets of belief. 'Meanings' is a generic term for these categories. Under one label or another, meanings are the central concern in all the various ways of thinking about culture. Meanings exist at various levels of consciousness and 'exert a powerful influence over what people think about, what they

perceive to be important, how they feel about things, and what they do (Kuh and Whitt 1988:25-6, citing Schein 1985).

Meanings are contextual, as the department-head issue illustrates, and are not 'objective readings' of the external world; they are subjective judgments about how things are and about what is important. Meanings are always invisible. Events, behaviours, and artifacts are directly observable; but their meanings can be known only by inference. The inferential nature of meanings implies that a cultural analysis offers plausible interpretations, not definitive conclusions. It also has implications for how one can learn about an organization's culture. To get at the meanings that underlie behaviour, one needs to observe the day-to-day functioning of a group.

> The characteristics of the culture being observed will gradually become evident as one becomes aware of the patterns of interaction between the individuals, the language that is used, the images and themes explored in conversation, and the various rituals of daily routine. And as one explores the rationale for these aspects of culture, one usually finds that there are sound historical explanations for the way things are done. (Morgan 1986:121)

Observing daily life in a college reveals what is expressed on the surface. Language use at Multisite College, for example, often includes metaphors of family and of hospitality. People 'invite' one another to discuss issues; 'revisiting' topics of discussion or earlier decisions is often suggested. There is frequent acknowledgment of accomplishment and contribution and frequent expression of thanks. Early periods in the college's history are described by 'old-timers' in such terms as: 'we were family' and 'we all knew one another and took care of one another.' When asked what they mean by saying they are family, people at Multisite talk about caring, connection, and community. Consistent with the metaphor of family, activities such as group meals and collective work are mentioned in stories of earlier periods. However, the family metaphor seems not to connote traditional authority relations. No one is designated as a parental figure, for example. This is consistent with what is presented as the historic pattern of Multisite College: an emphasis on participatory process and a lack of emphasis on hierarchical position (Owen 1993).

Observing daily life in a college also reveals what is missing on the surface. In the study at Brookview College, for example, Gawreluck (1993) notices the absence of two types of symbols. Each missing type can be seen to reflect an organizational theme. First, there are no symbols on the new campus that reflect the past. The current administrators appear uninterested or unaware of the college's history. For many members, the college's past identity was clear and valued; now, it is uncertain and changing. This obviously reflects an ambiguous institutional identity. Second, there are no symbols, like campus-wide ceremonies, that draw people together. This reflects isolation. The configuration of buildings physically separates people from one another. Gawreluck reports that many faculty and staff feel cognitively as well as physically isolated from colleagues and administrators.

Cultural meanings are rooted in experience. They are ways of understanding that emerge from the past and influence the present, and they are retained because they are seen as effective and, often, as inherently valuable. The related values of caring for one another and of building and maintaining a sense of community, for example, were established in Multisite's early years. These values seem important with respect to how the budget is handled. They account for the severe distress many people express at the possibility of some colleagues losing their jobs: 'We are supposed to take care of one another.' This is culture as a guide to interpretation and to action; culture as a description of 'how we do things here.' This is what is meant when one says that one of the functions of culture is to serve as an interpretive or sense-making device. This is also what is meant when one says that culture is a product of the past: 'Culture as product embodies the accumulated wisdom of the early members' (Bolman and Deal 1991:250).

Shared Meanings

All definitions of culture recognize the importance of shared meanings. Organized action requires the emergence and continued existence of consensually held interpretations of what to do and how to do it. Shared meanings allow day-to-day activities to be taken for granted, to become routine (Smircich 1983a, 1983b, 1983c). Shared meanings also underlie the interpretive or sense-making function of culture. People have to share a particular value or meaning, like the sense of being members of a community, in order to engage in collective interpretation or collective action.

Shared meanings provide the foundation for the other three general purposes of culture. In addition to the sense-making function, culture conveys a sense of identity, facilitates commitment, and enhances the stability of the social system (Kuh and Whitt 1988:10; Smircich 1983a:345). These purposes are frequently intertwined, as Multisite College illustrates. At Multisite, meanings concerning the college's values, goals, and history seem to be widely shared. Insiders (organization members) describe it as a 'good' college, 'a great place to work,' 'the nicest place I ever worked.' The value of an open and participatory way of interacting is frequently espoused, both in conversation and in meetings. This value is described as deeply rooted in the college's history (Owen 1993).

This sense of identity, of how we do things, seems to guide what happens and to provide stability in a difficult period. The college is faced with a budget shortfall. In an open forum, the president presents details of a draft plan to deal with this shortfall. The budget is discussed at a number of open (i.e., open to all members of the organization) meetings over a period of several weeks. It is difficult to decide where to cut costs. Using a participatory process, Multisite arrives at a budget plan which many participants seem to accept as 'about the best alternative.' The values of participation and openness seem to allow the expression of various perspectives with little overt conflict. These values are frequently articulated (Owen 1993).

Often, culture is defined solely in terms of shared meanings. In these definitions, culture is seen to exist only where there is consistency and consensus. Martin and Meyerson (1988) label these definitions as the integration paradigm. In their terminology, a cultural paradigm defines what culture is and, by implication, what it is not. It determines what is seen and what is not seen. A cultural paradigm is a 'subjective perspective that researchers and cultural members adopt when they perceive, conceive, and enact a culture' (p. 120). In the integration paradigm, culture excludes any meaning that is unclear, uncertain, or not a matter of consensus; that is, ambiguity (confusion, uncertainty, or contradiction) is denied.

In the integration paradigm, culture is the social or normative glue that holds together a potentially diverse group. Culture is an integrating mechanism, always emphasizing consistency, consensus, and (often) a specific leader as the primary source of culture. This monolithic view of culture seems to promise clarity, harmony, and a means of managerial control and organizational effectiveness. Top executives may find the harmony, the leader-centredness, and the implications for managerial control of this view appealing (Martin and Meyerson 1988). Integrationist views are generally appealing and pervasive; they dominate the popular press and have historically dominated the academic press. The most familiar views of culture, including those presented in bestsellers like *In Search of Excellence,* are integrative.

Diverse Meanings
Organization, 'being organized,' requires a degree of consensus concerning organizational routines. But diverse meanings, a lack of consensus on a range of issues, are a fact of organizational life. Martin and Meyerson's (1988) second perspective on culture, the differentiation paradigm, emphasizes lack of consensus, inconsistency, and the development of meaning by persons other than managers. In the absence of organization-wide consensus, there tend to be overlapping subcultures or other groupings.

Ambiguity is channelled; consensus is seen to lie only within subcultures, each of which is ambiguity free. This paradigm especially fits unionized organizations (Martin and Meyerson 1988). It also fits the dual (administrative and professional) authority structure that is often seen as characterizing institutions of higher education. Competing meaning systems can come to characterize identifiable groups (e.g., those in particular roles) within the organization. They also exist among individuals.

At Multisite College, a lack of consensus on various issues seems to be seen by many staff, faculty, and administrators as predictable and acceptable. During the budget process, there are faculty and staff who object to the specifics of the draft plan prepared by management. There are faculty and staff who object to the process itself, because most participants were reacting to the plan rather than shaping it. The participatory process allows diverse and sometimes dissenting perspectives to be expressed (Owen 1993). Events at Multisite seem consistent with the principle that openness to expressions of diversity tends to minimize conflict and to maintain or re-establish relative harmony. Re-establishing a degree of consensus on vital issues is essential to maintaining a sense of being organized. The processes that deal with differences, however, require time, patience, and a willingness to share power.

At Eastside College, a lack of consensus seems to be seen by senior administrators as a 'lack of support.' Many faculty say they think the new administrators are moving the college towards a highly bureaucratic style of management. Some faculty say that any comments inconsistent with the administrators' perspective places oneself and one's department at risk. They say that decisionmaking is increasingly autocratic and that people who object to it are seen as 'troublemakers' and dealt with punitively. The context is increasingly conflict-laden; efforts to negotiate improved relations fail. The conflict escalates over a period of several years. The publication of the administrators' program plan for the upcoming year triggers a series of events and processes, and a public hearing is demanded and scheduled (Owen 1992).

There are two sides at the hearing. One side consists of members of the board and senior administrators, while the other side consists of nearly forty speakers, representing faculty members, students, the faculty union, local employers, and other members of the community. The emphasis of some speakers is different from that of others; however, there is a striking consistency among the presentations. A number of speakers call for a public inquiry into the administration of Eastside. Some speakers object to how the college is being managed and to how power is used; they object to the decisions that are being made and to the process by which they are made. Other speakers focus on the plan, describing it as supporting a short-sighted, profit-oriented, political agenda. The event seems to underline the absence of shared meaning between the administrators and those represented by the speakers. 'A lack of a shared sense of purpose resulted in an intangible but pervasive sense of not being organized' (Owen 1992:280). Events at Eastside are consistent with the principle that attempts to repress diversity can lead to increased political activity, escalating conflict, and open confrontation.

Recognizing diversity means recognizing that conflict is inevitable. It means recognizing that people behave politically; they attempt to influence what is happening in the ways that seem to them to best suit their interests. Many people, including policymakers, college practitioners, and researchers, are uncomfortable dealing with political activity and with conflict. The appeal of integrative perspectives is the image of consensus and harmony they present. The merit of differentiating perspectives is that the image they present is consistent with much of our organizational experience. 'In organizations there are often many different and competing value systems that create a mosaic of organizational realities rather than a uniform corporate culture' (Morgan 1986:127).

Colleges as Mosaics of Meanings

College cultures are subdivided, complicated, and enriched by the development of subgroups around common roles, tasks, and problems. Many organizations have 'multiple organization subcultures, or even counter-cultures, competing to define the nature of situations within organizational boundaries' (Smircich 1983a:346).

Subcultures

'Groups of students, faculty, administrators, develop common beliefs, values, solutions, and norms as well as systems of symbols, rituals, and socialization processes to maintain their groups' (Kuh and Whitt 1988:93). These different subgroups may or may not be classified as subcultures, depending on how the latter is defined. Subculture, like culture, is a problematic notion. Like culture, subcultures are seen as highly salient in institutions of higher education (e.g., Kuh and Whitt 1988, among others), and there is no consensus on just what the term means. If the definition being used entails few criteria, any group with common problems can be seen as a subculture. With that definition, groups such as minorities, mature women students, and part-time faculty may constitute subcultures, even if the individuals never interact (Kuh and Whitt 1988:83). Typologies of subcultures may include groups that form according to discipline (e.g., humanities or natural sciences), role (administrator, faculty, staff, or student), proximity (different areas of a campus), and/or occupational/professional affiliation (e.g., welding, nursing).

More stringent definitions, consistent with the sociological origins of the concept of subculture, specify several criteria. One such definition is 'a group of people who have persistent interaction, a distinct group identity, and collective distinct understandings that form the basis for action' (Kuh and Whitt 1988:83). By these criteria, the 'extant typologies and other classification schemes purporting to identify subcultures tend rather to describe role orientation and ideal types' (p. 93). The advantage of the sociological definition is that the essence of culture (i.e., meanings) remains intact and is useful in understanding how the group interprets information and how it behaves (p. 37). Subcultures, like cultures, are sense-making devices, and are best understood as such.

The formation of subcultures is significant at Brookview College. Gawreluck (1993) explores the relation among organizational culture, structure, and leadership. Over time, the college changed dramatically in terms of mission; it increased greatly and rapidly in size; and administrators instituted more 'tightly coupled' (bureaucratic) policies and procedures. Successive administrators sought to manage, shape, and recreate an organizational culture. The current president is attempting to instil into the college's culture a renewed vision and mission, along with the values to support them.

The college culture responded, and continues to respond, by developing strong subcultures. Gawreluck identifies instructional staff and support staff as two second-level subcultures, respectively, and he describes the work units within these as third-level subcultures. Here, people find the values, cooperation, and caring they once found in the college as a whole during its earlier (and smaller) days. These subcultures are rich in 'local' (i.e., unit) culture; they have their own ceremonies, rites, rituals, stories, and norms; and they pose a challenge to the administration (Gawreluck 1993), for they threaten the existence of an integrative culture.

At least three types of subcultures (enhancing, orthogonal, and counter) can exist within a dominant culture, and each may pose a challenge (Kuh and Whitt 1988:50-1). Senior faculty may comprise an enhancing subculture, which fervently expresses and seeks to maintain the institution's core values. They may resist any initiatives that they think may change the mission of the institution. An orthogonal subculture accepts the core values of the dominant culture and maintains a separate set of values that does not conflict with it (nonetheless, they may become isolated from the rest of the institution). Any subculture may challenge aspects of the dominant culture. A subculture that poses a threat to the core values of the dominant culture is a counterculture (Kuh and Whitt 1988).

Countercultures

A counterculture opposes 'the organizational values espoused by those formally in control' (Morgan 1986:127). Implicit in Kuh and Whitt's (1988) definition, and explicit in Morgan's (1986), is the assumption that institutional goals are defined by senior administrators. The foremost countercultures are those fostered by trade unions. Unions exist because the interests of employer and employee may not be synonymous (Morgan 1986). 'The philosophy, values, and norms of union culture usually exert an important impact on the mosaic of culture, subculture, and counterculture that characterizes life in any organization' (p. 128).

At Brookview, the dominant culture was centred on the organization's efforts to implement the president's vision. The administrators did not realize the extent to which that vision was seen to change the emphasis from a focus on students to a focus on programs – a change which was seen to be in conflict with the values of many faculty. Faculty members and the faculty association see themselves as adversarial and critical of administrative decisions and process; that is, they see themselves as counter-administration (Gawreluck 1993).

At Multisite, an adversarial perspective emerged during consultations over the budget. It is expressed by a few people active in the union, although it does not seem to be the union position. It holds that it is a mistake to try to cut costs, to try to find ways to balance the budget. The idea is that doing so 'implies we are wasteful, reinforcing the public's perception there is always fat to cut' (an opinion expressed in the union newsletter). Instead, the college should shut down for a number of days, thereby making a public statement that 'underfunding generates less production' (Owen 1993). This perspective seems to be recognized as belonging to a minority, but it is accepted as a legitimate alternative view.

An adversarial perspective is consistent with the political principle that holds that those in power need to be held in check by some form of opposition. This principle is at odds with consultative and collaborative processes, as direct involvement in the management process is seen to reduce the power of dissent (Morgan 1986). 'Many advocates of labor rights have thus suggested that employee interests can best be protected through associations such as labor unions or professional bodies that adopt an oppositional role in order to shape policy without owning it' (p. 146).

At Eastside College's hearing, the speakers (representing faculty, among others) say they reject the managerial plan because it negates the mandate of a community college. They challenge the ability of the board to govern and of the administrators to manage. This event raises complex questions about the meaning of counterculture and, more generally, about politics in colleges. If the faculty are challenging the core values of the institution, then, according to Kuh and Whitt's (1988) definition, they constitute a counterculture. Some faculty, however, say it is the senior administrators who are challenging the core values of the community college. The faculty certainly are challenging the organizational values put forth by those formally in control; therefore, they are a counterculture, according to Morgan's definition (1986).

Our tacit assumptions about power and who has the right to exercise it underlie how we interpret events such as the Eastside public hearing. In a traditional view of power, faculty are likely to be seen as challenging legitimate authority and, hence, as engaging in malpractice. With respect to both the oppositional view of power and the tradition that accepts faculty authority with regard to instructional matters, however, faculty are likely to be seen as engaging in an appropriate demonstration of professional values. Among the questions that emerge here are: (1) who decides on the core values of the institution; (2) how is it decided when, if, and how those values change; and (3) by what processes, if any, are various constituents involved in such decisions.

The Four Cultures of the Academy

Bergquist's (1992) typology of four academic cultures provides a useful analytic framework for Canadian colleges. Two of these, the collegial and managerial cultures, have a long history in institutions of higher education. The collegial culture finds meaning in the disciplines faculty teach. The managerial culture finds meaning in work that is directed towards specified goals and purposes. The negotiating culture grew out of faculty opposition to the managerial culture, and it finds meaning primarily in the establishment of equitable and egalitarian policies and procedures. Finally, the developmental culture evolved primarily in response to faults associated with the collegial culture (which, traditionally, was not responsive to the needs of students or of the community), and it finds meaning primarily in programs and activities that further the personal and professional growth of all members of the college community.

Bergquist sees the four cultures as two pairs of opposites. A culture that is in opposition to another nevertheless shares with it many features and assumptions; each is understood best in terms of the other. He believes each of these four cultures is found in all institutions of higher education. One culture will be dominant in each institution, and the other three will interact with it and with one another (Bergquist 1992).

Gawreluck (1993), using Bergquist's typology, sees a conflict between the collegial and managerial cultures at Brookview. The managerial culture values management skills and fiscal responsibility, while the collegial culture values faculty research and scholarship along with the quasi-political involvement of faculty in the processes of governance (Bergquist 1992). The managerial culture is the dominant culture at Brookview. Administrators seek to manage the college by means of centralized policies and procedures. The president is attempting to embed a new vision into the college – a vision which is seen as threatening by many college members. The collegial culture at Brookview responded to the managerial culture with an anti-administration stance, exemplified by various political activities (Gawreluck 1993).

An increase in collegial-managerial conflict may be a trend in Canadian colleges. Gawreluck (1993) associates the rise in the managerial culture in recent decades with the demand for retrenchment in a period of declining resources. He sees management as being forced to reconcile institutional survival with the values and beliefs of the powerful collegial culture. Levin (1991) suggests that there has been a shift from collegial to managerial influence in the college system in BC. He notes a dramatic shift in the 1980s, a period of government restraint. Colleges that had been collegial institutions, characterized by employee participation, became bureaucratic and sometimes autocratic institutions, directed and controlled by senior administrators (Levin 1991).

The negotiating culture values confrontation and fair bargaining among constituencies which are seen to have vested interests that are inherently in opposition (Bergquist 1992). It developed as a reaction to the inability of the managerial culture to meet the personal and financial needs of faculty and staff (p. 129), and it shares with the latter the belief that anything with regard to educational programs and priorities is negotiable (p. 153). In this, it is at odds with both the collegial and developmental cultures, each of which believes that certain features of the academic enterprise are not negotiable. Its two dominant values, equity and egalitarianism, are also at odds with the collegial culture. It shares these values with the developmental culture but has quite different strategies for achieving them (p. 153).

The developmental culture values personal openness and service to others. It seeks to correct the lack of organization that often characterizes collegial culture, and it believes that teaching and learning, rather than research and scholarship, are at the heart of the academic enterprise. Developmental culture discourages the traditional authoritarian relationships between students and faculty and encourages student participation. Among the features and assumptions it shares with the collegial culture are a democratic spirit and the collegial values of deliberation and open communication (Bergquist 1992).

People at Multisite describe their college as collegial, and they see this collegiality as deeply rooted in their history. Multisite's culture would be better described, in Bergquist's terminology, as a developmental culture. People describe participation as a central value, embracing students, staff, faculty, and administration. This ideal of organization-wide participation is distinct from the faculty-centred governance processes that characterize the collegial culture. The collegial culture values the participation of faculty, but its sense of collegiality does not extend to other members of the college community. The values that people at Multisite frequently espouse and enact (openness, service, participation, a focus on teaching and learning and on personal and professional growth) are exactly the values that Bergquist describes as characteristic of a developmental culture (Owen 1993).

The different perspectives on culture reviewed to this point offer multiple and complex images of colleges. Each college has its own unique culture; each is deeply embedded in the common cultures that characterize all community colleges and all educational organizations. At first glance, a college may or may not present the homogeneous image of the monolithic culture of the integrative paradigm. On examination, any college will almost certainly reveal the texture, the multiple subcultures, and the channelled consensus of the differentiation paradigm. The culture of each college will include the four academic cultures in dynamic interaction. Every perspective on organizational culture is rooted in a particular way of thinking about organization. Exploring theories of organization allows for the better understanding and further development of different views of culture.

Culture and Organization Theory

What we mean by culture is closely linked to what we mean by organization. Theories of organization are often classified as either functionalist (often labelled traditional or instrumental) or interpretive (often labelled symbolic or expressive) theories. Functionalist theories are described as rational. They emphasize a specific (and limited) form of rationality, sometimes labelled ends-means, bureaucratic, or instrumental rationality. This means that the organization is designed to achieve predetermined ends as efficiently as possible. In functionalist theories, an organization is seen as an instrument for task accomplishment. The focus in functionalist research is on what an organization can accomplish and how effectively it can do it (Smircich 1983a). Functionalist theories emphasize shared meanings; some recognize diverse meanings.

In interpretive theories, rationality (in the functionalist sense) and objectivity are seen as myths. There is a basic uncertainty and ambiguity underlying values and action (Morgan 1986:135), and this ambiguity is inherent in organizational life (Kuh and Whitt 1988:5). Assumptions of order and control are set aside or at least questioned. In interpretive theories, an organization is seen as a network of meanings subjectively constructed by participants. Establishing and maintaining common interpretations of everyday practice, which is essential to being organized, is a part of an ongoing social process. The focus in interpretive research is on exploring organizational phenomena as subjective experiences and investigating the patterns that make organized activity possible – it is on how 'being organized' is accomplished (Smircich 1983a). Interpretivist theories emphasize the inherent ambiguity of meanings.

On the one hand, this either/or distinction is artificial, for theories of organization comprise 'clusters of schools of thought' which occur along a continuum rather than adhere to an extreme pole. On the other hand, the dichotomy is not entirely arbitrary, for two different sets of assumptions, often labelled objectivist and subjectivist, underlie two fundamentally different views on the nature of social reality and, hence, on the nature of organizations and of organizational culture.

Functionalist Views of Organization

Culture, when it first emerged as an analytic device, was seen as an emergent, contemporary notion and was often contrasted with more traditional or orthodox concepts (Petersen 1985). It was seen as a reaction against the image of organizations as objective, intentional, and rational systems, and it presented the more subjective, human, informal side of organization. Yet some views of culture are considerably less subjective, less emergent, than are others. The integrative perspective, for example, is quite consistent with functionalist theories.

Functionalist theories are rooted in objectivist assumptions. Social reality is orderly, objective, and external to the individual. Individuals are reactive, their behaviour being determined or at least shaped by the external world. Social phenomena, like norms, values, and roles, can be treated as hard, tangible 'facts' or entities, existing independently of the processes that created them (Putnam 1983:34). There is uniformity in philosophy, goals, and procedures. Action is purposefully and rationally consistent with a uniform mission (p. 45). Functionalist models of culture assume that it is composed of identifiable concrete elements, which can be analyzed by using quantitative checklists or questionnaires. Schein (1985), for example, describes culture in terms of a conceptual hierarchy of three levels: artifacts, values, and basic assumptions.

Metaphors of organizations as machines or organisms recur in functionalist theories – the organization is seen as tangible, as a thing. It could be represented in a diagram, for example, as a box-like object or as an attachment (like a handle or a lever) stuck onto a larger object. In this mechanical imagery, culture, the attachment, is seen as something that can be created, manipulated, and controlled. Culture is seen as a variable, as something an organization *has* (Smircich 1983a). It can be seen as the means by which the course of the organization is directed for managerial purposes.

Culture, as understood in functionalist theories, seems to be exemplified by Success College. Levin (1993) provides an account of events at Success College, based on long-term observations, extended discussions, and survey questionnaires completed by college administrators. A new president begins his tenure at a time when the college is experiencing considerable growth. The board gives him a mandate for change and considerable latitude in the exercise of his responsibilities, largely because his predecessor was seen as unsuccessful and because morale is poor. The president eliminates the decisionmaking authority of the other administrators and makes all decisions himself. He reorganizes the college structure and institutes new procedures; he initiates new rituals and ceremonies and abandons former practices. There is a shift in the ways in which members work and interact with each other. To many administrators, distrust, manipulation, and authoritarian control now define institutional life.

The administrators believe that the president intended to alter organizational life and action, and that the values and beliefs of members altered significantly during this period. They say that how members interpret organizational life and how they behave are intimately connected to the demands and behaviour of the president. Administrators who do not conform either behaviourally or ideologically leave the college. Levin (1993) concludes that the changes the president made were so sweeping and fundamental that the culture was changed to suit presidential purposes.

Interpretivist Views of Organization

Interpretivists see organizations as expressive forms (expressing feelings, meanings, needs) rather than as rational systems (efficiently achieving material outcomes). Interpretive theories are rooted in subjectivist assumptions. Social reality is seen as socially and subjectively constructed through the words, symbols, and behaviours of its members. Some interpretivists recognize a material (objective) reality as well and focus on the interaction between it and social reality. Individuals are proactive in that they act and interpret and have a critical role in shaping environmental and organizational realities. Social phenomena are ongoing, evolving social relationships and symbolic processes. For example, norms, values, and roles are dynamic and are constantly being recreated by the same interactive processes by which they were initially created (Putnam 1983). Interpretivist ideas are inconsistent with models that assume conceptual hierarchy. Culture is viewed as a holistic, contextual, and paradoxical phenomenon. One implication of this is that cultural dimensions (e.g., history, myths, values, norms) are seen to be mutually influential (as distinct from being separated into levels or layers). Interpretivists are likely to spend an extended period of time in the research setting, observing and interacting informally, in order to understand the meanings of participants in context.

Interpretivists compare an organization with another social phenomenon (i.e., culture) rather than with physical objects (e.g., machines). In a functionalist view, an organization *has* a culture; in an interpretivist view, an organization *is* a culture (Smircich 1983a). Culture is seen as a root metaphor rather than as a variable. 'The essence of metaphor is understanding and experiencing one kind of thing in terms of another' (Lakoff and Johnson 1980:5). In interpretivist views, the organization (one kind of thing) cannot be understood or experienced separately from the culture (another kind of thing). Culture is seen as the root (the heart or essential core) of the organization. All culture is likely to be seen as problematic and dynamic, constantly being created through ongoing interpretive processes (Smircich 1983a). Culture itself is seen as a process, continually being renewed and recreated (Bolman and Deal 1991:250). Because culture is now seen to be non-concrete, organization becomes an undertaking with greater room for ambiguity (Smircich 1983a).

The integration paradigm (which denies ambiguity) and the differentiation paradigm (which channels it) have so far dominated research in organizational culture (Martin and Meyerson 1988:95). In the ambiguity paradigm, ambiguity can be acknowledged and even made the focus of attention. Consensus and confusion coexist, making it difficult to draw subcultural boundaries. Individuals are connected by some shared concerns but not others. The pattern of connections that is relevant depends on what issue is salient at any given time. This is distinct from the organization-wide connections of the integration paradigm and from the subculture connections of the differentiation paradigm. Teachers and academics belong to occupational groups often described as comfortable with ambiguity, and educational organizations are often categorized as ambiguous (Martin and Meyerson 1988).

Each paradigm implies different ways of understanding what culture means. In the integration paradigm, culture consists of shared values at all levels, and consensus is clear and organization-wide. In the differentiation paradigm, culture is defined as both those values shared at the organizational level and those shared only at a subcultural level. There is clear consensus within subcultures and clear conflict across subcultures. In an ambiguity paradigm, the meaning of culture itself is ambiguous; it is unclear where, if at all, there is consensus and whether there are shared values. People may see similar problems but different solutions; they may have comparable experiences but with multiple meanings (Meyerson 1991). Culture may be less specific than shared values – it may be a general sharing of orientation or overarching purpose. Members of an organization may be held together by 'a common frame of reference or a shared recognition of relevant issues. There may not be agreement about whether those issues should be relevant or about whether they are positively or negatively valued' (p. 154). In the ambiguity paradigm, meanings are always ambiguous and multiple, often changing, and sometimes deceptive.

In the highly politicized culture at Eastside, ambiguous meanings seem to characterize much of what happens. In the organizational context, for example, the senior administrators advocate a highly bureaucratic style. They say this is to allow the college to be more effective in attaining goals. Some faculty say the administrators espouse efficiency so that they can personally wield more power in a college with top-down decisionmaking. At the hearing, there seems to be a dichotomy of 'sides,' with administrators and faculty apparently taking mutually exclusive positions on many critical organizational matters. That dichotomy, however, seems too neat to reflect the diversity of real people. It may be authentic, reflecting the blinders that can characterize open conflict; it may be strategic, showing unity against the 'enemy'; or it may be deliberately deceptive. One or both sides may express values which do not reflect their real intentions. Each side, for example, presents values likely to please its primary audience (Owen 1993).

The ambiguity paradigm also offers another way of looking at the events and processes at Multisite. On the one hand, there seems to be near consensus that 'the way we do things here' is by means of a participatory process. On the other hand, there is no consensus on just what participation means or on whether it is different from consultation, and there is no consensus on whether it has changed over the years. One opinion is that the truly participatory process of the past continues unchanged; another is that true participation was once the way things were done but it has been, or is being, lost; and still another is that some degree of participation may occur some of the time, to a certain extent, concerning certain issues. Some people recognize the uncertainty and contradiction in their own comments on the participatory process; that is, they acknowledge ambiguity. Some people express concern that what was once an effective democratic process may become a token consultative process, and they say they will try to prevent that from happening. These people recognize that they have a critical role in shaping organizational realities. In other words, they take an interpretivist view and see culture as needing to be monitored, sustained, and renewed on the basis of social processes (Owen 1994b).

Multiple Perspectives

Culture 'focuses attention on the expressive, nonrational qualities of the experience of organization. It legitimates attention to the subjective, interpretive aspects of organizational life' (Smircich 1983a:355). Culture offers an array of perspectives, of 'lenses for interpreting events and actions in colleges and universities' (Kuh and Whitt 1988:6). Martin and Meyerson's (1988) integration, differentiation, and ambiguity paradigms are one set of lenses with which to analyze culture. 'It is a misleading oversimplification to rely on a single-paradigm view of a culture. Instead, any culture can usefully be regarded from all three paradigmatic viewpoints' (p. 121).

Cultural perspectives can serve both the 'outsider' researcher and the 'insider' researcher. Levin (1993), for example, uses data collection techniques (e.g., extended on-site observation and conversation) that suggest an interpretivist perspective along with those (e.g., survey questionnaires) that suggest a functionalist perspective. Gawreluck (1993) develops two distinctive views on culture which he labels pragmatist and cultural purist, respectively. The pragmatic view (equivalent to what is referred to here as the functionalist view) denotes the goal of shared meanings and cohesion obtained through careful management. The purist view (equivalent to what is referred to here as the interpretivist view) sees culture as being an expression of members' needs; it cannot be created or managed by leaders. He uses both views, finding that each proves useful in understanding Brookview's culture.

In the case study at Multisite, both interpretivist and functionalist aspects of culture emerge. During the period of the study, people are dealing with a short-term budget shortfall and a long-term major organizational change. They frequently articulate and reiterate their values in meetings and in conversations. Their traditional participatory style of decisionmaking seems to allow for a satisfactory resolution of the budget problem. Culture functions as a guide to behaviour and interpretation. This is the functionalist aspect of culture, with culture being a product of past experience (Owen 1993).

There are also interpretivist aspects to this reiteration of values. Anxiety arises when people feel uncertain or ambiguous about what is happening. Ambiguity is inherent in organizations, and it is especially prevalent in periods of change. People often deal with uncertainty and ambiguity by creating symbols, for they can make it seem that the uncertainty has been resolved (Bolman and Deal 1991:244). Feelings of loss and threat seem a predictable response to major organizational change (Fullan and Stiegelbauer 1991). Value articulation is a form of symbolic action, an expressive way to deal with feelings. Values are frequently invoked when people perceive a threat to 'how things are done around here' (Kuh and Whitt 1988:106).

When the people at Multisite speak of how their participatory process has accounted for much of what they value, they are acting symbolically. This process is a central organizational symbol; it provides them with a sense of direction and of predictability. As people articulate and reiterate their values, their feelings of anxiety and loss are assuaged. They are acting symbolically to help create and recreate culture (Morgan, Frost, and Pondy 1982; Smircich 1983a, 1983b, and 1983c). They speak not only of the merit of the participatory process but of its apparent inadequacy in dealing with some aspects of the budget problems. They speak of the need to revisit and reshape the process so that such matters may be better dealt with in the future. This discourse is recreating the culture as it proceeds; it is exploring which meanings to revise or re-emphasize. Just what shape the revised participatory process will take remains ambiguous. This is the interpretive aspect of culture, with culture being a dynamic, ongoing process (Owen 1993).

Conclusion

It seems reasonable to say that many dimensions of college life will invite analysis in the years ahead. Colleges are already complex and difficult to understand. Many of them are highly politicized, and the future may be even more turbulent. Colleges and their cultures have been under pressure for some time, and this shows no sign of changing. One powerful source of pressure, for example, is the ongoing fiscal restraint that continues to characterize the postsecondary sector. Because colleges are dependent on government for funding, they are vulnerable to various direct and indirect pressures.

Continuing restraint has put pressure on the founding ideals of colleges. With the economic downturn of the early 1980s, for example, funding was reduced and there was a steady narrowing of access (Dennison and Gallagher 1986). The pattern of responses to this downturn included reducing public funding, passing more costs on to students, and evaluating programs in terms of cost-effectiveness. These responses, especially in combination, resulted in a reduction in accessibility. Concern with effectiveness, for example, often translates into admission requirements that decrease access and increase elitism. These and other responses to economic pressure reduce the capacity of colleges to pursue their traditional goal of accessibility (pp. 164-5).

In a related way, colleges' dependency on government for fiscal support has limited their autonomy and, hence, their ability to respond to community needs (Levin and Dennison 1989:43). The expectation, however, that community colleges should respond to rapidly changing economic and sociopolitical demands remains. Often, the response required is major organizational change. It is not coincidental that, in all the studies cited, colleges are dealing with significant structural change, and this, in itself, exerts a lot of pressure on them.

Levin and Dennison (1989:43) identify a range of pressures colleges faced in the 1980s. Political support for education diminished in an unstable economic climate, and there was increasing concern for accountability from public-sector organizations. Colleges are vulnerable to policy initiatives from provincial and federal governments as well as from various external agencies, other levels of education, and community services. They face great pressure from internal constituencies, including faculty organizations concerned with job security and the ordering of program priorities, a changing student clientele, administrators seeking managerial and technological innovation, and, in some cases, more politicized boards. These factors 'all contributed to the current level of instability in college operations' (p. 43).

The image of the colleges of the future that emerges from this discussion is troubling. It is an image of a culture under threat and likely to become more politicized. A number of factors suggest increased political activity and conflict. These factors will interact in complex, dynamic, and mutually influential ways, so that the effect over time may exceed what is currently anticipated. Limited funding generally means conflict about how available funds should be allocated. Restraint will continue to threaten the historic values of accessibility, adaptability, and responsiveness. The trend to a rise in bureaucratic management (i.e., an increase in the managerial culture) seems likely to continue, at least as long as restraint is with us. This will be experienced by many as a threat to college culture. There may be more pressure on the collective bargaining unit, the one form of faculty authority that is legitimate in the legalistic sense. The negotiating culture may become more powerful in many colleges, with a greater tendency to engage in confrontations.

There is, as well, a more optimistic image that emerges. It is an image of colleges as service-oriented organizations that remain value-sensitive and value-driven. Colleges developed strong and effective cultures quickly. Within the first decade of their being established, for example, they offered a range of courses and services that went well beyond what the original planners had intended (Dennison and Gallagher 1986:161). In a study that examines the current status of the original founding ideals, Levin and Dennison (1989) conclude that much of the idealism and innovation of earlier days still exists. They note that colleges are adjusting to pressures by means of various adaptive strategies, such as becoming more entrepreneurial. Colleges appear to be able to retain their strong cultures, probably for many of the reasons that made them possible in the first place. Committed faculty, staff, and administrators, many with long service, continue to contribute their expertise. Many members work at implementing strategies to improve service and to enhance survival. New members appear to become quickly socialized to college values. Factors that enhance this may include the criteria by which they are selected, their earlier socialization (e.g., as apprentices, graduate students, practising professionals), and the socialization they experience once they are hired.

People who understand the importance of organizational values and who can use a number of cultural perspectives, such as the three cultural paradigms discussed in this chapter, will understand what is happening in colleges. The integration paradigm, for instance, with its emphasis on consensus and consistency, is essential. It makes clear that critical values must be articulated and reiterated so that they gain the following necessary to create and maintain consensus. When the integration paradigm is the only one used, however, any lack of consensus is denied and conflict is likely to increase. When ambiguity leads to consensus being channelled into subcultures, as is the case in the differentiation paradigm, they tend to grow stronger and more isolated. When a lack of consensus is recognized as predictable and potentially constructive, people recognize the importance of participatory organizational processes. These processes can determine whether there will be an open and relatively harmonious negotiation of a new consensus or an open confrontation that rips an organization apart. The ambiguity paradigm recognizes that consensus and confusion coexist in organizations all the time. It emphasizes expressing and attempting to relieve the anxiety that comes from uncertainty and ambiguity as well as recognizing the importance of symbols and symbolic action (especially the activities that embody and sustain the most valued meanings).

People who understand that culture is a dynamic process understand the need to articulate, embody, and enact those values considered essential. They attempt to sustain those dimensions of the culture they value and to modify those dimensions they see as no longer appropriate. They know that everyday workplace 'reality' consists of that to which people pay attention, how they interpret it, and how they respond to it. They recognize and value the wide array of participative processes in which people share and negotiate interpretations, both formally and informally. They know that culture is created, negotiated, revised, and recreated through social interaction. Older members can teach and sustain what was and remains worthwhile, while older and newer members alike can work to redefine 'the way we do things here.' In the years ahead, community colleges are likely to experience profound challenges and changes. College members can be active participants in shaping and sustaining the cultures of their colleges during those demanding and exciting years.

Notes

1 The intention here is to illustrate the point that what is apparently the same issue is interpreted differently in different settings. This account consists of one observer's snapshots of this issue as it was expressed at a particular period in each college. As the respective interpretations around this issue continue to evolve, the snapshots do not accurately represent the current situation(s).

References

Bergquist, W.H. 1992. *The Four Cultures of the Academy: Insights and Strategies for Improving Leadership in Collegiate Organizations.* San Francisco: Jossey-Bass Publishers

Bolman, L.G., and T.E. Deal. 1991. *Reframing Organization.* San Francisco: Jossey-Bass Publishers

Chaffee, E., and W. Tierney. 1988. *Collegiate Culture and Leadership Strategy.* New York: Macmillan Publishing

Dennison, J.D. 1992. 'The University-College Idea: A Critical Analysis.' *Canadian Journal of Higher Education* 22:109-24

–.1994. 'The Case for Democratic Governance in Canada's Community Colleges.' *Interchange* 25 (1):25-37

Dennison, J.D., and P. Gallagher. 1986. *Canada's Community Colleges: A Critical Analysis.* Vancouver: UBC Press

Dill, D. 1982. 'The Management of Academic Culture: Notes on the Management of Meaning and Social Integration.' *Higher Education* 11:303-20

Fullan, M.G., and S. Stiegelbauer. 1991. *The New Meaning of Educational Change.* New York: Teachers College Press

Gawreluck, Robert S. 1993. 'Organizational Culture in a Community College and Its Interrelationship with Leadership and Structure.' Ph.D. thesis, University of Alberta, Edmonton

Hall, D.E. 1989. 'Interpretive and Adaptive Strategies in College Leadership.' Ph.D. thesis, University of Alberta, Edmonton

Kuh, G., and E.J. Whitt. 1988. 'The Invisible Tapestry: Culture in American Colleges and Universities.' ASHE-ERIC Higher Education Project No. 1, Association for the Study of Higher Education, Washington, DC

Lakoff, G., and M. Johnson. 1980. *Metaphors We Live By.* Chicago: University of Chicago Press

Levin, J. 1991. 'Power in the BC Community College.' Paper presented at Canadian Society for Studies in Higher Education, Learned Societies Conference, Queen's University, Kingston, ON

–.1993. 'Success Community College: An Examination of Organizational Change.' Paper presented at the Canadian Society for Studies in Higher Education, Learned Societies Conference 1993, University of Ottawa, Ottawa

Levin, J.S., and J.D. Dennison. 1989. 'Responsiveness and Renewal in Canada's Community Colleges: A Study of Organizations.' *Canadian Journal of Higher Education* 19 (2):41-57

Martin, J., and D. Meyerson. 1988. 'Organizational Cultures and the Denial, Channeling and Acknowledgment of Ambiguity.' In *Managing Ambiguity and Change,* edited by L. Pondy, R. Boland, and H. Thomas, pp. 93-123. New York: Wiley

Meyerson, D. 1991. '"Normal" Ambiguity? A Glimpse of an Occupational Culture.' In *Reframing Organizational Culture,* edited by P. Frost, L. Moore, M. Louis, C. Lundberg, and J. Martin, pp. 131-43. Newbury Park, CA: Sage Publishers

Morgan, G. 1986. *Images of Organizations.* New York: Sage Publishers

Morgan, G., P. Frost, and L.R. Pondy. 1982. 'Organizational Symbolism.' In *Organizational Symbolism,* edited by L. Pondy, P. Frost, G. Morgan, and T. Dandridge. Greenwich, CT: JAI Press

Owen, S.L. 1992. 'An Interpretive Approach to Leadership: Developing a Theme from a Case Study.' In *Educational Leadership: Challenge and Change,* edited by E. Miklos and E. Ratsoy, pp. 259-84. Edmonton: Department of Educational Administration, University of Alberta

–.1993. 'College in Transition: A Case Study in Progress.' Paper presented at the Canadian Society for the Study of Higher Education Learned Societies Conference, University of Ottawa

–.1994a. 'The University-College Idea: A Cultural Analysis.' Working paper

–.1994b. 'We've Always Run on Consensus: A Thematic Analysis in Progress.' Paper presented at the Canadian Society for Studies in Educational Administration Learned Societies Conference, University of Calgary

Peters, T.J., and R.H. Waterman Jr. 1982. *In Search of Excellence: Lessons from America's Best-Run Campuses.* New York: Warner Books

Petersen, M.W. 1985. 'Emerging Developments in Postsecondary Organization Theory and Research: Fragmentation or Integration.' *Educational Researcher* (March): 5-12

Putnam, L. 1983. 'The Interpretive Perspective.' In *Communication and Organization: An Interpretive Approach,* edited by Linda Putnam and Michael Pacanowsky, pp. 31-53. Beverly Hills, CA: Sage Publishers

Schein, E.H. 1985. *Organizational Culture and Leadership.* San Francisco: Jossey-Bass Publishers

Smircich, L. 1983a. 'Concepts of Culture and Organizational Analysis.' *Administrative Science Quarterly* 28:339-58

–.1983b. 'Implications for Management Theory.' In *Communication and Organization: An Interpretive Approach,* edited by Linda Putnam and Michael Pacanowsky, pp. 221-33. Beverly Hills, CA: Sage Publishers

–.1983c. 'Studying Organizations as Cultures.' In *Beyond Method: Strategies for Social Research,* edited by G. Morgan, pp. 160-71. New York: Sage Publishers

5
Values in the Canadian Community College: Conflict and Compromise
John D. Dennison

Introduction

As Burton Clark (1983b) noted in his classical essay, values in higher education is one subject which evokes both enthusiasm and despair. On the one hand, a debate over values tends to rise above the mundane and, in so doing, introduces the most fundamental questions: What is the organization trying to accomplish? Why? What is central to its mandate and must be preserved? What is peripheral and no longer essential? What should the organization seek to become? To what end? On the other hand, a debate over values can be painful, destructive, boring, cliché-ridden, rhetorical, and, perhaps worst of all, an invitation to cynicism. It is often wiser not to ask value-driven questions. Organizations continue to do what they do for a multitude of reasons, many of which may no longer survive the test of relevancy. Some strive to fill needs which might be better unfulfilled; others provide services which are no longer necessary; and still others measure success by criteria irrelevant or foreign to their purposes. Institutions of higher education, particularly universities, have been the subject of innumerable essays focusing on values. Much less attention has been paid to other components of the system, such as community colleges, technical institutes, vocational schools, and adult education centres. Furthermore, much of what has been written respecting the non-university sector is confined to institutions in the United States (Bok 1982; Kaplan 1991; Sloan 1980; Wilson n.d.; Hunter 1977; Collier, Tomlinson, and Wilson 1974).

This chapter will address the question of values in the context of the Canadian community college. It will examine which values are appropriate, how they translate into polices and practices, and how day-to-day college operations are judged by the values they espouse. Finally, through the examination of some case studies, I demonstrate how decisionmaking is often plagued by value conflicts and how this attests to the complexity of the college as a contemporary social organization.

Values in the Canadian Community College

As a point of departure, it is useful to examine the fundamental values in higher education as delineated by Clark (1983a). These values may or may not adequately reflect those of Canadian colleges.[1] Canadian colleges did not, and do not, determine their own fates. They are products of history, and political, sociocultural, economic, and educational imperatives converged to result in their creation. Hence, they are characterized by organizational diversity not only within the various provinces and territories but even within single jurisdictions (Dennison and Gallagher 1986). In the process of their development, various groups imposed their values upon colleges. Governments, in particular, as the major sponsors of the college idea, have always held a large stake in determining what they shall be and how they shall undertake their mission. And in Canada, governmental pressures upon colleges are further complicated by the fact that federal and provincial governments are not always in agreement. Other societal groups which press their values upon the college sector include employer organizations, unions, community agencies, ethnic and minority groups, local governments, and other components of the educational spectrum. All of these groups are powerful, and all are motivated by self-interest. All exert their influence through both formal and informal structures, and rarely do they share the same values.

Further complicating this scenario are the ever-present pressures exerted by internal constituencies, support staff, instructors, administrators, and students. Instructor organizations have little difficulty in expressing what is important to them, and they exert considerable influence upon college policies. Administrators and students usually express different but, in their view, equally crucial priorities.

It might seem that, with such diverse forces attempting to direct the college, no succinct set of fundamental values can be described. Clark, however, concludes that 'three basic sets of values are inescapable in the expectations of an attentive public in the modern period, the interests of government officials themselves, and the attitudes of academic workers' (1983a:241). To these three value sets – social justice, competence, and liberty – he adds loyalty, which he sees as 'powerfully developed' by government. The question which must be addressed is, how appropriate, either in their present or in an amended version, are Clark's value sets when applied to the Canadian community college? The primary locus of Clark's thesis is the university sector. In the discussion which follows, however, the four fundamental value sets will be developed in the context of the community college.

The first value set, social justice, is concerned with equality/equity and fairness/parity in the policies and practices which apply to students, staff, and the external community. To be consistent with this value set, a college would adhere to equality of student access, equality of treatment after admission, and equality of opportunity with respect to outcome. Utilizing a broad-based admission policy, a college would seek to attract students from a wide range of backgrounds without regard to extraneous factors such as age, gender, socioeconomic/sociocultural status, or disability. As an agent of social justice, a college would, perhaps through the application of affirmative action policies, actively encourage the participation of those traditionally unable to continue their education. A college would adhere to the concept of democratization of opportunity and promote practices which would ensure student success.

With respect to instructional and other staff, a commitment to social justice would be reflected in fair and equitable employment and in promotion and retention policies. The college would provide equitable access to decisionmaking and policymaking bodies, to professional development opportunities, and to the promotion of an environment of civility and respect for all employees. In its relations with its community, a college would ensure access to all groups who wished to express their views or to offer advice. It would also seek to ensure equity of representation with respect to advisory bodies. It would listen to both the powerful and the less powerful voices in the wider community.

Clark's second value set, competence, might, for the purposes of this chapter, better be termed 'quality.' Community colleges are, first and foremost, educational institutions; as such, they are beholden to meritocratic principles. Colleges aspire to achieve a high quality of student performance in both classrooms and workshops and a high quality of graduate performance in the workplace (in part to protect the public interest). To accomplish these ends, colleges measure, assess, and evaluate students with respect to admission, retention, and graduation. Colleges also promote quality with regard to the performance of their personnel (i.e., they strive for excellent teaching, competent support services, and capable administration). To this end, most institutions evaluate the performance of instructors, presidents, and board members. A college will insist that quality be a distinguishing characteristic of all its programs, be they credit or credit-free, part-time or full-time, academic or vocational.

The third value set, liberty, refers to those aspects of college education which link together 'choice, initiative, innovation, criticism and variety' (Clark 1983b:247). The value of liberty is expressed in the freedom of instructors to think, write, and teach within their fields of competence. It allows a college teacher to determine how a subject will be presented, which standards for student performance will be set, and how the curriculum will be ordered. Academic freedom has long been a hallmark of postsecondary education. It has been rooted largely in the university sector, and, while its application may differ, it is not out of place in the college sector. College teachers are professionals in the broadest sense of the term. Their expertise is the product of both study and experience. The shop, laboratory, and/or classroom is where that expertise is expressed. College students are also entitled to liberty. As independent and mature learners, they are granted, and expected to exercise, the freedom to question, to explore, to challenge, and to debate the issues endemic to their training as nurses, technicians, tradespeople, and adult learners generally.

Colleges, as educational organizations, enjoy certain privileges not shared by many other publicly funded agencies. In most provinces, governing boards exercise corporate authority with respect to setting program and instructional priorities, allocating internal budgets, hiring personnel, and so on. While institutional autonomy in the college sector is more limited than it is in the university sector, colleges are nevertheless accorded a degree of freedom from government control concomitant with their status as postsecondary educational institutions. As Clark (1983b) notes:

> The subvalues of this complex [i.e., liberty] interact: a variety of institutions extend the range of choice for students, teachers, and administrators alike: extension of choice on the demand side tends to lead to more innovation and variety on the supply side, as institutions respond differently to a wider set of demands and carve out different niches. (p. 248)

The fourth value set, loyalty, is more difficult to interpret in the context of the community college.[2] In essence, loyalty concerns the relationship between the institutions and their primary funding source, the state. As a condition for fiscal support, governments expect colleges to perform certain tasks perceived to be politically desirable. Colleges, for example, are charged with the task of preparing individuals to contribute to the economy through the exercise of skills in the workplace. Colleges are also expected to assist in the realization of political goals, such as greater access to advanced education, preparing students for citizenship, enhancing social opportunity, eradicating illiteracy, and contributing to the general well-being of society. While the state promotes education as a wise investment, colleges must, in turn, meet state expectations. Among postsecondary institutions, the connection between colleges and government is relatively strong, certainly stronger than it is between universities and government.

Aside from institutional loyalty to the goals of the state, colleges share many loyalties which characterize other postsecondary educational institutions. Faculty members are affiliated with their professional fields, trades, or disciplines. Their allegiance extends to their departments, their students, their colleagues, and to the organization in and for which they work. Collective loyalties are also crucial if the college is to effectively pursue shared goals and objectives. Departments have obligations to the central administration, the central administration to the president, and the president to the board. While the formal requirement of loyalty is overtly present in structures of higher education in other Western societies (particularly those which operate within a national system), it is more muted in North America, although state and provincial governments exercise many subtle controls over the operation of colleges, which, in effect, legislates loyalty.

The Applicability of Clark's Four Value Sets

Are Clark's four value sets applicable to the Canadian community college? This chapter agues that they are. Of all postsecondary educational institutions, the community college has borne the most responsibility for the promotion of social justice. At the time of their establishment during the 1960s and 1970s, the literature was filled with assertions that the new institutions would redress charges that Canadian higher education was the privilege of the economic middle class, of young, male, full-time, anglophone learners with the necessary social credentials.

Quality is a term which has long been associated with the college idea. Previous studies reveal that virtually all colleges emphasize their commitment to excellence in teaching and student services, to the competence of their graduates, and to the value of advisory bodies which will ensure the relevance of their curricula (Dennison and Levin 1989). Of more recent vintage is a concentration upon strategies to improve student retention and success.

At first glance, the value sets of liberty and loyalty may be less apparent than the value set of quality. The particular relationships which prevail between government and colleges have a major bearing upon the relevance of these value sets. Caught between pressures to respond to the wishes of their various communities and the expectations of provincial, territorial, and federal agencies, real conflicts between liberty and loyalty inevitably arise. This challenge is exacerbated by the existence of targeted funding. Another source of conflict is to be found in the various arrangements that many colleges make with universities, secondary schools, and technical institutes to ensure program articulation and transfer of credit for those students who elect to continue their studies. Loyalty to formal agreements inevitably imposes constraints upon curriculum choice, evaluation procedures, and, in some cases, selection of instructors, all of which are fundamental to any notion of academic freedom.

Similarly, colleges contracts with community agencies, industries, government departments, and other local, national, and international organizations to offer 'tailor-made' programs may result in difficult situations.

Understandably, the client often wishes to influence the curriculum, the criteria for participating in the program, and the format for delivery of instruction. Loyalty to the contracting organization (in terms of meeting the conditions of the agreement) may well compromise the institution's freedom to train or educate according to its accepted standards. While universities also face this dilemma, traditional concepts of academic freedom tend to protect them.

Are there other, and perhaps equally appropriate, value sets which are associated with the community college idea? Probably yes. A review of missions, goals, and strategic plans for Canadian colleges reveal both explicit and implicit references to values.[3] Commitments to integrity in matters of human relationships, to openness in decisionmaking, to the avoidance of conflict of interest, to sensitivity to community needs, to respect for individual learners, and to the optimal development of student abilities are all to be found in college publications. Nevertheless, although clearly open to challenge, it is my view that virtually all of these can be subsumed within Clark's four value sets.

Conflict and Compromise

It requires neither great imagination nor detailed explanation to recognize that the four fundamental values sets, social justice, quality, liberty, and loyalty are in constant conflict in the community college milieu – conflict which is exacerbated by the political and fiscal environment of the 1990s. Not only are they in conflict in practice, but they may be logically in conflict as well.

The notion of social justice, a predominant force among the establishment of the community college sector, is consistent with a policy of open admissions, mass education, and equitable access to disadvantaged groups. However, in a climate of limited resources, quality becomes an increasingly important criterion, as the demand for seats in a program may exceed the supply. Instructors, committed by training and inclination to encouraging high-quality work from their students, face the consequences of having to deal with high-risk applicants. And both social justice and quality are in conflict with liberty and loyalty, as is attested to by the following dilemmas:

- The freedom of departments to select applicants to programs for which there is high demand may be complicated by the institution's public commitment to equity of access.
- Loyalty to an institution and its preservation may well limit constructive criticism of its inadequacies. The results of an honest internal evaluation may cast doubts upon the wisdom of continuing to fund particular programs.

- A college's freedom to set standards for graduation is in conflict with the demand of employers, and often governments, for greater program standardization. Clark (1983a) refers to this issue in more colourful language: 'Institutional liberty carries with it the likelihood that institutions will vary all over the map in what they do, including the marketing of shoddy goods to uninformed customers in the soft underbelly of a diverse system' (p. 7).
- Conditions applied to fiscal support from government, often exercised through formula funding, may well compromise an institution's requirements for quality, both in the selection of students and in the instructional environment.
- Contracts made by colleges with private industry, while financially rewarding, may compromise both academic standards and principles of equity of access.
- Attempts to provide for full and effective participation in decisionmaking for all stakeholder groups may present an obstacle to a college's freedom to respond effectively to emerging needs for particular programs.

All of the foregoing examples demonstrate the kinds of conflicts which arise when a college attempts to adhere to Clark's four value sets. Without any clear understanding of the complexity of value conflicts, and in the absence of any prior discussion of priority setting, most resolutions are ad hoc and are designed to do the least harm to all parties involved. While such resolutions may solve the immediate problem and allow a particular practice to proceed, inevitably the same conflicts will arise again.

In searching for integrity, it is incumbent upon the community college to address the issue of values, to determine those to which it adheres, to undertake the contentious task of seeking agreement on priorities, and to establish a code of conduct which will guide future action. None of these challenges is without risk, nor can they be met with ease. There are, however, practical ways for an organization to come to grips with these challenges. The first of these is through debating value statements, the second is through utilizing case studies.

Value Statements

Value sets may be given a more practical orientation when embodied in value statements. Each statement will express an aspect of policy or practice common to a particular college setting. They may be extracted from its mission and goals, its operational policies, or simply as philosophical positions taken by its members. The technique then involves asking board members, administrators, instructors, support staff, students, and representatives of the wider community to respond to each of these statements by indicating the extent of their agreement along a continuum from 1 (totally disagree) to 5 (totally agree).

As these statements reflect attitudes towards policies which are fundamental to the operation of the college, wide disagreement, particularly among those who establish policy, those who administer it, and those who are directly affected by it, will reveal a level of dissonance which could have important implications for decisionmaking. Furthermore, a wide range of responses to these statements among and between various college constituencies may provide dramatic evidence of a lack of shared values (the latter being essential to the attainment of the college's mission/goals). Of even more importance than responses to value statements are the discussions which follow them. Experience has shown that the reasons individuals respond as they do tend to expose even deeper conflicts. When these individuals work in the same departments, form part of the same management team, or serve on the same board, the implications of their diverse attitudes assume major proportions.

Some examples of value statements are:

(1) Community colleges should be used as a means of increasing social equity and mobility.

(2) Affirmative action respecting student admissions policy is defensible even in the most competitive of programs.

(3) Admission of academically unqualified applicants to college programs will ultimately jeopardize the reputation of the institution.

(4) An open admissions policy is antithetical to the culture of any institution committed to quality education.

(5) In assessing the performance of a student in a college course, consideration should be given to any language or sociocultural obstacles with which he or she must contend.

(6) The mission and goals of the college must always take precedence over the mission and goals of individual departments.

(7) The individual instructor is responsible for setting the grading standards in his or her course.

(8) As the public interest must be protected, a failure rate of 50 per cent is acceptable if it is necessary to ensure competence in the graduates of a college program.

(9) Having admitted a student to a program, a college must accept responsibility for ensuring that he/she achieves his/her goals.

(10) When entering into a contract with industry to offer a program, a college must retain full authority over its content and delivery.

Each of the foregoing reflects one or more of Clark's four fundamental value sets. In these examples, the issues raised are abstract.

Case Studies

The case study approach to conflict entails an extension of the value statement approach. After responding to the value statements, participants are asked to consider these cases in specific contexts. The three cases presented here involved community colleges in various regions of Canada. In each example, two or more of the fundamental value sets converge and require a resolution. In considering these cases, a participant is confronted with three tasks: (1) to determine which value sets are integral to the case, (2) to propose and then rationalize a resolution to the problem, and (3) to examine the extent to which his or her original responses to the value statements relevant to the case were consistent with the action proposed as a resolution. A description of three case studies and a brief comment on each follows.

Case One

The business administration program at Happy Valley College invariably has many more qualified applicants than places available. The head, Dr Elizabeth Capital, is very careful about the application of criteria for admission, which she feels can be fully justified. The president, Constance Smooth, has been under pressure from community groups to provide seats in several programs for First Nations students. The intent is to raise the quality of life in First Nations communities by encouraging the creation of role models in a number of professional fields. Smooth has sent a memo to Capital, notifying her that eight of the forty places in the business administration program must be reserved for First Nations applicants. None of the latter meets the full criteria for admission, but Smooth contends that her request is in the spirit of 'affirmative action' and 'social responsibility.' Capital has just received Smooth's memo. What action should she take?

Comment

This case introduces the dilemma of a college attempting to maintain its commitment to social justice while, at the same time, striving to ensure quality and fairness in its student admissions policy. Furthermore, the freedom of a particular department to enforce appropriate policies is compounded by its responsibility to adhere to the values of the institution of which it is a part. In this case the relevant value statements are (1), (2), (3), (4), (6), and (9).

Case Two

As part of his course in environmental studies, James Green has taken his students on a field trip along the Red River. At various points the class sampled the water for levels of pollution. It became evident that certain industries were prime offenders in the polluting of the river. Hence, Green and his students prepared a report which summarized their findings. The report was submitted by Green to Power, the college president, for information and comment before being published in the student newspaper.

After discussing the report with the board of governors, Power informed Green that the report must NOT go beyond the class, as some board members have objected to the naming of industries which they regard as 'major tax generators' and 'friends of the college.' Furthermore, they suspect that Green's motives are, to some extent, political. Green has just received the president's memo. What action should he take?

Comment

Case two involves aspects of all four value sets. In particular, the conflict arising between the professional freedom of an individual instructor and his or her responsibility to the institution, as represented by the board and the president, constitutes a personal dilemma.

Case Three

The business department at Big City Community College has been contracted by Oldine Industries to prepare and offer a program designed to give some of their employees an opportunity to attain current 'management and organizational' skills and, hence, to qualify them for advancement. Although not stated explicitly, the department's understanding was that the selection of students, and the content, length, and design of the curriculum, would be by joint agreement between the college and Oldline Industries.

The business department has submitted its proposal and, from fifty-eight employee applicants, has selected those it considers to be the twenty best qualified students. However, the personnel director at Oldline, Herbert Chauvin, has responded by (1) striking all women from the list and (2) removing instructional time slots devoted to business communication skills and business ethics. By way of explanation, Chauvin notes that 'this business is not yet ready for women in management positions' and that Oldine 'does not have the money to pay for non-essential frills.'

The head of business, Simon Shares, recommends that you, as president of the college, reject the contract outright. However, Conrad Campeau, your vice-president in charge of contract services, advises you to remember that 'he who pays the piper calls the tune,' and that the college would lose both money and its reputation for cooperation by rejecting the contract. What should the decision be?

Comment

This case dramatizes the political difficulties for a college when it enters into a contractual arrangement with an outside agency. The need to pre-serve values which the institution sees as essential to its integrity are placed under pressure when attempting to honour a contract. Statement (10) is of relevance in this situation.

College and University Cultures

As noted earlier in this chapter, Clark's four value sets were originally pre-sented in the context of the university sector. A particular characteristic of higher education in the US is the differentiation in mandate and mission which has developed among those institutions which fall under the general rubric of universities. In the inexorable post-Second World War trend to-wards mass higher education so well documented by, among others, Trow (1973), universities have accommodated the inevitable conflict between social justice and quality by creating cadres of institutions, ranging from research-intensive multiversities to four-year colleges with a primary focus upon teaching. Given the extensive galaxy of postsecondary institutions in the US, which encompasses public and private sectors of almost unlimited variety, intense competition for clients translates into educational opportu-nities for a wide range of students. The result is a highly differentiated uni-versity system, which, through diverse institutional mandates, is able to meet the challenge of providing maximum access while sustaining quality.

In Canada, largely due to the small number of institutions, almost all of which are in the public sector, and partly because of a conventional view of what constitutes quality, universities display far less differentiation than they do in the US. While the emphasis upon research may vary among Canadian universities, its importance in terms of gaining status is present in all of them (Smith 1991). Similarly, selectivity in admissions policy re-mains a significant characteristic of universities, although some recent at-tempts have been made to encourage greater access for disadvantaged groups. One outcome of this is that Canada's universities tend to give less promi-nence to the value set of social justice, particularly when it is judged to be in conflict with quality. In fact, the role of social justice tends to fall, both by design and by default, upon community colleges. As noted earlier, the value conflict over social justice and quality is an ongoing issue which is far more prominent in the college sector than it is in the university sector.

With respect to the two other value sets, liberty and loyalty, there are also some important distinctions between the college and university sec-tors. Canadian universities enjoy a degree of autonomy rarely equalled in industrialized societies (Skolnik 1991). It may be argued that the ever-present constitutional debate regarding federal as opposed to provincial jurisdiction with respect to fiscal support tends to ensure that Canadian education does not experience the kind of central government influence found in countries such as the United Kingdom, Australia, Germany, and France. Liberty, as conceived by Clark, is rarely under direct threat in Canada's universities. Conversely, however, it continues to be a major source of debate in the twelve college systems. Colleges, through their connections with government on the one hand, and through their connections with local and/or regional communities on the other, maintain a far more limited degree of institutional autonomy than do universities. At the same time, their responsibility to become directly engaged in the realization of both government priorities and community needs highlights the significance of loyalty.

Another important distinction between the college and university sectors is reflected in governance. In universities, the independence of departments, faculties, schools, and institutes in the pursuit of their respective research agendas places central management in a different role from that of its counterpart in the college sector. Colleges emphasize unity – they seek a broad commitment to institutional missions from each component of the organization. A college instructor's primary responsibility is to student learning rather than to the acquisition of knowledge in his or her particular field of study. Loyalty to the organization and its values, rather than loyalty to one's discipline, distinguishes the college instructor from the university professor. Academic freedom has an important place in both organizations, but it is interpreted somewhat differently in each and, consequently, is exercised in a different manner in each.

All of the foregoing reinforces the argument that the four fundamental value sets in postsecondary education are even more applicable to the community college sector than they are to the university sector, a conclusion which provides an interesting addendum to Clark's university-focused thesis. At the same time, this discussion throws additional light upon the complications which can arise from new organizational initiatives in higher education, such as the university-college experiment in BC (Dennison 1992).

When the values integral to the cultures of the conventional Canadian university and the more pragmatic community college are brought together into a single operational identity, it is not surprising that a variety of issues arise. An analysis of organizational values, such as that presented in this chapter, provides a useful tool for understanding the consequences of creating new models from old organizations.

Conclusion

This chapter has attempted to accomplish two tasks. First, to open a predominantly theoretical dialogue on the subject of values in the Canadian community college and, second, to describe how Clark's four fundamental value sets (social justice, competence, liberty, and loyalty) may be adapted to the college sector. It has been demonstrated that these four value sets are not only applicable, but that they are also integral, to the policies and practices which colleges formulate to accomplish their missions. As a means of further demonstrating the important role which values play in the operation of colleges, the second part of this chapter describes a practical exercise in value clarification. The four value sets are translated into examples of statements, which reflect both policy and practice, and to which members of the wider college community indicate the extent of their adherence. This also reveals the congruence between these value statements and the apparent values of those responsible for setting and implementing policy. Furthermore, the exercise emphasizes the difficulty in reaching institution-wide agreement upon a common, comprehensive mission. Finally, the case studies demonstrate the importance of assigning priorities to values if conflicts are to be resolved.

A knowledge of values and the role they play in the college community is an important prerequisite to productive debate about why the institution exists, the principles which guide its operation, the bases upon which it resolves conflicts, and the yardsticks by which it measures its accomplishments. While agreement upon certain fundamental values is usually achievable in the abstract, it is far more difficult to agree upon priorities when these values are in concrete conflict. Nevertheless, in the interests of preserving institutional integrity and consistency, the often contentious task of value analysis seems crucial. Furthermore, by so doing, those committed to the community college concept will also gain insight into the difficulties inherent in transforming a group of somewhat idiosyncratic postsecondary institutions into a system. As described in Chapter 3 of this book, one current debate is over how the educational and training needs of the wider population may be better served by a more coordinated system of institutions, both public and private. If the idea of lifelong learning is to be realized, greater access and mobility for those seeking further education must be achieved. This goal will require universities, colleges, technical institutes, and other centres of adult learning to better coordinate curricula, transfer/ admission policies, and program planning.

As described in this chapter, however, the values which underlie and ultimately determine such policies are integral to the culture of each organization. If institutions are to work together in an effective manner, some resolution of their value differences must be found. The functional difficulties apparent within BC's university-colleges, the University College of Cape Breton, or the protracted efforts to bridge the philosophical gap between Ontario's colleges and universities are all examples which bear testimony to this argument. The first step in creating an overall system is to clarify the values which determine the role of each institution. By so doing, both the roots of organizational culture and an agenda for change may be brought to light. This chapter has attempted to begin this task.

Notes

1   While several models for classifying values in higher education exist in the literature, Clark's version was deemed to be the most succinct and the most applicable to the broad spectrum of institutions falling under the rubric of postsecondary education. However, it must be acknowledged that there are many different values between which Clark draws no distinction (e.g., values may also be classified as moral, prudential, economic, social, etc.).
2   Loyalty, as used by Clark, is a concept to which it is difficult to assign a succinct meaning. In the context of this chapter, loyalty is broadly equivalent to responsibility (in the sense of an organization being responsible for using funds according to the purpose for which they were granted). Loyalty may also be seen as equivalent to accountability (in the sense that a college is accountable for serving the needs of its community in the manner defined in its mandate).
3   It is instructive to note two examples of value statements which have been extracted from Canadian documents. The first is from Ontario and is a background paper which was prepared for *Vision 2000: Quality and Opportunity*, a review of the mandate of Ontario's colleges commissioned by the Ministry of Colleges and Universities in 1988. It was written by Susan Wismer and is entitled 'Ontario's Community Colleges: Values for the Year 2000':

> Ontario's Community Colleges should provide accessible, high quality services and programs which are available on an equitable basis to diverse groups within the communities they serve; and with special emphasis on those groups who are least well served by other public and private sector educational organizations and institutions. In all their policies, programs, structures and services, Ontario's colleges should model for their communities the peaceful, equitable and viable world for which they educate. (Wismer 1990:ii)

The second example is from the mission statement of Malaspina University College in Nanaimo, BC.

> The Mission of Malaspina-College is to:
> • Develop the full potential of students in every program
> • Promote the development of analytical and creative thinking skills in all students
> • Maintain excellence in all instructional activities and services
> • Collaborate with the community in providing programs and services that respond to regional needs

- Provide the broadest possible access throughout the region to the university-college's programs, services and facilities
- Balance community education, developmental, international, career, technical and academic offerings to reflect regional needs and provincial priorities.

References

Barnett, R. 1990. *The Idea of Higher Education.* Milton Keynes: Open University Press

Bok, D.C. 1982. *Beyond the Ivory Tower: Social Responsibility of the Modern University.* Cambridge, MA: Harvard University Press

Bowen, H. 1982. *The State of the Nation and the Agenda for Higher Education.* San Francisco: Jossey-Bass Publishers

Clark, B. 1983a. *Values in Higher Education: Conflict and Accommodation.* Tucson: Center for the Study of Higher Education

–.1983b. 'Values: Academic Organization in Cross-National Perspective.' In *The Higher Education System,* edited by B. Clark, pp. 240-62. Berkeley and Los Angeles: University of California Press

Collier, G., P. Tomlinson, and J. Wilson, eds. 1974. *Values and Moral Development in Higher Education.* New York: Wiley

Dennison, J. 1992. 'The University College Idea: A Critical Analysis.' *Canadian Journal of Higher Education* 22 (1):109-24

Dennison, J., and P. Gallagher. 1986. *Canada's Community Colleges: A Critical Analysis.* Vancouver: UBC Press

Dennison, J., and J. Levin. 1989. *Canada's Community Colleges in the Nineteen-Eighties: Responsiveness and Renewal.* Toronto: Association of Canadian Community Colleges

Hunter, J.O. 1977. *Values and the Future.* Sherman Oaks, CA: Banner Books International

Kaplan, A. 1991. 'Moral Values in Higher Education.' In *Moral Values and Higher Education,* edited by D.L. Thompson. Albany: State University of New York Press

Skolnik, M. 1991. 'Odd Country Out: A Speculative Commentary on Possible Causes and Consequences of the Absence of a National Policy Toward Higher Education in Canada.' Paper given at Annual Meeting of the Association for the Study of Higher Education, Boston, MA

Sloan, D. 1980. *Education and Values.* New York: Teachers College Press

Smith, S. 1991. *Report of the Commission of Inquiry on Canadian University Education.* Ottawa: Association of Universities and Colleges of Canada

Thompson, D.L., ed. 1991. *Moral Values and Higher Education: A Notion at Risk.* Albany: State University of New York Press

Trow, M. 1973. *Problems in the Transition from Elite to Mass Higher Education.* Berkeley, CA: Carnegie Commission on Higher Education

Wilson, O.M. n.d. *Values in Higher Education.* Tucson: Center for the Study of Higher Education

Wismer, S. 1990. 'Ontario's Community Colleges: Values for the Year 2000.' Paper prepared for *Vision 2000.* Toronto: Council of Regents

6
A Matter of Survival: Emerging Entrepreneurship in Community Colleges in Canada
Janet Knowles

Introduction

The Chinese character for 'crisis' is composed of two elements: one symbolizing danger, the other opportunity. This serves as a metaphor for the funding crisis facing community colleges in Canada today, as it captures both the negative and positive aspects of their current reality. Although the funding crisis threatens to undermine the institutional base of most colleges, it also provides the impetus to pursue new opportunities.

The current fiscal crisis is the result of changes in the external environment within which colleges operate. Evidence of the extent of this crisis can be seen in decreasing operating grants, rising costs, outmoded funding formulas, and program constraints that severely limit the ability of colleges to adequately respond to changing enrolment patterns and new educational needs (Kapraun and Heard 1993). Recurrent funding problems threaten existing programs and operations and are leading many colleges to reconsider their size, mission, purpose, and structure.

The current fiscal crisis is also giving rise to entrepreneurship as a means of sustaining, and in some cases transforming, the college.[1] In organizational terms, entrepreneurship is a means of employing productive labour and organizing expenditures in ways that maximize a return on investment. It is increasingly valued as an appropriate response to the growing need to 'do more with less' and as a means for generating new sources of revenue (Kapruan and Heard 1993).

This chapter explores some of the external factors that are causing colleges to adopt a more entrepreneurial approach to how they operate. Some organizational models and educational responses are described, along with various approaches to risk-management. It is noteworthy that a review of current literature shows that, unlike the case in US colleges, entrepreneurship in Canada's colleges has yet to be fully explored (only three Canadian sources were uncovered [Muller 1992; Thom 1987; Ontario Council of

Regents 1990]). As a result, research for this chapter relies primarily on secondary sources and on the direct experience of the author, first as a community programmer in Saskatchewan and BC between 1980 and 1981, and 1991 and 1993, respectively, and currently as the manager of Centre 2000, a newly created contract services unit at Douglas College in New Westminster, BC.

Threatening Times
'When a change in the weather makes a difference to your living,
You keep one eye on the banker, and another on the sky.'
– Connie Kaldor

As was mentioned in the introduction, emergent entrepreneurial activity in colleges is largely a reactive response to changes in the external environment. Some trends dominating this climate include: (1) international competition, (2) new technology, (3) changing demographics and demands in program mix, and (4) changing federal and provincial government commitments to postsecondary education and labour market training.

International Competition
The emergence of a global economy is shifting our attention away from a national economic strategy and towards a strategy geared towards increasing local and regional participation in world markets. In the world market, the economy for primary products (e.g., petroleum, wood, and steel) is being separated from the industrial manufacturing economy. In turn, the industrial manufacturing economy is shrinking (Wilms 1987). 'The movement of capital [rather than trade] has become the driving force' in the economy (Drucker 1986:768). Local recessions, sparked by fluctuations in supply and demand, are no longer easily remedied through regulation, tariffs, or price. Instead, in many industrial and manufacturing sectors seasonal lay-offs are being replaced with permanent plant closures.

Although comparable data for Canada is unavailable, Drucker (1986) estimates that in the US, for every $1 billion lost in trade, 25,000 jobs are also lost. As a result, 'doing more with less' in order to increase productivity and competitiveness has become the new modus operandi for both business and government.

Public-sector community colleges are particularly vulnerable to this trend, partly due to their close links to the labour market. Their primary dependency on government support also makes them obvious instruments for implementing public policy. As a result, they are extremely vulnerable to changing funding priorities and commitments.

Perhaps at no other time in the relatively short history of community colleges has the reality of 'doing more with less' been more profoundly expressed than in 1992 and 1993. In some provinces, most notably Ontario and Alberta, 'less' meant a 5 per cent reduction in salaries and an overall decrease in base operating funds. Historically, while overspending in colleges was frowned upon, the system accommodated it through slippage, deficit budgeting, modest reductions in program expenditures, and attrition. In the 1990s, however, public demand to reduce both the federal and provincial deficits has resulted in a real decline in investment in the community college system across the country. It has also created an intolerance for deficit financing.

Although public sector investment in colleges is declining, the demand for educational services and training is continuing to grow. As a result of technological change and the adoption of new processes and practises, business and industry are requiring skill-training for employees. Many industrial/business sectors are not being adequately supplied by the local labour market.

In response to declining public investment, many colleges are engaged in some process of consolidating programs and reducing program expenditures. As a result, there is increasing competition for scarce resources. To counter this trend, colleges are actively pursuing ways to diversify their revenue base by pursuing new educational markets (such as international education) and by increasing links to business and industry through the provision of contract training and other services (Kapraun and Heard 1993; Teitel 1991; Winter and Fadale 1990; Hetzler, Roberts, Anderson, and Clark 1989). In this environment, colleges can either choose to continue to downsize and to realign their operations, or they can seek to diversify their resource base and program offerings through participating in new markets. Most colleges are doing both.

New Technology
The introduction of new technology in all economic sectors is creating new demands for employee training and retraining. Initially, some of the larger companies expanded their own in-house training resources. More recently, the trend has shifted to out-sourcing or contracting out for this training. Arguably, much of the growth in private-sector training during the past decade resulted from the market gap created by a public-sector college system lacking the capacity to respond to training needs. This gap is beginning to close, as colleges adopt a more entrepreneurial approach to their operations and become more attentive to the training needs of industry.

Until recently, a buoyant economy and the sheer size of the training market has obscured the tardy entry of many colleges into the technology training market. Administratively, the artificial separation between credit and non-credit continuing education programs has contributed to a fragmented, and often uncoordinated, college response. For example, in some colleges, continuing education operations have been able to capitalize on their operations, acquiring new technology through revenue generated from market demand for computer applications training, while their counterparts (delivering credit programs within the institution) have remained hostage to annual budget allocations with respect to satisfying their hardware and software requirements. In a climate of declining public investment, most capital programs fall short of the growing demand for applied technology training in all fields of study.

In colleges that invested in technology and in an entrepreneurial approach to the market, the benefits have been substantial. The Community Computer Education Centre established in Regina in 1984,[2] the CIAMM (Applied Computer Science Centre) associated with the Enterprise Development Centre at Collège Édouard Montpetit at Longueuil (near Montréal), and the downtown Business Training Centre at Algonquin College in Ottawa are all the result of this kind of investment. With respect to the Community Computer Education Centre, extensive capitalization and resources were acquired through the purchase of microcomputer training by several large corporations. These training contracts enabled the centre to acquire computer hardware and software which, in turn, allowed it to offer training to smaller companies and individuals in the community. Revenue generated from these markets has been reinvested in new hardware and software, as needed, in order to maintain a timely response to new training needs.

It is noteworthy that the financial success enjoyed by these centres is the result of an approach to continuing education programming that is grounded in adult education theory and practice. Specifically, it was the need to improve access to technology training, coupled with the awareness that knowledge of computer technology will continue to be a required skill, that stimulated the adoption of an entrepreneurial approach to meeting technology training needs locally. This approach involves utilizing the resources and revenue acquired by one segment of the market to serve its less affluent sectors. In this case, the population at large represents the underserved market.

At Collège Édouard Montpetit near Montréal, a provincial consortium has been formed with several collèges d'enseignement général et professionnel (Cegeps). Consortium members have been able to acquire hardware and software at reduced costs, thereby enabling these Cegeps to participate in meeting the training needs of business, industry, and government across the province. At Algonquin College's Business Training Centre, and at other centres across the country, colleges are entering into partnership agreements with suppliers to become authorized training centres for specific industry products. Both the Business Training Centre and CIAMM boast that they are authorized Novell education training centres. In these partnerships, training delivery is provided by the college, but the curricula, materials, examination, and evaluation materials are all controlled by the supplier. In some instances, even the price to the consumer is pre-established, thereby limiting the operating margins for the college.

The availability of fibre-optic cable networks, interactive video, satellite conferencing, widespread access to the Internet and other related telecommunications networks, all providing educational products and services, will result in greater competition among colleges in the future. Colleges can expect increasing demands from business for 'the best training products and services at the best price,' irrespective of local jurisdictions or geography. If colleges want to increase their overall market share in the technology training market, then a greater integration and blurring of credit and non-credit activities is necessary across a continuum of training that serves both full- and part-time credit programs as well as the training needs of business. Revenue generated will be necessary to meet the hardware and software requirements of both delivery systems.

Those colleges that are established providers of technology training to business and industry will have a competitive edge with companies which are now demanding customized training in project management computer applications, open systems architecture, client/server systems, network management, telecommunications, and administration. They are well situated to begin forming provincial and national consortia as vehicles for responding to training tenders that are provincial or national in scope. They are also well positioned to take a leadership role in developing training standards and certification processes that meet industry's demand for evaluation, certification, portability, and transferability.

Shifting Demographics
The changing demographics and economic structure of most communities are affecting local demand for educational services. As a result, college populations are increasingly drawn from beyond the local region. Where local participation rates were once 75 per cent to 80 per cent of the total student body, in some colleges participation has declined to below 50 per cent.

In most Canadian communities, the average age of the population is also increasing. As the demographic make-up of most communities continues to change, the average age of students and the number of students who reside outside the local college region will continue to increase. This is particularly true in urban areas, where the number of colleges from which to choose spans several regions. The choice of one institution over another depends more on its particular program offering and available space than on its location.

The increased competition for a limited number of spaces in most programs is an additional barrier to newly graduated high-school students who wish to attend their local college. Many find themselves competing for access with students from outside their college region; in some cases, with students from a variety of socioeconomic backgrounds and from school districts with varying resources and educational standards.

The structure of the Canadian workforce is also demanding a new training response from colleges and institutes. In BC, for example, only about half the workplace population is working in regular full-time jobs. Furthermore, of these, only about one-third is working in jobs which offer dental plans and related benefits. This means that many people are either working one or more part-time jobs or are working as contractors and self-employed entrepreneurs. Many people are successfully finding ways of generating income but not necessarily by following traditional employment patterns.

The views of educators are also changing. Although most colleges assert a primary commitment to serving local needs, resource allocations are increasingly determined by perceived provincial, national, and international demands for vocational and occupational training. These occupation and employment training demands extend beyond business and industry demands in any one region. In Canada, government sponsors of education and training are looking for programs that offer learners transferable generic skills. These skills include critical thinking and problem-solving, communications, positive attitude and workplace behaviours, computer skills, numeracy, literacy, and the occupational skills essential to the specific occupation being pursued. Governments want to ensure that the skills acquired by their program trainers are transferable. Employers want a broad-based, well-trained workforce from which to draw. Historically, educators have supported a liberal rather than an applied approach to postsecondary education. However, it is likely that it is those programs which demonstrate their applicability in the workplace that will flourish in the 1990s.

Labour Force Development

The federal Labour Force Development Strategy (LFDS) is Canada's national policy initiative for countering the effects of ongoing labour market dislocation and adjustment. The combined effects on the economy of economic globalization and the North American Free Trade Agreement led to the creation of this initiative. The LFDS will continue to have a profound effect on college operations in the future.

The LFDS represents a number of economic policy initiatives that are changing both the amount of federal resources and the means by which they are allocated for training. In turn, they demand that colleges adopt new ways of working with industry in order to access these resources. The LFDS emerged from recommendations from the Canadian Labour Market Productivity Centre (CLMPC) in the late 1980s, following consultations with business, labour, education, and equity interest groups. It involves increasing the participation of both business and labour with respect to creating a 'learning culture' in Canada. In practical terms, this means giving business and labour a more direct voice in determining expenditures for training dependent on UI and other training funds. This process, in turn, led to the formation of the Canadian Labour Force Development Board (CLFDB) in 1991. Implicitly, the LFDS assumes that industry should assume greater responsibility for the retraining and maintenance of a trained workforce.

The CLFDB is the organizational vehicle responsible for advising the minister of human resources development (formerly Employment and Immigration Canada) on labour force development policy. The board advises the minister on labour market development issues and recommends the annual expenditures for training that should be drawn from UI funds. The CLFDB is comprised of representatives from business, labour, education, and designated equity groups.

The LFDS also calls for the creation of provincial and regional (local) boards. Since 1991, although consultations have been extensive, only five provincial boards have been formally established. The Newfoundland Labour Force Development Board was established on 21 September 1992, the Nova Scotia Labour Force development Board was established on 24 March 1993, and the Ontario Training and Adjustment Board was officially established in 1993. The BC Labour Force Development Board was announced as part of the provincial government's new Skills Now! initiatives in May 1994.

Across the Prairies, provincial board formation has been uneven. Manitoba signed a Labour Force Development Agreement with Canada in March 1993. A six-month consultation process will be completed prior to further development of its provincial board. In Saskatchewan, a steering committee was established in September 1992 to develop terms of reference for a provincial board. To date, Alberta has declined to develop a provincial board. Québec has established its own version of a labour force development board called La Société Québécois de Développement de la Main d'oeuvre (SQDM). The SQDM was announced in April 1993. The remaining provinces and territories are just beginning discussions with various stakeholders and with the federal government.

During the past two years, the provincial board formation process across the country has evolved against a backdrop of fluctuating federal and provincial interests and speculation. Provincial interest in forming labour force development boards was initially stimulated by the anticipated transfer of powers that would have ensued had the national referendum on the Charlottetown Accord been favourably passed in October 1992. This initial flurry of interest subsided following the defeat of the accord. Although consultations were ongoing, most provincial action continued at a snail's pace as speculation increased over the anticipated outcome of the federal election of October 1993.

In August 1993, Conservative prime minster Kim Campbell's recognition of the SQDM served to rekindle provincial interest in labour force development boards. The agreement-in-principle between Canada and Québec fell just short of a direct transfer of federal money and resources to Québec for labour force development initiatives and training. Since the federal election, however, more attention has been focused on the internal restructuring of the new Department of Human Resources Development (HRD) and on assessing the extent to which the LFDS will be a priority of the new Liberal government. The February 1994 announcement by Lloyd Axworthy, minister of human resources development, that the delivery of social security and income support programs will be reorganized has, by creating a climate of uncertainty, mitigated against the continued development of provincial boards.

In June 1994, the federal government proposed to pilot the transfer of programs and staff to the provinces. Since then, there has been renewed discussion as to the role provincial labour force development boards might play, if any, in this process. At the provincial level, policy and program emphasis has been on harmonizing programs and services to ensure that limited resources are directed towards training and retraining an underemployed workforce. Behind the rhetoric of these federal and provincial policy and program initiatives lies an assumption that business and industry, organized labour, and the population at large will increasingly pay a greater share of the costs of training and retraining Canada's workforce. In BC, for example, in announcing the Skills Now! training initiative the government clearly views itself as one of many 'partners' responsible for the development and maintenance of a skilled workforce. All provinces are cautious about, and remain vigilant against, what they refer to as federal off-loading of clients, programs, and services without a corresponding commitment of resources to meet growing demands for training and retraining.

According to critics of these policy and program shifts, current trends indicate that the federal government is continuing to divest itself of responsibility for postsecondary education and is focusing, instead, on meeting the immediate and short-term labour force training demands of industry. The impact of these policy shifts at the federal level can be seen in the types of training programs that are supported, who receives access to them, and who provides the training.

Since before the CLFDB was formed, there has been a continuing decrease in the amount of guaranteed federal funds made available to the provinces for training programs. Historically, these funds were transferred directly to the provinces and then spent by HRD to purchase seats in training programs in colleges and institutes. Now, however, although some federal transfer funds are provided through government-to-government purchases, the bulk of federal funds available for training are accessed locally through the Canada Employment Centres (CECs) in each college region.

It should also be noted that both the total amount of guaranteed funds available to the provinces through transfer payments and the amount of funds for training available under the Canadian Jobs Strategy (CJS) program fund have declined. However, the total amount of UI funds available and revenue from the Consolidated Revenue Fund for other training and related program initiatives have remained steady and, in some cases, have increased. An additional $280 million of public funds, for example, was committed to the Sectoral Partnership Initiative in 1992. This initiative includes $30 million spent in 1992-3 and another $250 million expected to be spent over the next five years (McWhinnie 1994). With the recent announcement by Lloyd Axworthy concerning the review of social programs (including UI), current priorities and funding commitments could change in early 1995.

It is important to note that these shifts in programs and funding have sometimes been detrimental to the specific populations they were meant to serve. For example, members of designated equity groups, who benefited from training offered to them under CJS funding, have not fared as well in securing access to training resources under current programs. Although there are more designated equity group members represented in program statistics, the amount of training time received is frequently shorter, and the type of training received is usually in traditional occupations (which are in decline or low-paying, or both).

The reallocation and decentralization of federal training funds to local CECs is forcing colleges to market their programs more effectively and to compete with private-sector suppliers in the delivery of training. Previously, colleges received direct access to federal funds for training through program purchases from the provinces. Now, federal funds to colleges are mostly received through training purchases and other project-based training that is purchased directly from local or regional CEC offices. CJS funding for training is accessed locally or regionally (depending on the region) either directly or through a coordinating group.

Changing funding relationships are also affecting program training and delivery formats. To participate in these new training markets, colleges submit training proposals to their local CEC offices. The training provided must conform to the delivery parameters set by HRD. This UI-sponsored training is full-time and consists of a minimum of twenty-five student contact hours of supervised instruction per week. Students on UI who have been approved as fee payers (i.e., who pay their own tuition but continue to receive UI benefits) cannot have more than a three-week interruption or break in their studies. Currently, most college programs and delivery formats are not designed to accommodate the specific needs of UI clients.

The avenues that training providers must pursue in order to secure federal training revenue are circuitous and complex. In some circumstances, employers with fewer than 100 employees can participate in industrial adjustment programs designed to help small- and medium-sized enterprises to become more competitive. These programs assist small and medium enterprises (SMEs) by providing funding to help them increase their investment in human resource development within their respective companies. In some instances, these programs assist employers with up to 75 per cent of the training costs (depending on the location and type of training required). As of April 1994, access to training under these programs has become more restrictive, often limited to designated equity groups and/or industry coordinating groups.

In order to participate in this training market, colleges must develop and market their training services directly to companies, which, in turn, apply for training assistance directly from their local CECs. To date, most program activity in this area has concentrated on the delivery of specific workplace-based training to specific companies and on the delivery of owner development programs that provide training to several local businesses. The owner development programs developed by the former Enterprise Centre at Okanagan University College and by the Business Development Centre at the University College in the Fraser Valley are examples of this type of training. These are programs developed in close consultation with industry associations, which provide both marketing assistance, sponsorship, and curriculum advice.

The five-year federal Sectoral Partnership Initiative is an important development for Canadian colleges.[3] The intent of this initiative is to create partnerships between labour, management, and government in order to develop comprehensive human resources development strategies within the various industrial sectors by: (1) building a consensus among all labour market partners, (2) establishing a forum for cooperation, (3) developing clear occupational/skill standards through an industry, and (4) promoting high-quality training and leading-edge skills for workers (McWhinnie 1994).

Initially, the Sectoral Partnership Initiative called for the creation of approximately fifty-five national sectoral councils comprised of representatives from management, labour, and business. Recently, the federal government has indicated that it will pursue a more modest venture that could result in the formation of between nineteen and twenty-five councils. The formation of these councils begins with a four-step process that includes: (1) a national sector study, (2) formation of the sector council, (3) identification of national occupational standards for the industry, and (4) skills training and upgrading. The sheer magnitude of the federal investment, which represents only 50 per cent of the total revenue expected to be matched by private-sector investment over five years, is without precedent – and colleges ignore it at their peril.

Until recently, representatives from education were notably absent in the formation of these councils. However, in 1994, the Association of Canadian Community Colleges signed an agreement with HRD to participate in the formation of future sector councils, including identifying representatives from colleges across the country to sit on them.

The sector councils have a mandate to determine occupational and training standards for industry. However, federal expectations that each council become self-sustaining within three to four years are, in turn, causing some councils to incorporate an entrepreneurial approach into their public service endeavours. Some councils (notably the Forum on International Trade Training [FITT] and the Software Human Resource Council [SHRC]) are moving beyond the development of occupation and certification standards to the development of curricula and programs for delivery. Having secured a mandate to determine desirable occupational training standards and certification requirements, these councils are developing and delivering educational products in an attempt to generate revenue. The councils need this revenue in order to support themselves once federal assistance is diminished.

Clearly, the federal initiative is not without its sceptics. Critics anticipate that the councils' need to generated revenue may compromise the intent of the original policy objective. Critics maintain that by investing in curriculum development projects for market resale, while at the same time investing each council with a mandate for developing and maintaining national occupational training standards, leads to a potential conflict of interest. Maintaining the councils' financial investment in curriculum development runs the risk of favouring returns to the council over returns to other public- and private-sector suppliers (who have already invested in the development and design of training infrastructure, products, and services to meet the training needs of industry). It is likely that the Sectoral Partnership Initiative could change significantly in both its magnitude and its scope in the coming year.

The Entrepreneurial Response

Responding to these external challenges requires a response from colleges that is oriented to market demand; that is, it requires an entrepreneurial response. This response is market- and revenue-driven. Generating revenue includes both identifying new sources of revenue within the organization and pursuing new educational markets. Current entrepreneurial activity in colleges can be broadly grouped into the following areas of activity: advocacy and lobbying, fiscal management, fund-raising, and revenue diversification through the pursuit of new markets (Kapraun and Heard 1991; Hetzler et al. 1989).

Advocacy

Advocacy and lobbying of federal and provincial officials is a form of entrepreneurial activity when it is focused on securing resources and favourable funding policies. In most provinces, umbrella organizations, such as educational councils, do this work.

Fiscal Management

Fiscal management strategies are designed to reduce costs. Ideally, they also facilitate the development of new revenue-generation opportunities. This approach assumes that internal capacity can be increased by streamlining internal processes and discontinuing program offerings that are redundant or too costly. Developing effective fiscal management strategies involves evaluating budget practices and creating new cost-accounting practices and management information systems. This process involves both centralizing accounting systems and increasing accountability by decentralizing decisionmaking (i.e., putting it in the hands of department administrators).

Fund-Raising

Fund-raising is another entrepreneurial activity being pursued by most colleges. This includes establishing alumni organizations, foundations for the generation of educational scholarships, and creating institutes for educational programs and research. Other methods include accessing non-cash donations (e.g., equipment, facilities, and services) and creating and marketing auxiliary services (e.g., book stores, parking, food services, and audio-visual equipment and printing shops to serve both the college and the community). The money to support rising program costs is primarily being acquired through the pursuit of educational grants for program development and research. The bulk of this activity comes from raising funds for student scholarships and research.

The concept of the specialized training institute, as created through a foundation (or other subsidiary organization) within the college itself, will continue to gain popularity. As colleges work closely with business and industry to develop specialized market niches, they will require the formation of organizational entities and structures that support their activities. These initiatives will include joint venture and shared investment schemes as well as ownership of curricula and assets. The use of foundations in creating highly specialized training institutes as vehicles for delivering programs and services may become instrumental in creating investment strategies for program development and delivery (e.g., joint ventures such as educational partnerships between suppliers, business, industry, and government). These structures are set up to facilitate the flow of revenue into the organization. They can also offer tax receipts and other benefits to contributors.

Although foundations and institutes can create vehicles for revenue generation to support college programs, more often the entrepreneurial efforts entail the pursuit of new educational markets. In colleges to date, this activity has primarily been in the areas of international education and business and industry training.

International Education
With increased globalization, the demand for educational services from foreign students remains strong. This demand is also creating opportunities for colleges to participate directly in international development activities through organizations like the Association of Community Colleges (ACCC), the Canadian Bureau for International Education (CBIE), the Canadian International Development Agency (CIDA), or the World Bank. In some colleges, international education is a highly lucrative business. It is not uncommon for the revenue from international education activities to represent between 10 per cent and 20 per cent of the entire college budget. Revenue generated from the participation of foreign students in college programs represents the largest portion of international education activity. Additionally, colleges benefit from the professional development opportunities for faculty and students who participate in international exchanges. They also gain from the value-added quality of their educational programs when their curricula become more internationalized and, hence, more marketable.

Colleges are creating consortia and other new organizational structures that are designed to strengthen their capacity to participate in international markets. For example, the BC Centre for International Education (BCCIE) is a consortium of colleges and institutes that was created for the express purpose of strengthening the capacity of all participating institutions in foreign markets. Until recently, most international education activity has been focused on recruiting foreign students into Canadian colleges, faculty exchanges to foreign institutions, and various educational training projects. In future, it is likely that this activity will expand to include the sale of curricula and other educational products and services to companies which are expanding into foreign markets.

Business and Industry Training
One of the most significant developments in higher education over the past decade has been the establishment of increased linkages between colleges, other organizations such as labour and community agencies, and business and industry. One such prominent and fast-growing linkage is in the area of contract training.[4] Contract training programs and services can generally be clustered around the following areas: apprenticeship training, community-wide collaboration, training for industry, labour market adjustment, and faculty return-to-industry programs.

Apprenticeship Training
Historically, apprenticeship training has provided the most direct link to industry, in that a significant portion of the training is provided on the job. Certification is regulated by the industry. Recently, the Total Quality Management and Customer Service movement within certain industrial sectors has stimulated even closer links between industry and training. Apprenticeship programs themselves are being customized to serve specialized market niches. The Modified Automotive Apprenticeship Program at Centennial College in Ontario is an example of this kind of programming.

Centennial College has accelerated the rate of certifying automotive mechanics by forming partnerships with automotive manufacturers and local dealers. The manufacturers provide cars and instructional support to college staff and carry the costs of both designing and renovating teaching space within the college. The local dealers agree to hire the apprentices before they enter the program and, during it, are responsible for assessing their employment skills. The college is responsible for providing reading and writing skills and mechanical and technical skills. Currently, the college has agreements in place with Ford, General Motors of Canada, Nissan, Honda, Canadian Tire, and the Truck Coach/Association. The Honda service bay at Centennial College is exactly like those found at dealerships across the country, complete with company logos and interior layout.

All parties benefit from this partnership. Automotive manufacturers are committed to Total Quality Management as a means for developing and maintaining market share for their products. To serve this commitment, dealers need trained mechanics who are knowledgeable and able to service their manufactures' products. The students benefit from the commitment they receive from their employers in training, and in the opportunity to learn in an applied training environment. Other students in the regular program also gain by having access to a fleet of contemporary vehicles on which to work. The relationship with the industry manufacturers and the dealers provides an additional benefit and lobbying voice when it comes time for the college to negotiate with government on the apprenticeship training needs of the industry.

Community-Wide Collaboration

Other examples of entrepreneurial activity can be found across the country in the community-wide partnerships that are emerging between colleges, school districts, and industry. The growth in the number of these ventures has been rapid during the past five years, and the Conference Board of Canada has been instrumental in encouraging it. Since 1990, the board has sponsored an annual conference called 'Reaching for Success: Business and Education Working Together.' The goal of the conference is to 'build a shared vision of education and learning for all Canadians, and to generate a sense of opportunity and optimism about public education in Canada' (Nininger 1994). Each year, the conference brings together all stakeholders in a forum designed to build a common purpose that cuts across geographic boundaries. Successful industry and education partnerships are highlighted and receive awards. Promoting industry and education partnerships remains a central theme of the board's activities. Also encouraging closer links between colleges and industry is the current trend favouring private-sector over public-sector bids for supplying services to the federal and provincial governments. In some instances, colleges must become subcontractors to private-sector industries in order to participate in these tenders.

Business and Industry Training

Providing customized training to business and industry represents a new market for colleges – one that is changing the role of the institution. Historically, most colleges, through their continuing education departments, have provided professional development courses that were of interest to individuals and small business. Traditionally, participants register for these programs individually, although sometimes they are sponsored by their companies. In either case, the primary relationship is between the college and the individual learner. Increasingly, however, companies are purchasing entire programs for their employees. Training programs are customized and delivered to groups of learners. As the company pays for all of the direct and indirect costs of training, the primary relationship is between the company and the college. In the end, the recruitment and selection of participants, course content, and delivery formats are most often determined by the company. Frequently, the curriculum is owned by the trainer, who is contracted to deliver the customized service. Rarely is an existing institutional program suitable (without substantial modification) for delivery in the workplace. The certification and credentials offered by the college are sometimes secondary in value and importance to those recognized by professional accreditation bodies or industry.

As the growth of contract training over other traditional modes of training continues, many Canadian colleges have designated a department to be responsible for the delivery of contract training to business and industry. Similar responses have been noted in the US (Kapraun and Heard 1993; Kapraun and Heard 1992; Lynch, Palmer, and Grubb 1991; Updike 1991; Hetzler et al. 1989; Deegan 1988). Warford (1989) reported an increase in contract training programs at select US colleges between 1980 and 1987 (from less than 54,000 in 1980 to close to 684,000 in 1987).

For most colleges, initial forays into the contract training market began in the 1980s in the area of technology training (specifically, in microcomputer applications training). Since then, colleges have diversified their range of training services to include business management training, human resources development, strategic planning, communications, and occupational health and safety programs. It is important to note that most contract training activity falls outside regular college activities and so is not supported by base funding. In most institutions, contract training initiatives are required to cover all of the direct and indirect costs of their delivery and are expected to generate a profit. Expectations for a 20 per cent return annually over all direct and indirect expenses is not considered unusual, even though the extent to which colleges are actually attaining this target has yet to be fully researched and documented. However, a 1987 study of seventeen league for innovation colleges in the US did find that, although contract training programs have increased dramatically over the past decade, most institutions surveyed indicated that they did not profit significantly from these programs. Nonetheless, most believed that they contributed significantly to the fulfilment of their mission statement (Warford 1989).

Labour Market Adjustment Training
One value-added advantage which colleges bring to the contract training market is the capacity to provide training which will lead to certified credentials that are aligned to both business needs and employer skill development and that also meet industry standards. As such, they have an important role to play, with industry, in labour market adjustment training and the retraining of workers who are displaced as a result of economic

restructuring. Colleges are currently serving this market through providing it with transitional training programs for displaced workers, human resources training for small- and medium-sized enterprises, and training designed to promote the participation of new and re-entrants to the labour market (including women, visible minorities, First Nations peoples, and persons with disabilities). Frequently, this training is provided on a project basis through direct contract with a local CEC or through the training department of provincial ministries of social services.

Colleges also have the potential to customize their program offerings and to tailor them to meet the ongoing skill development needs of employers while at the same time offering participants opportunities to gain recognition for their learning in non-traditional ways. Providing credit for prior learning and the delivering workplace-based training are some of the ways in which colleges are responding to the needs of this new market as well as extending training beyond the confines of the workplace. Other benefits include the opportunities to increase their assets through increased capitalization and no longer being dependent on a single source of funds. Increased linkages to industry are also benefiting colleges in terms of their own human resource development. Industry links not only provide opportunities for student placement in cooperative education programs, they also create new opportunities for faculty to return to industry as part of their own professional development.

Entrepreneurial responses that require new organizational structures, a reordering of administrative accountability and practices, and, perhaps more important, a realignment of educational purpose threaten the status quo. For some, the pursuit of overt entrepreneurial activity in educational programs and services is viewed as detrimental to the interests of educators and learners alike. Some critics predict that the trend towards contract training and industry-specific vocational training will result in the continued erosion of the liberal arts education needed by employees and supported by research (Pincus 1987). Critics also predict that the increased revenue gained by colleges in the short-term will be offset by a loss of educational autonomy in the future. Some view the delivery of contract training through subcontracts as an erosion of potential faculty employment opportunities.

While community college leaders support contract training because it is seen to service all sectors of the community, some feel that profit-making corporations have the most to gain, particularly in terms of reduced employee-training costs. For those colleges which are actively engaged in the pursuit of new markets, investment in this process is sometimes characterized by conflicting expectations. Conflict can arise, for example, between expecting to achieve an immediate and high return from the provision of contract training and attempting to achieve needed institutional renewal, acquisition of new equipment, an overall increase in productivity, and/or organizational stability. It is against this backdrop that colleges must balance ongoing tensions in the process of institutional development.

Managing the Risk

Responding quickly to new and diverse education markets that are dynamic, competitive, and that demand both program customization and market relevance is challenging for most institutions. In some colleges, declining investment from provincial sources and the threat of job loss have resulted in an entrenchment of traditional labour management relations, with all its ensuing tensions. Institutional self-preservation and the need for personal job security contribute to a resistance towards any redirection of existing resources in ways that might satisfy new external demands for education and training. As a result, efforts to initiate new programs and services designed to strengthen the overall capacity of the institution are often, initially, met with scepticism and mistrust. Balancing these internal tensions is a daunting task for even the most adept college administrators.

Despite these limitations, colleges across Canada are creating new organizational entities and processes to accommodate their entrepreneurial activities. These models can be grouped into the following categories: (1) an integrated approach, (2) single division responsibility, (3) a college-wide unit, (4) a subsidiary organization, and (5) regional or national partnerships and consortia. A number of organizing principles are common to all these models. First, all emphasize that their primary purpose is serving the training needs of business, industry, and government agency organizations rather than the needs of individuals. As a result, they are highly service-oriented and client-centred. Second, they are all operated as profit centres, with varying degrees of financial independence from their parent college in terms of both revenue and expenditure. Third, they all operate with considerable autonomy; in most instances, this means they operate outside traditional governance systems or collective agreements. Fourth, they all view their function and role as fulfilling an integral part of the college mission and mandate. And fifth, they all view restructuring as necessary in order to function effectively in the markets they are attempting to serve.

An integrated approach to the development of contract services intermeshes contract training with other educational services provided by the college. No separate organizational unit exists within the college – participation in the contract training market is pursued by all its divisions/departments. Contract training, however, is usually secondary to those departments' primary educational activity, which is the delivery of credit programs, and, as a result, market participation can become fragmented. This approach relies primarily on existing faculty to service the needs of the market. The use of external contractors is generally frowned upon. Usually, a portion of the net revenue acquired through contract training accrues to the department.

Another popular model for accommodating entrepreneurial activities is the single-division responsibility model. In this case, a single unit within the college is given responsibility for contract training. These units have generally evolved either under the auspices of continuing education departments (e.g., the former Enterprise Centre at Okanagan University College and the Business Management Centre at Algonquin College) or as separate divisional units (e.g., the Business and Industry Services Division at Humber College), and they tend not to be involved in mainstream college activities. Faculty participation in the development and delivery of training is minimal, and this can result in the creation of two solitudes within the college. These units tend not only to have extensive autonomy from the college with respect to their financial operations, but they are also heavily taxed by it. They are sometimes viewed as cash cows, offering training of lesser quality than that offered in other parts of the institution but providing revenue that is necessary to support college operations.

The college-wide contract services unit is a hybrid of the first two models. Under this model, a central unit is created to facilitate, coordinate, and promote the participation of all divisions in contract training activities. In this case, however, the delivery of training services may be either direct or through partnerships. These partnerships include other divisions within the college as well as other delivery partners and subcontractors in the community. Various financial structures are in place to support this type of model, which includes units ranging from those that are centrally supported to those that work on a line of credit. In either case, they are expected to cover all of their direct and indirect operational costs as well as to turn a profit for the college. Douglas College's Centre 2000 is an example of this type of contract training unit.

Another organizational model that is being adopted by some colleges to support their contract training activities is the subsidiary organization, usually a non-profit corporation. These models offer training activity that is completely separate from college operations and governance. They also provide opportunities for members from the business community to participate directly in their development. These subsidiary organizations are also becoming increasingly important with respect to participating in sectoral development initiatives and other ventures where the direct participation of educational suppliers is restricted. The non-profit corporation serves to promote the college's interests while protecting it from potential conflicts in the marketplace. Malaspina College, located in Nanaimo, BC, was one of the first colleges to experiment with this strategy.

While each college is wrestling with the creation of its own model for contract services, many are pursuing market opportunities by adopting an interinstitutional approach to collaboration with other educational providers. The Canadian Transportation Institute (CTI) and the Consortium for Canadian Energy Management and Environmental Training were two of the first consortia of this type. It is important to note that these structures have a lifespan that is determined by the market. They are not conceived to be permanent structures, but organizations that grow, decline, and evolve into something else as needs change.

At one time, CTI, which was created in 1990, represented a consortium of nineteen colleges across Canada. Corporate clients included Navistar, Midas, Ford, General Motors, and DeHavilland, to mention a few. The consortium served to create a national delivery network for training for the transportation industry. Some national contracts were coordinated centrally through CTI; in other instances, individual colleges took the lead in coordinating training. Delivery was subcontracted, as required, through each college.

Colleges are finding the creation of consortia an effective way to expand their resources and to manage the risks of participating in the contract training market. Consortia are non-permanent structures that come together for a specific educational purpose and for an undefined period of time. The degree of formality in organizational structure also varies, as membership increases and decreases according to changing need. They are also fluid in the sense that a single college can belong to several consortia simultaneously. Most consortia identify a lead college to represent the interests of its members, and most also develop memoranda of understanding that outline the terms and conditions of their association.

Effective participation in the contract training market is complex and requires specialized skills. In the world of contract training, this includes mastering the politics, learning the companies' and funders' plans and priorities, and knowing the other suppliers in the market. Successful interorganizational collaboration is the key, according to Beder (1984), and it includes the following: the adoption of flexible, adaptive structures; openness to the external environment; a sense of commitment that engenders trust; and adherence to principles of reciprocal benefit.

An extensive program of business and industry training also requires support from the college president, the board of trustees, the administration, and the faculty. Maintaining this support requires that colleges establish networks that include all constituencies in order to foster a team concept and to ensure that the program has knowledgeable spokespersons and supporters throughout the institution. A leader, according to Parkhouse and Lapin (1980), should also be chosen for his or her skills in academe as well as for his or her skills in program planning, implementation, administration, and evaluation. He or she must be given authority to act and be credible in the eyes of funders. The future of contract training is bright. The challenge for most institutions is to find ways to use the expertise of those involved in contract training as catalysts for institutional renewal across the system.

Conclusion

This chapter has reviewed the trends leading to entrepreneurship in Canadian colleges. The external pressures on colleges to continue to accommodate new educational demands in a climate of decreasing public investment demands that they adopt an entrepreneurial approach to their current endeavours and pursue new training markets. However, although often driven by the need to generate revenue, contract training is, in fact, necessary if community colleges in Canada are to meet the educational and training needs of the community as a whole.

The rise of entrepreneurship in colleges can be seen in both the development of internal cost-saving measures, the development of alumni and foundations, and the development of new educational markets as means of generating revenue. These new educational markets include the development and expansion of international education and contract training services to business and industry. Although international education and contract training are not new approaches to the delivery of adult education services, current trends demand that they be expanded. This expansion is necessary not only to meet market demand but also to generate revenue to support the existing infrastructure. These trends, in turn, require the creation of organizational structures and processes within colleges that will support the demands of the marketplace.

Although the approach taken by each college varies, a number of organizational models with similar characteristics are emerging. Unfortunately, to date, there is very little published research on the experiences of Canadian colleges. As a result, Canadian colleges must rely on the experiences of US colleges. It is likely that adult education research will command greater attention in the future. Until then, the external pressures on colleges to adopt an entrepreneurial approach to the management of their affairs will continue, and it will increasingly permeate all spheres of college activity.

Notes

1 By definition, an entrepreneur is a person who organizes and manages an enterprise, especially a business, involving considerable initiative and risk.
2 Formerly Regina Plains Community College, now part of the Saskatchewan Institute of Applied Science and Technology (SIAST).

3 The definition of a sector is based on the Canadian Occupational Projection System-Groups of Standard Industrial Classification (SIC) Units. The 'operational definition usually consists of a national group of companies, organizations or workers which share some relevant combination of products, services or technology which results in their having common human resource concerns' (McWhinnie 1994).
4 Contract training refers to an arrangement in which a business, government agency, or community association contracts directly to the college for the provision of instruction for its employees, clients, or members.

References

American Association of Community and Junior Colleges. 1991. 'Community College Involvement in Contracted Training and Other Economic Development Activities: A Report of a National Survey.' ERIC Document Reproduction Service No. ED 292 502. American Association of Community and Junior Colleges, Washington, DC

Anderson, Richard E. 1985. 'The Continuing Education Market: Financial and Structural Issues.' ERIC Document Reproduction Service No. ED 254 178. American Association for Higher Education, Washington, DC

Beder, Hal, ed. 1984. 'Realizing the Potential of Interorganizational Cooperation.' *New Directions in Community Colleges*. San Francisco: Jossey-Bass Publishers

Bragg, Debra D. 1990. 'Building World-Market Competitors: Technology Transfer and the Illinois Community College System, 1990 Status Report.' ERIC Document Reproduction Service No. ED 322 741. Illinois University, Urbana Department of Vocational and Technical Education, Urbana, IL

Catanzaro, James L., and Allen D. Arnold, eds. 1989. 'Alternative Funding Sources.' *New Directions for Community Colleges*. 17(4):128

Deegan, William L. 1986. *Should Your College Start a Center for the Delivery of Contract Training Programs?* Washington, DC: Office of Educational Research and Improvement

–.1988. 'Managing Contract Training Programs: Progress and Proposals.' Policy paper no. 2, Institute for Studies in Higher Education Policy, Florida State University, Tallahassee

Deegan, William L., and Ronald Drisko. 1985. 'Contract Training: Progress and Policy Issues.' *Community and Junior College Journal* 55 (6):14-17

Drucker, P.F. 1986. 'The Changed World Economy.' *Foreign Affairs* 64 (4):768-91

Doucette, Don. 1993. 'Community College Workforce Training Programs for Employees of Business, Industry, Labor, and Government: A Status Report.' Survey conducted by the League for Innovation in the Community College with support from the Student Loan Marketing Association and with assistance from the National Computer Systems Corporation, League for Innovation

Hetzler, Robert L., Donna J. Roberts, Andy Anderson, and Gary O. Clark. 1989. 'Toward the Year 2000. Delta College Committee of 100 Report 1989.' ERIC Document Reproduction Service No. ED 324 069. Delta College, University Center, Michigan

Hines, Thomas E. 1990. 'Creative Alliances with the Business Community: Pima Community College.' Paper presented at the Annual International Conference on Leadership Development of the League for Innovation in Community Colleges, San Francisco, CA

Illinois Community College Board. 1985. 'Economic Development Grant Report, Fiscal Year 1985.' ERIC Document Reproduction Service No. ED 267 862. Springfield, IL

Kapraun, E. Daniel, and Don Heard. 1991. 'Financing Community Colleges: Review of Trends and Annotated Bibliography, 1976-1991.' ERIC Document Reproduction Service No. ED 351 076. Arkansas University, Fayetteville, AR

–.1992. 'Assessing the Financial and Institutional Concerns of Arkansas Community Technical Colleges: A Model Approach.' ERIC Document Reproduction Service No. ED 352 088. Arkansas University Department of Educational Leadership, Counseling, and Foundations, Fayetteville, AR

–.1993. 'Financing Community Colleges: Threats and Opportunities.' Opinion papers, Arkansas University, Fayetteville, AR

Lynch, Robert, James C. Palmer, and W. Norton Grubb. 1991. 'Community College Involvement in Contract Training and Other Economic Development Activities. Report of a National Survey Conducted by the American Association of Community and Junior Colleges and the National Centre for Research in Vocational Education.' ERIC Document Reproduction Service No. ED 339 434. American Association of Community and Junior Colleges, Berkeley, CA

McWhinnie, John. 1994. Presentation to BC Colleges and Institutes Contract Training Network, February, Vancouver

Muller, Jacov. 1992. 'Education and Work, Education as Work: Canada's Changing Community Colleges.' *Canadian Journal of Education* 17 (2):244-6

National Employment and Training Consortium of Two Year Colleges Dedicated to Putting Americans to Work (NETWORK). 1990. 'Results of the 1989-90 NETWORK Survey of Two-Year College Involvement in Employment, Training, and Literacy.' ERIC Document Reproduction Service No. ED 330 380. Cleveland, OH

Nininger, James R. 1994. 'Reaching for Success: Business and Industry Working Together.' Conference brochure. Reaching for Success Conference, Vancouver

Ontario Council of Regents for Colleges and Applied Arts and Technology, Vision 2000 Steering Committee. 1990. 'Some Empirical Features of the College System: Responding to Quality, Access, and Funding Trade-offs.' *Study Team Final Report.* Toronto: Ontario Council of Regents

Parkhouse, Bonnie, and Jackie Lapin. 1980. *The Women in Athletic Administration: Innovative Management Techniques for Universities, Colleges, Junior Colleges, Highschools, and State Highschool Associations.* Santa Monica, CA: Goodyear Publishing Company

Pincus, Fred L. 1987. 'Customized Contract Training in Community Colleges: Who Really Benefits?' Paper presented at the Annual Convention of the American Sociological Association, Washington, DC

Powers, David R., Mary F. Powers, Frederick Betz, Carl P. Aslanian. 1988. *Higher Education in Partnership with Industry.* San Francisco: Jossey-Bass Publishers

Ramirez, Kevin M. 1989. 'Economic Development and the Role of Community Colleges: Contract Education in Review.' ERIC Document Reproduction Service No. ED 326 277. California Association of Community Colleges, Sacramento, CA

Scott, Robert A. 1987. 'The $40 Billion Question: Who Will Train for the Corporate Future?' Paper presented at the Annual Meeting of the American Society for Training and Development, Long Island Chapter, Bethpage, NY

Smith, Norman D. 1983. 'An Identification of Effective Practices in Contact Education Programs in Selected California Community Colleges.' Ph.D. thesis, Pepperdine University, Malibu, CA

Stanley, P. and John Prentise. 1992. 'Economic Development Program Funding Plan: 1992-1993.' ERIC Document Reproduction Service No. ED 351 062. California Association of Community Colleges, Sacramento, CA

Suchorski, Joan M. 1987. 'Contract Training Community Colleges.' Paper delivered in a graduate seminar, University of Florida, Gainesville. ERIC Document Reproduction Service No. ED 291 425

Taylor, Lyndon E., and Fred L. Head. 1988. 'Restructuring the Community College at the Yorba Linda Education Center.' ERIC Document Reproduction Service No. ED 292 502. North Orange County Community College District, Fullerton, CA

Teitel, Lee. 1991. 'The Transformation of a Community College.' *Community College Review* 19 (1):7-13

Thom, G.A. 1987. 'Employer Interaction with Public Colleges and Institutes in Canada.' Discussion paper, Science Council of Canada, Ottawa

Thor, Linda M. 1987. 'Performance Contracting: Successfully Managing the Risk.' *New Directions for Community Colleges* 60:23-32

Updike, Katherine May. 1991. 'A Comparative Study of Contract Training in Select Community Colleges.' ERIC Document Reproduction Service No. ED 336 161. Office of Corporate Training and Development, Phoenix, AZ

Warford, Larry J. 1989. 'A Study of Customized Contract Training Programs at Selected Community Colleges.' Ph.D. thesis, University of Oregon, Eugene

Wilms, Welford W. 1987. 'Marching to the Market: A New Tune for Training Organizations.' *New Directions for Community Colleges* 60:5-14

Winter, Gene M., and LaVerna M. Fadale. 1990. 'Impact of Economic Development Programs in SUNY Community Colleges: A Study of Contract Courses.' *Community Services Catalyst* 20 (2):3-7

7
Aboriginal Education in Community Colleges
Douglas Baker

One of the most significant challenges facing Canadian colleges in the 1990s is how to respond to the needs of aboriginal adult learners. This challenge will confront college missions, structures, curricula, and governance. How effectively colleges transform themselves to meet aboriginal peoples needs and demands will be a measure of how capable they are of dealing with change. To maintain relevance during the next decade, responsive institutions must internationalize, form community partnerships, facilitate interinstitutional collaboration, enable multimode admission, strengthen retention rates, and simplify transfer. To be competent in a culturally diverse world, Canadian college personnel must be prepared to value aboriginal peoples' cultures and expectations. When the educational attainment levels of the aboriginal population reach those of the general population, and when employment and income equity is achieved, a good measure of the credit for those accomplishments may be given to the efforts of responsive community colleges.

Aboriginal peoples have found a place on the Canadian social and political agenda in the past two decades. However, acknowledgement is not accomplishment, as was seen in the ill-fated Charlottetown Accord. When the needs of equity groups are raised, every recent report recommends improved access and quality of service for aboriginal peoples. Virtually every provincial and federal ministry has developed aboriginal support programs. The Department of Indian Affairs and Northern Development (DIAND) allocates over $190 million annually to the postsecondary education assistance program. The Canada Employment and Immigration Commission (now Human Resources Development) spends over $30 million on training through regional aboriginal management boards and the Pathways to Success Programme. Each of the western provinces, Ontario, and the two territories maintain aboriginal postsecondary programs, for which they provide funding allocations of $5 to $10 million per year. In each college region with an aboriginal population of more than 3 per cent, there are some programs or services to encourage access to and completion of courses. As well, many aboriginal organizations have developed their own programs and/or institutions.

The aboriginal population of approximately 700,000 comprises slightly more than 2 per cent of the population of Canada. Three-fifths of this number are non-status Indians and Métis, who fall outside the jurisdiction of the Indian Act. The remaining two-fifths are status Indians and Inuit. Of this group, approximately half live on reserves or in Inuit communities, while the remainder reside in small towns or larger urban centres. The geographic distribution of non-status Indians and Métis shows that 60 per cent of them reside in urban settings.

A combination of factors, including isolated geographic locations and small population densities, constitute formidable barriers to a college education. Nevertheless, from 1986 to 1992, federal sources reported a 30 per cent increase in adult aboriginal participation in postsecondary education. The 1991 census data place the educational attainment levels of status Indians at 3 per cent for degree completion and at 8 per cent for some postsecondary education, while the educational attainment level of the general population was at 15 per cent for degree completion and 25 per cent for some postsecondary education.

Issues in Aboriginal Education

The belated but rapid increase in both aboriginal adult participation in, and completion of, advanced educational programs is primarily the result of a growing assertiveness by indigenous leaders and educators. By giving voice to the causes of failure and by identifying the ingredients necessary for success, they have found a responsive audience during the last decade. The seminal policy paper, 'Indian Control of Indian Education' (National Indian Brotherhood 1972), prepared by the National Indian Brotherhood (NIB) (the predecessor of the Assembly of First Nations [AFN]), provided the guidelines and stimulus for an educational self-determination movement. From this document came the impetus to support the training of aboriginal teachers, to create band and community schools, to develop tertiary institutions, and to negotiate master tuition agreements and the postsecondary assistance program. This movement towards empowerment brought with it a collective aboriginal initiative to create changes which would encourage more children to matriculate from both community-owned and public schools and for adults to begin to attend colleges and universities. While a good deal of attention has been drawn to the accomplishments of universities with respect to the provision of aboriginal programs, a larger role can be attributed to community colleges, aboriginal affiliates, and independent institutions.

The major barriers to participation by aboriginal adult learners fall into a classification system developed by Patricia Cross in 1981. These barriers may be grouped under the following headings: geographic, situational, dispositional, and institutional.

Geographic
A large proportion of aboriginal people live in rural and isolated small communities. For them, participation in advanced learning requires either moving to larger centres or availing themselves of distance education programs and/or those subject to local delivery.

Situational
A legacy of forced assimilation, racism, and abusive residential schools has created both alienation and mistrust of mainstream education systems. Many rural aboriginal peoples speak only their own language. Urban adults are largely members of the social and economic underclass and have no positive experience with mainstream social and employment systems. Educators' lack of cultural sensitivity has led to inhospitable environments, continued low academic achievement levels, and high illiteracy rates.

Dispositional
Pepper and Henry (1991) report that chronic low self-esteem has contributed to educational failure, withdrawal, and/or lack of application. With a high incidence of personal abuse and family dysfunction, expectation of improved life chances is reduced. Cultural and lifestyle differences and a strong attachment to family and community reinforce a reluctance to participate in mainstream educational institutions. Fear of isolation and prejudice are well justified, given the experience of parents and peers.

Institutional
Lack of social, emotional, and cultural support is prevalent in our colleges and other institutions. An unwillingness to adapt delivery systems, instructional methods, and curriculum content to accommodate cultural and ideological diversity has been characteristic of traditional tertiary education systems. Their values, rituals, and physical structures have seldom reflected those of Canada's aboriginal peoples. A lack of respect, reciprocity, and aboriginal representation in staffing and governance has been systematic, and this has reduced aboriginal students' expectations of either welcome or success.

Studies of Aboriginal Students and Graduates
Studies of aboriginal students and graduates conducted by Athabasca Uni-

versity, the University of British Columbia/First Nations House of Learning, the Saskatchewan Institute of Indian Technologies, and the Ontario, Alberta, and BC ministries of advanced education/colleges and universities have identified the following factors which contribute to higher levels of aboriginal participation/retention/success in postsecondary education:

(1) *Location:* access to adult education near home and community (particularly crucial for students at lower academic levels or having their first educational experience).

(2) *Assessment and advising:* sensitive recruitment and accurate academic placement at the appropriate skill level. Aboriginal advisors are essential, and assessment instruments should be free from cultural bias.

(3) *Transition:* emphasis on life and study skills in an orientation process. Preparation/support for life and family transitions related to the postsecondary regimen, with an emphasis on building self-esteem and celebrating cultural heritage. Elders are critical participants in student counselling.

(4) *Academic preparation:* assigning students to upgrading/GED or college preparatory programs which support indigenous languages, histories, and cultural/spiritual practices. Teaching methods, based on oral communication and experiential learning, are essential.

(5) *Community linkages:* resource people, faculty, staff, and those involved in governance must be linked to the aboriginal community in order to be seen as part of the educative process and as an extension of positive community life and values. An active role should be played by indigenous educators and holders of tribal wisdom in decisions affecting curricula. Community and family should participate in events and celebrations.

(6) *Relevant curricula:* aboriginal languages must be taught in credit courses. Positive treatment must be given to aboriginal history and its impact on Canada's economic and social development. Equal value should be placed on traditional aboriginal wisdom and learning methods.

(7) *Culturally hospitable environment:* physical facilities should reflect aboriginal art, images, architecture, and values. Traditional or popular aboriginal art and spiritual practice should be included in social events and celebrations. On large campuses, there should be aboriginal student meeting places and support services. It is important to create a sense of community when aboriginal students constitute a majority in their own settings.

(8) *Peer support:* program design and assignments should emphasize group projects and peer tutorial systems in which aboriginal students work and study collaboratively.

(9) *Student support:* there should be aboriginal and elder counselling (both

personal and academic) in order to support healing, to confront racism, and to assist in resolving issues of dislocation and family stress. Special support programs improve grades and increase retention.

(10) *Family and child:* the majority of current aboriginal participants in postsecondary programs are women with children. Services and co-operative housing and child care programs contribute to retention rates and completion of courses/programs.

(11) *Financial assistance:* advocacy and intervention is often required in order to assist students in obtaining financial aid appropriate to their family and community obligations. Existing programs are often either difficult to access or are subject to arbitrary limitations based on eligibility, program type, or Indian status classification.

Summary of Issues

Most issues requiring attention by adult educators are summarized by Richard Atleo in his study of aboriginal education in British Columbia. This study addresses the self-image and academic achievement of primary and secondary aboriginal students, and its analysis can be reasonably extended to adult learners. Atleo (1993) states that

> orientational improvement around Native culture is required of the school system ... [and must] include values that are important to the Native community ... teach from where the student is ... understand the potential benefit [to mainstream] society of a resource that has been kept down, oppressed and misunderstood since the early 1600's. (p. 3)

Biculturalism works both ways. Aboriginal peoples must master English and employ contemporary methods and technologies in order to successfully participate in the Canadian social and economic system. And when non-aboriginals learn from aboriginals, environmental, interpersonal, and community benefits will follow. The education system is the best medium of bicultural exchange, and the postsecondary system is slowly coming to realize its key role in facilitating it.

Key Changes in the System

In order to include aboriginals in postsecondary education, governments, institutions, and aboriginal organizations have made a number of major adjustments over the past two decades. Some of these are itemized below.

Policy and Programs

The provinces of British Columbia, Saskatchewan, Manitoba, and Ontario have developed strategies and initiatives to encourage special programs, curricula adaptation, and access-support services to enable aboriginal adults to participate in post-secondary education. The territories have gone much further; they have created legislative mandates which require institutions to be bicultural in both curriculum emphasis and delivery methods. Only BC and Saskatchewan have aboriginal-owned educational institutions. All western provinces (and Ontario) require aboriginal representation on college/institute boards of governors. All of BC's colleges/institutes have engaged aboriginal coordinating staff in order to ease entry and to attempt to ensure both retention rates and completion of programs. Funding initiatives provide between $5 and $10 million per year in each provincial jurisdiction for targeted aboriginal programs and services. Programs such as the Vocational Training Program (Alberta), the Non-Status and Métis Program (Saskatchewan), the Access Program (Manitoba), and the Native Education and Training Strategy (Ontario) provide support to public institutions or partnership projects with aboriginal organizations. The products of such initiatives include special academic entry courses, aboriginal management courses, student counsellors, student centres, special professional preparation courses in health and education, and support for cultural events.

Only Saskatchewan has legislated aboriginal institutions into existence by creating the Saskatchewan Indian Community College (now the Saskatchewan Institute of Indian Technologies) and the Dumont Institute (formerly the Native Services Branch of SIAST). The two territories have established comprehensive bicultural institutions (i.e., Yukon College and Arctic College) respecting the political power of large aboriginal populations (30 per cent and 60 per cent in the Yukon and the Northwest Territories, respectively).

Leadership

Many college boards and presidents have demonstrated a commitment to aboriginal equity. A few colleges in Canada have defined goals, policies, and equity targets for aboriginal participation. Yukon College requires that there be three aboriginal members on its board of governors, promotes goals supporting self-government, develops culturally relevant curricula, and encourages aboriginal-oriented research and economic development. It also has a mandate to provide learning centres in isolated communities, and it maintains a ratio of 25 per cent aboriginal participation in both student enrolment and in staff membership.

In other regions, colleges with aboriginal populations of over 20 per cent have developed similar goals. Northwest College in BC has made a commitment to 'facilitate the efforts of First Nations organizations to establish educational enterprises and increase access ... within their communities, in keeping with their goals of self-determination' (Northwest Community College 1994: iv). Alberta Vocational Centre at Lesser Slave Lake offers band social service workers and aboriginal child care programs in rural centres, and it also offers aboriginal languages to its 40 per cent aboriginal population. Similarly, Northlands College in Saskatchewan has created spaces for aboriginal students (constituting a minimum of 50 per cent of the total student population) in its resource extraction and management programs. Keewatin College in Manitoba has a band administration program for its aboriginal population (40 per cent of the total student population), as does Cambrian College in Ontario. Assiniboine College has participation targets of 5 per cent aboriginal enrolment in every program – a standard which it meets through recruiting on reserves, delivering extension programs, and creating partnerships with aboriginal organizations. Over 50 per cent of Canadian colleges, while not having officially committed to providing access to aboriginal students, do provide extension programs to reserves and do offer aboriginal student services on their campuses. Fewer than 20 per cent of colleges, however, have affiliation or accreditation agreements with aboriginal colleges.

Infusion and Integration of Aboriginal Values and Images
Several colleges have aboriginal names (Kwantlen, Keyano, Keewatin, Nippissing). A few, such as the Ayamdigut campus of Yukon College, are architecturally designed according to an aboriginal theme or display symbols similar to the Nisga'a logo of Northwest Community College. Representation of aboriginal people on staff and teaching faculty is the most tangible way to integrate values and images. Unlike most northern institutions, very few southern colleges have affirmative action staffing targets. For those institutions which have stated targets, aboriginal staffing ranges from 30 per cent at Arctic College to 5 per cent at Assiniboine. Other symbolic or cultural demonstrations of integration include involvement of elders on the counselling staff and the featuring of art, theatre, and traditional dances. The hosting of events such as pow-wows, feasts, and presentations by aboriginal leaders are all components of the infusion process.

Cross-Cultural Training
Cross-cultural training is provided by some institutions as part of professional development and orientation. For college staff, the learning of aboriginal histories, cultures, and economic practices encourages them to use them during instruction and improves their tolerance and sensitivity. Growing levels of awareness are stimulated through the application of bicultural instructional methods.

Curricula

'Native People of Canada' has become a standard university anthropology course in BC. Aboriginal studies is also an important part of adult basic education for aboriginal preparatory students. The Native Community Economic Development Program, the Band Management Program, and the Indian Social Work Program are but a few of the aboriginal-specific programs found in both colleges and institutes. Literature courses on aboriginal writers as well as university-level aboriginal art courses are common. Aboriginal languages are replacing European languages in several liberal arts curricula, and aboriginal teacher training programs (with university articulation) are offered by most college jurisdictions. Aboriginal management methods are found in college resource technology programs, the student population of which is 20 per cent aboriginal. The development of inclusive curricula reorients mainstream values and strengthens aboriginal identity and self-esteem.

Strategic Planning and Evaluation

Linking aboriginal demographics to institutional missions, and connecting student outcomes to program plans, are major problems in all jurisdictions. Planning for inclusion, biculturalism, increased life choices, and occupational mobility for aboriginals is also problematic. Yukon College and Arctic College, together with some colleges in Saskatchewan and Manitoba, are the only institutions which have set student and staffing participation targets. Universities such as the University of Alberta are involved in establishing affirmative participation targets. Information and assessment of data on aboriginal student participation, retention, completion, academic performance, and employment placement are largely uncollected, and the available data have not been adequately analyzed. Evaluation of individual programs is required by some government agencies (e.g., Employment and Immigration Canada), but provincial monitoring of special funding initiatives is at a very early stage.

Resource Allocation

Most institutions are committing very little of their base operating funds to aboriginal programs. In many cases, colleges provide access staff and outreach programs on a self-sufficient basis or only if they receive special grants. The exceptions occur where the aboriginal portion of the student body exceeds 30 per cent. In northern colleges, the bicultural mandate has become central and is supported with appropriate financial commitments.

Aboriginal Institutions

One of the critical outcomes of the aboriginal movement to create self-determining systems is the development of community or tribal adult education agencies. Aboriginal postsecondary institutions come in three basic models: (1) the integrated, (2) the affiliated, and (3) the independent.

The integrated aboriginal postsecondary institution has some form of governance or advisory board but is essentially part of a larger college or university. The First Nations House of Learning at the University of British Columbia has a meeting place, provides student advisors, and offers two degree programs, but its admission requirements, curricula, and accreditation remain under the authority of the university. There are similarly integrated organizations at several universities.

The affiliated aboriginal postsecondary institution (e.g., the Saskatchewan Indian Federated College [SIFC]) has financial autonomy, a board of governors, and numerous culturally relevant diploma and degree programs. But it has no academic autonomy. For example, SIFC's admissions, accreditation, and course content require the approval of the senate of the University of Regina.

The independent aboriginal postsecondary institution is discussed by Barnhardt (1992). There are between thirty and fifty independent aboriginal institutions in Canada, ranging from small learning centres serving a dozen or so basic education students in remote reserves to multicampus institutions with several hundred students enrolled in vocational, diploma, and degree programs. While many independent aboriginal colleges operate their own cultural and language programs, their academic and technical courses are all accredited by public colleges or universities. The large independent institutions have a full range of student services, residences, highly qualified faculty and staff, and multimillion dollar self-administrated budgets. Governance is provided by an elected or appointed board representative of the aboriginal peoples being served. Aboriginal institutions are incorporated under various provincial acts, such as the private institutions acts of BC and Alberta. Only Saskatchewan and the two territories have legislated public postsecondary mandates for aboriginal institutions.

Aboriginal colleges have developed a variety of accreditation arrangements with public institutions. These extend from simple brokerage (providing a delivery site) to complex protocols which permit the aboriginal institutions to control all elements of the educative process (including curricula, instruction, and evaluation), with the public institution providing a guarantee of standards and credentials.

DIAND provides funding for aboriginal institutions intended to service those First Nations peoples covered by treaties. In most situations, this funding is supplemented by other federal programs, such as Pathways for Success (an HRD program for aboriginal basic education). Financial contributions from the provinces take the form of special aboriginal grants. In BC, two aboriginal institutions receive formula allocations through affiliated public colleges. As is the case with their US counterparts, the tribal colleges, Canadian aboriginal institutions receive approximately half of their financial support from the federal government. There is growing provincial participation in the funding of capital projects for equipment and facilities.

Aboriginal colleges attempt to provide the hospitable environment necessary for student retention and program completion. Culturally comfortable facilities along with the majority of students and staff being aboriginal form part of identity-reinforcing student support systems at these colleges. Curricula and methods celebrate aboriginal peoples' traditions, languages, and socioeconomic contributions. The completion/transfer/graduation rates are double those that exist for aboriginal students enrolled in public institutions. For a student's first experience, aboriginal institutions are making major contributions to equity of opportunity and are setting examples of how to redress past educational policies.

The development of more aboriginal-controlled institutions must be seen as a priority. The trend towards more specialized and diverse types of colleges should provide an opportunity to invite aboriginal members to join the postsecondary system as unique but equal partners. Rather than requiring curricular, programmatic, or structural conformity from these organizations, they should be valued for their capacity to respond to the current and future social and economic demands of aboriginal communities. Programs which promote a holistic model of training (embracing spiritual and cultural values, sustainable economic development, non-hierarchical decisionmaking, and equity of value for different types of work) should be celebrated for the example they provide to our entire postsecondary education system. Sensitivity to the employment of prior learning assessment and more open articulation mechanisms should provide greater recognition of the skills, knowledge, and credentials of graduates from aboriginal institutions.

While the portability of credentials is important, the greatest contribution of aboriginal institutions will be their efforts to revitalize the cultural, social, and economic activity of aboriginal cultures. Providing appropriately skilled, socially conscious, and artistic technical and managerial personnel to operate healthy, prosperous, self-governing communities is the highest purpose of aboriginal postsecondary education. If this education takes place in a racism-free, culturally invigorating environment (as opposed to in alien and socially integrative institutions), it is likely to be successful. Aboriginal institutions need to have legislated mandates which respect their cultural and educational differences, which foster equitable funding, and which recognize them as equal partners.

Conclusion

There is good reason to be optimistic about the possibilities of improving the representation of aboriginal adults in postsecondary education and the workforce. Self-determination and strong aboriginal economies are noble goals – goals which also provide benefits for mainstream Canadian society. It may well be necessary to legislate the inclusion of aboriginal institutions in the public postsecondary system. Increased participation of aboriginal students will follow increased institutional respect for aboriginal values, images, and contributions to society. The creation of a system of college/institutional governance which is open to communicating with and attempting to understand aboriginal cultures will result in higher levels of success on the part of aboriginal students.

References

Alberta. 1991a. *The Secondary and Post-Secondary Transition Needs of Native Students*. Edmonton: Ministry of Advanced Education

–.1991b. *Students of Native Ancestry in Alberta Public Post-Secondary Institutions*. Edmonton: Ministry of Advanced Education

Arctic College. 1991. *Calendar, 1991/92*. Yellowknife, NWT

Atleo, E.R. 1993. *An Examination of Native Education in British Columbia*. Native Brotherhood and Sisterhood of BC

Baker, D.A. 1993. 'Aboriginal Post-Secondary Education in Canada: A Survey.' Paper, Department of Adult, Administrative and Higher Education, University of British Columbia

Barnhardt, Ray. 1992. 'Higher Education in the Fourth World: Indigenous People Take Control.' *Canadian Journal of Native Education* 18:199-231

Battell, Evelyn. 1991. 'ABE First Nations Students: Delivery Styles and Curriculum in BC Ministry of Advanced Education.' Paper, Ministry of Advanced Education, Training and Technology, Victoria

Boyer, Paul. 1989. *Tribal Colleges: Shaping the Future of Native America*. Princeton, NJ: Carnegie Foundation for the Advancement of Teaching

British Columbia. 1990. *Report of the Provincial Advisory Committee on Post-Secondary Education for Native Learners*. Victoria: Ministry of Advanced Education, Training and Technology

–.1992a. *Recommendations of the Report of the Provincial Advisory Committee on Post-Secondary Education for Native Learners: Status Report*. Victoria: Ministry of Advanced Education, Training and Technology

–.1992b. University of Northern British Columbia Act, 1992

–.1993a.'Aboriginal Post-Secondary Education.' Unpublished policy paper, Ministry of Advanced Education, Training and Technology, Victoria

–.1993b. *Aboriginal Post-Secondary Education Funding, 1992/93*. Victoria: Ministry of Advanced Education, Training and Technology

Brown, Doug. 1993. 'Dene Training Network.' Project proposal no. 27. Unpublished. College of New Caledonia, Prince George, BC

En'owkin Centre. 1992. *Calendar, 1992-93.* Penticton: En'owkin Centre

First Nations House of Learning. 1993. *Newsletter*

Francis, A.M. 1993. *Facing the Future: The Internationalization of Post-Secondary Institutions in British Columbia.* Vancouver: British Columbia Centre for International Education

Hampton, Eber. 1988. 'Toward a Redefinition of American Indian/Alaskan Native Education.' Ph.D. thesis, Harvard University, Boston

Joseph, Shirley. 1992. 'Vision of First Nations Education.' Paper, Vancouver Community College, Vancouver

Kirkness, Verna J., and R. Barnhardt. 1991. 'First Nations and Higher Education: The four R's — Respect, Relevance, Reciprocity, Responsibility.' *Journal of American Indian Education* 30 (3):1-15

McGivern, Ronald N. 1990. 'Communities of Learners: A Study of Models of Brokerage and Affiliation between Native Organizations and Public Post-Secondary Institutes.' Paper, Simon Fraser University, Burnaby

National Indian Brotherhood. 1972. 'Indian Control of Indian Education.' Policy paper presented to the Ministry of Indian Affairs and Northern Development, Ottawa

Nis'ga'a House of Learning. 1992. 'Mission Statement.' Nis'ga'a Tribal Council, New Aiyansh, BC

Northwest Community College. 1994. *Calendar.* Terrace, BC

Oddson, Lori, and Lynda Ross. 1991. 'Athabasca University's Role in Native Education Programmes.' Paper, Athabasca University, Athabasca

Oike, N., and D. Baker. 1993. 'Aboriginal Post-Secondary Education and Open Learning in BC.' Paper, Department of Administrative, Adult and Higher Education, University of British Columbia

Ontario. 1991. *Native Education and Training Strategy: Report of the Native Advisory Committee.* Toronto: Ministry of Colleges and Universities

Pepper, Floy C., and S. Henry. 1991. 'An Indian Perspective of Self-Esteem.' *Canadian Journal of Native Education* 18 (2):145-60

Private Colleges Accreditation Board. 1990. *Private and Independent Colleges in Alberta.* Edmonton: Ministry of Advanced Education

Ross, Rupert. 1992. *Dancing with a Ghost: Exploring Indian Reality.* Markham, ON: Octopus Publishing

Saskatchewan Department of Education. 1991. *Annual Report, 1990/91.* Regina, SK

Saskatchewan Indian Institute of Technologies. 1990a. *Aboriginal Literacy Action Plan: A Literacy Practitioner's Guide to Action.* Saskatoon

–.1990b. *Aboriginal Literacy Action Plan: Regional Validation Workshops Report.* Saskatoon

Secwepemc Cultural Education Society/Simon Fraser University. 1991. *The Third Year: A Year of Consolidation, 1990-91 Annual Report.* Kamloops, BC

University of Alberta. 1992. *General Faculty Council Policy Manual.* Edmonton

University of British Columbia/First Nations House of Learning. 1993. 'Graduate Survey, 1993.' Vancouver

Wright, Bobby. 1985. 'Programming Success: Special Student Services and the American Indian College Student.' *Journal of American Indian Education* 24 (1)

Yukon College. 1991. *Yukon College Calendar, 1991/92.* Whitehorse, YT

8

Accountability: Mission Impossible?

John D. Dennison

Introduction

From the critical review of the evolving roles of Canadian community colleges presented in Chapter 1, it is apparent that certain common themes (such 'restructuring,' 'entrepreneurship,' and 'accountability') seem destined to influence the future of college education. This chapter focuses upon accountability and the way in which it has become increasingly applicable to the mandate of the community college.

While accountability is not a new concept in the literature of higher education, it has become more prominent since the mid-1980s. It is used in many senses in a variety of contexts, and, while it appears to be a term which is broadly understood, it has no common definition. For example, a recent report from Ontario (Task Force on University Accountability 1993) provided no precise definition, although it did offer meanings ranging from 'strict' accountability (re the allocation of public funds under explicit regulations) to 'responsiveness' (re universities being accountable to their communities for the provision of sociocultural leadership). The report also makes clear that accountability applies far beyond a fiscal relationship and extends to management of human resources, the fulfilment of social policy, and the effectiveness of external communications.

Conrad and Blackburn (1985) associate accountability with three other terms: 'efficiency,' 'effectiveness,' and 'excellence' – all components of a yet wider concept, 'quality.' In so doing, these authors state that 'accountability implies that a program is at least adequate: a program that meets some minimum set of standards and achieves its goals is said to be an accountable one' (p. 286). Quality, however, they regard as suggesting complete goal fulfilment, well beyond simply being acceptable. Conrad and Blackburn also note that demonstrating a program's accountability implies legitimizing its existence to others.

Another report, *Reporting on Effectiveness in Colleges and Institutes* by the Canadian Comprehensive Auditing Foundation (1993), will be discussed in more detail later in this chapter. Suffice it to say that while this report proposes an 'accountability framework' for a college system, its primary concern is with the accountability relationship between senior management and the governing board, which has become part of a general pattern of increasing scrutiny of all public institutions.

A wide and popular application of accountability is embodied in the recommendations of both Elton (1988) and the *Human Resources Development Project (1992): Report of the Steering Committee* (British Columbia 1992). These recommendations are based on the view that organizations (both public and private) have goals and objectives which are either assigned or self-determined and which are widely understood and accepted. It is the demonstrated and documented realization of these specific goals and objectives that comprises accountability. The tasks are then to agree upon what are valid indicators of performance and how they are to be measured. As discussed later in this chapter, neither task is easy, and the consequences of attempting them can be highly controversial.

Accountability in the Community College

Although a substantial literature on accountability in postsecondary education has emerged, particularly since 1980, it is generally associated with related concepts such as quality, outcomes assessment, performance indicators, value-for-money auditing, and program evaluation. Nadeau et al. (1993) reported finding over 800 items related to quality and excellence, but, with two or three isolated exceptions, none referred to Canadian examples. In the general area of accountability, while there are some published references to Canadian universities (e.g., Cutt and Dobell 1992; Cutt 1988; Canadian Association of University Teachers 1993; Task Force on University Accountability 1993) in addition to several addresses at professional conferences, there are few items which refer to community colleges (Canadian Comprehensive Auditing Foundation [1993] being one exception). Actually, most of the relevant material on colleges may be found in numerous graduate follow-up reports (which tend to remain buried in ministerial or institutional archives).

This chapter critically examines accountability within the community college context. As demonstrated in Chapter 1 of this book, colleges play a distinct role in the public education sector. Their relationship to government, on the one hand, and to their respective communities, on the other, distinguishes them from universities; and the variety of clienteles which they attempt to serve gives them a unique responsibility. In preparing this review, it also became clear that accountability, if it is to be broadly applicable to colleges, must necessarily involve questions of quality, evaluation, program relevance, and performance indicators.

Why has the subject of accountability earned so much prominence during the past decade? The intensity of debate over fiscal matters, specifically regarding operating and accumulated deficits at both federal and provincial levels, has put the spotlight upon publicly supported services, health, social welfare, and education as possible targets for restraint. In the public policy agenda, each of these services is being required to document its contribution to the public good in order to justify its continued support. And while the public good is usually interpreted by government, opinion polls often suggest that the population at large has a quite different agenda. The message for publicly supported social organizations of all kinds is that they had better inform and enlist the direct allegiance of their various clienteles if they are to earn the confidence of the public and the political support which they hope will follow.

Education in general has become a target of intense scrutiny. Accounts in the media and formal reviews by task forces and other agents (see Chapter 1) often result in the recommendation of relatively drastic reforms. As described earlier, many highly developed nations are generally disillusioned with the perceived inability of schools, universities, and colleges to deliver on their promises. The breadth and vagueness of many of the goals which governments prescribe for colleges (e.g., to develop individual potential or to contribute to economic growth and diversity) are so vague that precise reporting with respect to their achievement is impossible. But in the 1980s this explanation, or excuse, is no longer acceptable to either government or society. It is interesting to recount that, in the past, acknowledgments of this problem have been expressed quite uncritically. Comments such as those by Tuchman, 'Quality is achieving or teaching for the highest standard as against being satisfied with the sloppy or fraudulent' (1980:38), and Glendenning, 'Quality is in the eye of the beholder and like charity it begins at home' (1990:6), tended to be accepted at face value.

Another problem related to assessment of quality, and certainly having implications for accountability, has been the practice of allowing institutions themselves to gather and summarize the evidence relevant to their performances. Applied more particularly to universities, the concept of autonomy, so characteristic of higher education in Canada, has contributed to the view that self-assessment is more acceptable than external assessment. As detailed by the Task Force on University Accountability (1993), there is a growing concern that accountability, documented internally, is less than fully convincing. The community college sector practice of 'proving' its accountability through self-generated annual reports, most of which are both positive and uncritical, is also being looked at askance by government.

The thrust in many recent provincial reports has been to state explicitly that community colleges should contribute to economic growth and renewal and, ipso facto, ways to accomplish this should be established. The recommended process is usually for more direct government intrusion into the management of colleges, assisted by provincial training boards, in which labour and management representatives play prominent roles. The ultimate scenario resulting from this trend would be the creation of a quite different college model from that used in the past. While some may argue in support of this trend, in my view it would not produce a more desirable result. Having said that, however, it is important to acknowledge that, if colleges wish to continue to contribute significantly to their own destinies, they must better demonstrate their accountability.

To return to a point made earlier in this chapter, government and societal expectations of performance do not necessarily coincide. An interesting example may be found in Saskatchewan, where the 1970s idea of the college as an agent of the local community was much amended by the government of the 1980s, which viewed colleges as direct contributors to economic growth. A recent review by the Regional Colleges Committee of the Saskatchewan college system suggests that the public was far from satisfied by the second scenario and was anxious to have the colleges return to being more directly responsive to community needs.

Accountability to Whom?

Given the role of community colleges as responsive institutions, the inevitable first question is: To whom are colleges actually accountable? The relevant literature on colleges provides a number of answers (e.g., students, faculty, staff, employers of their graduates, institutions to which the students transfer, communities, and government, their most obvious paymaster). Also classified as stakeholders, each of these groups hold different expectations as to what colleges can and should do. While all stakeholders would express agreement on, for example, quality, they would place quite different priorities upon skill readiness, preparation for citizenship, and productivity. Clearly, it would be impossible to satisfy all groups by using the same criteria for accountability.

Accountability to Students

Colleges are educational and training institutions which exist primarily to serve those who engage their services (i.e., their students). Unlike universities, most colleges offer a wide range of programs with an equally wide range of objectives; hence, they have a highly heterogeneous student body.

Some come expecting to upgrade their basic numeracy and literacy skills, others to qualify for immediate employment in a selected field, and some simply to supplement the quality of their lives by taking courses in their special fields of interest. While each student might list his or her objectives in a different order, all would agree on one common expectation – that whatever instruction they receive should be of the highest quality. But, yet again, there are variations as to what quality might mean. For those wishing to continue their studies at a university or technical institute, quality means receiving preparation which will ensure success in advanced learning; for those seeking employment after college, quality means ensuring an excellent performance in the workplace; and for others, instructional quality means creating ongoing enthusiasm for, and appreciation of, learning for its own sake. Only the student is in a position to determine whether his or her particular objective has been adequately met. It is incumbent upon a college, therefore, to ensure that students are afforded the opportunity to accurately and fully record the quality of their experience.

In more general terms, a community college which wants to offer high-quality instruction must establish a way of measuring its success or failure. As Paul Gallagher comments in Chapter 10, it is much easier to claim commitment to quality instruction than to document its existence. Although individual institutions will wish to develop criteria of instructional excellence which will apply specifically to their program objectives, there is a good deal of advice available in the literature. For example, the work of Chickering and Gamson (1991) merits consideration. Based upon extensive research, these authors offer seven principles on which to base undergraduate education: (1) encourage student-faculty contact, (2) encourage cooperation among students, (3) encourage active learning, (4) give prompt feedback, (5) emphasize time on task, (6) communicate high expectations, and (7) respect diverse talents and ways of learning.

In the community college milieu in most Canadian jurisdictions, the diversity of student backgrounds, the essential role of student support services, and the belief in lifelong education all give credence to these seven principles. Furthermore, the current concern over efforts to better ensure student success, reduce drop-outs and failures, and attend to disadvantaged and high-risk students also points to the relevance of Chickering and Gamson's principles. Most of Canada's colleges, by both design and intent, admit many students with undistinguished academic backgrounds. By admitting such students, the college's commitment to furthering their educational advancement is unquestionably heightened, as is the evidence of its accountability to the community. Instructors are faced with the unenviable but essential task of providing these people with a supportive learning environment and with recognizing that learning may take many forms.

One additional form of accountability to students may be found in a policy established by Holland College in Prince Edward Island. This policy guarantees graduates from certain programs that, if their education or training is found to be unsatisfactory in the workplace, they may return for further education at no cost to either themselves or their employers. A similar policy is being explored in a number of Ontario colleges.

Accountability to Staff

The idea that colleges are accountable to their instructional and support staff might be seen as arguable at best. However, colleges, as noted earlier, have a primary responsibility to educate and train those who engage their services. Hence, the predominant task of administration (and the first measure of its performance) is to support the teaching-learning process. Every policy discussion taken by the board should ultimately translate into improved teaching or learning. First and foremost, the college must ensure that its staff is competent and able to provide the direct instruction and the indirect support necessary to facilitate student learning. This means having teachers who are up to date in their fields, working conditions that encourage commitment to the instructional task, administrative practices which assist rather than frustrate student access to classes, libraries, shops, and laboratories, and advice to learners which is both accurate and easily available.

Naturally, staff will argue that better salaries, improved facilities, smaller classes, and greater opportunities for professional development are essential to maintaining high-quality performance of duties – but fiscal realities will assuredly work against this. Nevertheless, the task of administration is to demonstrate, be it only by word and attitude, a continuing recognition of the essential role of faculty and staff in the teaching-learning process. Community colleges, unlike universities, tend to enshrine career administrators, a practice which can produce a we/they relationship with faculty and staff. Once such a gulf develops, it becomes increasingly difficult to demonstrate accountability. (It should be noted that accountability is a two-way street, and that staff are accountable to the institutions in which they work.)

Accountability to Employers

Demonstrating the accountability which a college owes to the employers of its graduates is an ongoing challenge. Most institutions depend upon the assistance of program advisory committees to keep curricula relevant and to maintain contact with the field. As potential employers of the graduates of specific programs tend to be well represented on advisory committees, this relationship often leads to employment opportunities. While employer representatives offer a useful service to program managers, they often tend to reflect the status quo of the workplace and, consequently, do not encourage innovation and experimentation in program design. But one major issue which has arisen in recent years is the standards of performance exhibited by graduates. In the deliberations that accompanied *Vision 2000: Quality and Opportunity,* a review of Ontario's colleges (Council of Regents of Colleges of Applied Arts and Technology of Ontario 1990), employers expressed a concern that standards varied from college to college and were reflected in the performance of graduates.

Respecting this issue, which is essentially one of accountability, *Vision 2000* made several specific recommendations which were designed to lead to increased program standardization. Furthermore, the idea of accreditation was raised (a topic which will be discussed later in this chapter). Two of most significant recommendations in *Vision 2000* were as follows:

> There should be system-wide standards for all programs leading to a college credential. Such standards must focus on the learning outcomes expected of graduates from a program.
>
> All programs leading to a college credential should be subject to regular, system-wide review for the purposes of accreditation. (p. 170)

In response to the above, Ontario's Ministry of Colleges and Universities initiated a provincial College Standards and Accreditation Council (CSAC), a body whose influence has yet to be determined. There is little doubt that this decision will meet with controversy. Some will argue that a regulatory agency such as CSAC will ultimately intrude into the traditional autonomy of colleges in curriculum development and evaluation of students. Others will insist that pressures to standardize ultimately produce a level of mediocrity in which no program is any better than another. It is instructive to note Michael Skolnik's essay, pointedly entitled, 'How Academic Program Review Can Foster Intellectual Conformity and Stifle Diversity of Thought and Method in the University' (Skolnik 1988). Skolnik sees a program appraisal system as a form of 'paradigmatic ethnocentrism' in that it gives one group the authority to impose uniform definitions and standards of quality across all institutions. While the context here is the university, the principles which Skolnik enunciates apply equally to the non-university sector.

Thus, the question is whether accountability to employers is best realized by greater program standardization, in spite of the disadvantages which might follow. In Ontario particularly, where preparation for the workplace is the primary function of college education, the interests of both graduates and those who employ them must be highly influential. In other provinces, such as Newfoundland, Nova Scotia, and New Brunswick, where colleges play a similar role, program standardization is an equally dominant issue.

Quite apart from the above, maintaining accountability to employers creates other difficulties. Program evaluation activities usually call for employer feedback, which, based upon this writer's experience, is often plagued with contradictions. Many employers ask for graduates which are 'generally educated.' Usually, this means employees with good literacy and numeracy skills, who are able to think critically and creatively, and who have both a good understanding of human relationships and a 'work ethic.' In addition, there is often an assumption that graduates will also have specific job skills, be flexible, and be able to adapt to technological change. All of this poses a dilemma for program managers in colleges. Given the less than finite time they have to prepare graduates as well as the cost of adding items to the curricula, college planners are often forced to make decisions based on contradictory advice. There is little doubt as to why the maintenance of program relevance, being a primary component of accountability, constitutes an ongoing challenge to conscientious college administrators and faculty.

Accountability to Transfer Institutions
For community college systems which involve a 'university transfer' function as part of their mandate (notably, those in Alberta, BC, and Québec), accountability includes a recognition that preparing students for transfer entails certain responsibilities. A similar requirement exists where students transfer to technical and other specialized institutions. Transfer agreements, by which credit is granted under specified conditions, are negotiated largely on trust. The college is trusted by the receiving institution to engender skills in its transferring students, although there is no formal process for regulating or supervising instruction. In this respect, the college is accountable to the university for ensuring that the necessary standards of student performance will be maintained, that grades awarded will accurately reflect their accomplishments, that instructor credentials will be as stated, and that course curricula will reflect the content of the agreement. To fail in any of these conditions would not only compromise a relationship with the university but would also do a serious disservice to those students who transfer.

Some college personnel believe that the university, through the transfer exercise, exerts undue influence upon curricula and/or assessment procedures. Admittedly, university departments in various disciplines are sometimes insensitive to the instructional difficulties which colleges often face. Nor do university academics always recognize the serious implications for colleges when the university makes curriculum changes without prior notice or when it creates new prerequisites which affect transfer credits. Under these circumstances, accountability works two ways and often requires the diplomatic skills of individuals from both parties to the agreement.

Nevertheless, the critical component in all of the above arrangements are the students, to whom all institutions have a primary responsibility. Too often, it is forgotten that the priority target in the entire accountability debate is the student, whose academic success is the responsibility of the institution in which he or she is enrolled. But, however noble the motive, students are not well served when standards of performance are relaxed or when a curriculum is not fully covered. Too often, students transfer with false confidence (based upon their success in college), only to face failure in the university. Quite apart from the disillusionment experienced by the students, the reputation of the college is damaged in the eyes of all concerned.

Accountability to the Community

Few would disagree that colleges in all provinces and territories were founded on the assumption that they were accountable for responding to the multitude of educational needs in the regions in which they were located. While their immediate communities are not their sole constituencies (provincial, national, and international programming has expanded rapidly in recent years), most college managers place a major emphasis upon the needs of their regional clienteles. It must also be acknowledged that the organizational and governing structure of each college system determines, in large part, how much, and in which form, community involvement in college affairs will occur. In Saskatchewan, Newfoundland, and Alberta, for example, communities have an ownership role in their local colleges; but in other regions they play a far less prominent role.

Maintaining accountability to communities has become a somewhat difficult task for colleges. Small communities often demand services which would be hard to justify in terms of cost-effectiveness. Many people are primarily interested in credit-free recreational and cultural courses which usually receive minimal or no recognition by government within the operating budget, and, hence, they have to be supported almost entirely from the instructional fees paid by participants. When frustrated in their efforts to enlist satisfactory responses to their requests, some community groups begin to view colleges as becoming more centralized and as having lost touch with local needs.

In theory, lay board members chosen from college regions are expected to ensure that community interests are given a high profile in the planning process. But, as described later in this chapter, board members have to deal with several dilemmas in carrying out their roles. All in all, it may be said that the 'community' in community college is more rhetoric than reality. Funding constraints, program priorities set by the federal government, and a lack of direct community involvement have all contributed to making it difficult for colleges to remain accountable to their communities. At a time when public support for colleges is vital if they are to hold their place in the public policy agenda, any failure to maintain local support could be seriously damaging.

Accountability to Government

The issue of how colleges are, and must be seen to be, accountable to government usually tends to dominate other aspects of accountability. Often, the context of this debate is fiscal. As colleges are funded from the public purse, how do they demonstrate good stewardship? Are public funds being expended in ways consistent with the objectives set by the funding agency? The intensity of these questions grows in concert with financial pressures. But, for a variety of reasons, neither models nor methods of accountability are easy to construct.

One problem is that colleges in most regions of Canada have either an unclear or an incomplete template on which to design accountability measures. Rarely does the provincial government spell out in precise and measurable terms its objectives for the college system. Policy statements from provincial ministries often refer to colleges as tools for 'economic renewal,' 'accessibility,' 'community outreach,' 'an adaptable workforce,' 'social development,' and so on; and all these expressions are reproduced in institutional mission statements and plans. As stated in the report of the Auditor General of British Columbia (British Columbia 1993) in its value-for-money audit of the then Ministry of Advanced Education: 'While there is, in everyday activities, a significant congruence of goals and objectives between the ministry and colleges, the lack of clear operational objectives makes it difficult for colleges to know precisely what they should do in support of the goals' (p. 41).

Nevertheless, in many provinces the relevant ministry initiates follow-up studies of college graduates as a way of measuring the extent to which certain goals have been realized (i.e., to demonstrate accountability). Many of these studies are referred to in the provincial reports in Chapter 1 and will not be discussed in detail here. Not surprisingly, these studies tend to generate responses in relatively straightforward and measurable terms, such as job placement results by program, completion rates, student satisfaction with college experience, relationship between college training and job requirements, and so on. While it may be argued that these data reasonably reflect the contribution of colleges, definitive conclusions must be reached with caution. For example, many graduate follow-up reports not only have poor response rates but display high response bias (i.e., those with jobs tend to respond in higher numbers than do those without jobs). Furthermore, even with respect to high retention rates (which most regard as positive), some may well argue that high standards in college programs will inevitably translate into a fairly high level of non-completion.

As will be noted later, attempts to gain more sophisticated, and perhaps more reflective, indicators of the effects of a college education (such as value-added studies and performance evaluation in the workplace) are expensive, time-consuming, and difficult to design. While it has been argued (Bowen 1977) that many of the benefits which accrue from higher education, both for the individual and for society, are not necessarily monetary, the economic and political climate of the 1990s calls for tangible evidence that the public's investment in college education is both wise and productive.

In this context, it is instructive to refer to the series of reforms instituted in 1993 by the Minister of Education in Québec after an extensive review of the performance of the Cegep system. Among several actions designed to revitalize the system was the requirement that each college review its evaluation procedures respecting student learning, programs of study, and performance of personnel. Specifically, each program was required to implement a final examination in order to validate the learning that had occurred. Nor did this new emphasis on accountability in Québec end with these internal procedures. In addition, the government was to establish a semi-independent, three-person commission with a mandate to evaluate program quality and internal review measures in each institution. The commission was then to prepare recommendations (which were to be made public) for the provincial government. This constitutes the most comprehensive review of accountability in a college sector yet taken in any region of Canada. The Québec minister's exercise of authority, while indirect, leaves little doubt that individual institutions will be expected to fully document their performances; and the creation of the semi-independent commission ensures that colleges will conduct their affairs in concert with the public interest.

While no such sophisticated accountability procedures have yet emerged in other provinces, colleges in every region have grown increasingly aware of the consequences of inaction. They are concerned that if they do not demonstrate satisfactory performance, the government will impose evaluation procedures upon them. This would be unlikely to be received with enthusiasm in the college community, as the latter commonly hold that ministerial policies respecting evaluation would not adequately reflect the college's mission as a comprehensive educational agency.

Reporting on Effectiveness in Colleges and Institutes

One notable attempt to establish an accountability framework was outlined in a study supported by the Canadian Comprehensive Auditing Foundation (CCAF) and conducted by a group representing institutional managers in BC. Entitled *Reporting on Effectiveness in Colleges and Institutes: A Proposed Accountability Framework for the British Columbia Public System,* this study 'offers potential to improve management and accountability, not only at the institutional level, but also in the manner which these institutions demonstrate the effectiveness of their stewardship to the communities and governments which fund them' (Canadian Comprehensive Auditing Foundation 1993:1). The essence of accountability, according to the report, may be found in the answers a college provides to seven basic questions:

(1) Does the institution have an adequate mission statement and a plan that clearly states its objectives, and are these clearly communicated to its community?
(2) Does the institution offer programs and other services that best meet the needs of its community?
(3) Does the institution attract and keep an appropriate number and mix of students?
(4) Do students achieve appropriate outcomes?
(5) Does the institution obtain, organize, and administer resources so that student outcomes are achieved at a reasonable cost?
(6) Is the institution maintaining and building its intellectual and physical resources, including the quality of its employees, curriculum, and physical plant?
(7) Does the institution have systems that produce information that enables management to answer the above questions?

Few would argue against the relevance of these questions. They are undoubtedly the kinds of questions which, if they are to fulfil their responsibilities as representatives of the wider community, boards of governors should be posing.

Inevitably, however, due to their subjective nature, questions such as these are extremely difficult to answer. Almost all institutions prepare mission statements which are carefully constructed and comprehensive. Impressive as they may be, however, the extent of their adequacy is essentially subjective. Does 'adequate' mean complete, or accurate, or realistic, or all of these? And under what circumstances may a plan be considered to be 'communicated clearly'? On what basis does one conclude that an institution's programs and services 'best' meet community needs? Is 'best' to imply relevancy, comprehensiveness, efficiency, or cost-effectiveness? The authors are not unaware of concerns such as these, and they do attempt to provide further interpretation, much of which, however, is also subjective. But the biggest problem with regard to the effective application of these seven questions lies in the interpretations of critical terms such as 'appropriate' (question 4), 'reasonable' (question 5), and 'maintaining and building' (question 6), all of which call for judgements which extend well beyond what may be based on so-called objective data. Presumably, it is in the answers to question 7 that the real worth of the accountability framework will rest.

Performance Indicators

Many of the concerns expressed above reappear in a recent report by Nadeau et al. (1993) which attempted to delineate 'criteria and indicators of quality and excellence in Canadian colleges and universities' (p. 1). In this ambitious exercise, the authors focused upon two dimensions of excellence, the external environment (which is influenced by economic, social, and political factors) and the internal environment (which is influenced by the general climate of morale within the college and the governing structures). The methodology involved eliciting the views of a panel of expert Canadian educators – views that were later validated through being reviewed by an even more extensive panel. Using this consensus-development technique, the study produced criteria (as domains) and indicators (as measures) of excellence for students, faculty and administrators, programs, and services in community colleges and universities.

The final list of criteria extended to several hundred items, which, through a process of validation, eventually resulted in the priority ranking of specific indicators. Prominent in the final list in each category were the following criteria:

Students:
Commitment to learning
Ability to synthesize, analyze, think critically
Effective study skills as habits
Performance on the job

Faculty:
Teaching competence
Up to date in subject matter
Effective communication skills

Administrators:
Concern for quality, excellence
Interpersonal and leadership skills
Planning and innovating activities

External environment:
Public support for postsecondary education
Institutional image/reputation
Accessibility

Internal context:
Clarity of institutional mission/goals
Student satisfaction with institution
A climate of openness

Programs:
Development of independent learning
Clearly identified goals and objectives
Appropriate performance standards

The extent of support from the college community established for these indicators, while not surprising, is certainly reassuring. The real difficulty arises when the application of criteria becomes necessary. How, for example, is 'commitment to learning' expressed and measured? How will a faculty member's knowledge of subject matter be assessed as being 'up to date'? In which ways can the administration demonstrate concern for excellence? What is the evidence of a 'climate of openness'? What are 'appropriate performance standards' for programs? Do these standards vary from program to program? Finding answers to these questions extends, in both complexity and commitment, well beyond the mere listing of criteria, be it ever so carefully produced. Generating performance indicators is a challenging project, but using them to produce definitive measures of accountability is even more challenging.

The Value-Added Approach to Accountability

The value-added, or talent-development, approach to accountability with respect to student learning has been expounded by a number of authors, notably Astin (1985). The primary theme in Astin's *Achieving Educational Excellence: A Critical Assessment of Priorities and Practices in Higher Education* is that few educators are precise about what is meant by quality and are, hence, unable to fully demonstrate accountability. Astin identifies four ways in which quality is conceptualized in higher education: (1) reputation, (2) resources, (3) student outcomes, and (4) talent development.

The first two conceptualizations, although commonly used, are open to challenge. High-prestige institutions attract excellent students and accumulate a wealth of resources largely on the basis of reputation. Gathering information on the third dimension of quality, student outcomes, has become more popular in recent years, particularly in the community college sector. Nevertheless, this is not devoid of problems. Job placement rates, for example, while a convincing measure of student outcomes, might well be more dependent upon the state of the market. Furthermore, other graduate outcomes, such as securing employment, are also related to institutional reputation. Assessing the performance of graduates as employees is a task which involves innumerable difficulties, not the least of which is the problem of trying to gather objective data from representative numbers of qualified respondents.

However, it is through talent development that colleges have a real opportunity to make their case. Community colleges enrol many marginal students, most of whom have been rejected by more prestigious institutions. In the process of developing a variety of demonstrative skills (both generic and specific) in these students, colleges have an excellent opportunity to document their performance. The notion of talent development is based upon the assumption that colleges will enhance intellectual, psychomotor, and affective qualities in their students as a consequence of exposure to the curricular and extracurricular experiences gained while attending the institution.

The assessment of talent development involves regular pre- and post-testing of students in the specific areas of knowledge and skills which colleges claim to be consistent with their missions. Astin is able to support his value-added thesis by referring to a large number of studies in this arena which have been conducted under the aegis of the American Council on Education. Similar attempts to assess talent development have been conducted in several US constituencies (e.g., Florida and Washington). The important point in this discussion, however, is that the value-added approach, which is particularly applicable to colleges, can and should be utilized. While there are several problems inherent in carrying out such studies (cost, time, sampling difficulties, selection of testing material, etc.), the contributions which it makes to ensuring accountability, at least with respect to student performances, well outweighs any obstacles.

The Role of Boards of Governors

Central to any debate on accountability is the part played by the respective governing boards of each institution. With regard to their authority, boards are often in a complex situation. In its value-for-money audit of the Ministry of Advanced Education in BC (British Columbia 1993), the Office of the Auditor General noted that, given the legislated authority of the board of governors, 'the ministry is not responsible for the operation of colleges' (p. 4). Ultimately, it is the board who is accountable, not only for the proper expenditure of public money, but for the entire operation of the institution. In a similar vein, in its report on university accountability in Ontario, the Task Force on University Accountability (1993) judged the governing board to be 'the primary and most effective locus of institutional accountability,' and, in consequence, many of its recommendations were designed to strengthen these boards.

In most Canadian community college systems, governing boards are composed largely of lay persons appointed by the minister of education and charged with setting policy and managing the affairs of the institution. Board members, particularly those from the public arena, inevitably depend upon the advice of management in the performance of their responsibilities. In this regard, the Ontario study reiterated that, if university accountability were to be strengthened, governing boards would have to become more involved in the monitoring of institutional performance. In addition, the report recommended the need for an external provincial monitoring agency. This would, in effect, contribute to the notion of accreditation – an issue discussed elsewhere in this chapter.

Board members face a dilemma. While they are essentially volunteer, part-time participants with limited backgrounds in the complex field of higher education, they bear considerable responsibility, both legal and moral. Furthermore, it may well be asked to whom they are primarily accountable – to the college? To the minister who appointed them? To the wider community? To themselves? Board members, if they are to perform their legislated duties, must be prepared to ask difficult questions, to demand complete answers, and to ensure that their advice respecting policy is heeded. Board members must make sure that they not become so beholden to the administration that their objectivity is compromised.

At the same time, board members often face the charge of being political appointees and, hence, of being unable to effectively challenge the government to honour its responsibility to fund and maintain the college. The advice which they may receive, formally or informally, from the wider community could well be in conflict with either governmental or institutional priorities. If full accountability is to be the responsibility of boards of governors, then members should be well advised of, and fully oriented to, that role rather than simply appointed and left to deal with things. If this kind of support is not provided, perhaps governments should dispense with boards of governance and manage the affairs of institutions directly. Under such conditions, accountability would assume a much different dimension. The government would be in a position to establish its own criteria for performance and to take appropriate action if and when individual institutions were not meeting prescribed standards.

Accreditation

No discussion of accountability in postsecondary education is complete without a reference to the argument that if institutions were required to be accredited, some measure of accountability, at least, would be ensured. Under such a regimen, government and society could rest assured that programs, faculty, and other services would meet acceptable standards of performance.

In the Canadian tradition of postsecondary education, the term 'accreditation' has very limited application, partly because no national governing system or regulatory body exists, and partly because institutional autonomy, in the university sector at least, has become a dominant characteristic of the system. Indeed, as Skolnik (1991) observes, no public universities in the world are as autonomous as are those in Canada. While academic autonomy is rarely associated with the college sector, governing boards are awarded substantial authority and responsibility for managing college affairs in most jurisdictions. Private denominational colleges in Canada are often subject to accreditation by outside agencies such as the Association for Theological Colleges, which is based in the US. Private vocational schools in many provinces are also accredited by a provincial regulatory body.

Fundamentally, public colleges and universities in Canada are given the right to award credentials and to offer programs of study when the appropriate provincial ministry determines that they can do so. From that point on, hiring faculty, designing curricula, establishing standards of admission, and setting the conditions by which students qualify for a particular credentials are all the responsibility of the institutions. There are, of course, important exceptions, and these involve the role played by professional and semi-professional accrediting agencies. It is acknowledged that professional accrediting bodies also require certain institutional conditions as a prerequisite to granting its graduates admission to particular professions. However, as noted in *Governance and Accountability: Report of the Independent Study Group on University Governance* (Canadian Association of University Teachers 1993), they also function as lobby groups for increased university spending on particular professional programs.

Professional accrediting bodies are primarily concerned with specific programs; they rarely focus their activities upon the institution itself, its management, its mission, or its fiscal situation. In fact, formal accreditation of institutions is not practised in Canada. The closest equivalent to institutional accreditation, although restricted to the university sector, is admission to membership of the Association of Universities and Colleges of Canada (AUCC). This is a professional body which plays an advocacy role for its members vis à vis government and the business community. While AUCC imposes certain conditions for membership, these conditions fall well short of an institution's having to pass a comprehensive assessment of its overall performance.

Cognizant of the current emphasis upon accountability, in a 1993 report the Canadian Association of University Teachers (CAUT) proposed the creation of an independent national system of institutional accreditation which would review the active operations of each university (CAUT 1993). With remarkable candour, this report argues that continuing autonomy can be preserved only if the 'current skepticism in the land about self-policing professionals' is allayed by 'combining local accountability measures with a national system of accreditation' (p. 67).

Another important reason for CAUT's proposal is the growing heterogeneity of the postsecondary education system in Canada. The small number of formally recognized degree-granting institutions which existed in the 1960s has been supplemented by open learning agencies, university-colleges, cooperative degree programs offered through special arrangements, and a variety of private institutions (both inside and outside Canada) which often offer degrees via unconventional delivery methods. While a number of provinces (e.g., BC and Alberta) have established structures to deal with these new developments, the CAUT report argues that provincial-level accreditation will lead to the balkanization of Canadian higher education.

How is this discussion applicable to the community college system? Colleges are much more provincial in their orientation than are universities and, consequently, are much more variable in all respects. Unlike AUCC, the college equivalent, the Association of Canadian Community Colleges (ACCC), plays no part in accreditation, either formally or informally. But while provincial and territorial college systems conduct their affairs independently, graduates of their programs move freely across provincial borders in search of further education or employment. In a few selected 'red-seal' trades, there are provisions for having credentials recognized nationally; but the great majority of college programs are not recognized beyond provincial borders.

Under current circumstances (not excluding constitutional impediments), it would be unrealistic to propose any national college accreditation system in Canada. However, an argument for a provincial-level accreditation system might well be made, particularly in the context of a larger concern over accountability. The more pertinent questions respecting provincial accreditation of colleges, however, are: How? and By whom? Given that the main point of the exercise is to supply documented evidence that public money is being spent wisely, effectively, and in a manner consistent with established economic and sociocultural priorities, would it be the institution, the government, or an independent agency which would be most able to earn credibility?

A practice common in the US is to maintain accreditation through regionally based bodies in which colleges participate voluntarily. This policy is reviewed in some detail in Mayhew et al. (1990), where it is given a mixed reception. The authors note the traditional resistance of educational institutions to be monitored by outside agencies, particularly governments. Rather, they are inclined to support the idea of self-monitoring, essentially through the process of voluntary accreditation. This practice, beginning as early as the late nineteenth century, involves the establishment of regional associations which, in theory at least, protect the public interest by passing judgment on the quality of education offered by their members. Mayhew et al., however, document numerous concerns about the policy and the process itself. For example, there is the ever-present danger of imposed standardization of institutional operations, particularly with respect to curricula. Innovations may well be discouraged, particularly if they are not practised by other members of the association. Furthermore, strong institutions feel confident of their ability to set standards, irrespective of the approval of others. Another concern is with the effectiveness of self-studies, which are normally a prerequisite to external review. Mayhew et al., for example, ask whether self-studies conducted for accreditation would truly find institutional weaknesses, or whether they would always be self-serving, even cosmetic, efforts. Furthermore, they ask whether accreditation could help to improve strong institutions, particularly since it is a process which is influenced by weak institutions, which wanted approval rather than improvement.

But perhaps the weakest aspect of accreditation, voluntary or otherwise, has been the limited criteria upon which approval has been based. Rarely have either self-reviews or external reviews examined students' learning or intellectual growth, knowledge in major fields, or generic skills such as analysis, synthesis, or problem-solving capacities (Kells and Kirkwood 1979, reported in Mayhew et al. 1990). Generally speaking, such reviews focus upon admission criteria, organization, quality of teaching, and/or planning policies.

Finally, if accreditation is to truly protect the public interest, it seems inevitable that some institutions will be denied approval while others will receive it. As Mayhew et al. note, this is rarely the case. Indeed, they report that, since the end of the Second World War, only one publicly supported institution has lost its accreditation. They go on to state, in a somewhat cynical vein, that they 'can predict safely that, under current procedures, if an institution has a reasonable longevity, a definite campus, and reasonably recognizable programs and it is not in danger of imminent bankruptcy, it will continue to receive accredited status regardless of how its graduates

perform' (p. 226). In fact, while acknowledging the development of creative programs by many institutions in the 1980s and 1990s, Mayhew et al.
insist that these are due to outside funding opportunities rather than to
accreditation practices.

Based upon the foregoing, a number of issues arise. Is there value in the
overall concept of institutional accreditation? What form, if any, should
accreditation take? Will accreditation ensure, or even allow for, improved
accountability? As the primary focus of this debate is upon the community
college, comments are generally restricted to those institutions.

For essentially practical reasons, including the mobility and future educational aspirations of college students who are confronted by a complex galaxy of programs (leading to an even more complex array of credentials),
provincially based institutional accreditation should now be considered.
For more altruistic reasons, potential students and the general public need
assurance that programs are of recognized relevance and quality. Given the
growth of both public and private institutions (many regarded as unortho-
dox in program content and delivery), this need for assurance is exacerbated. The design of college education in Canada precludes national accreditation, thus making provincial accreditation the only logical alternative.

While voluntary accreditation associations have a certain appeal, the deficiencies disclosed by Mayhew et al. must be acknowledged; however, the
notion of direct government involvement in the accrediting process is even
less appealing. While government plays a dominant role in directing college education in most provinces, there is a need to separate the powers of
judge and jury with respect to determining how well institutions perform.
The most attractive model of accreditation is that offered through the offices of a quasi-independent agency, comprised essentially of qualified individuals with no college affiliation but including representatives from the
university and the private sector. As described earlier, a similar model has
been proposed in Québec.

If the task is to be carried out effectively, if the activities of this agency are
to earn wide-based credibility, and if accreditation is to serve as a basis for
public accountability, it will require a substantial investment of both human and material resources. To address the most significant aspects of institutional performance, such as assessing changes in the generic skills of students or evaluating graduates in the workplace, both management expertise
and budgetary support are essential. Nevertheless, given the enormous investment of public money in college education, the expectations of the
thousands of students who enrol in colleges, and the importance of colleges with respect to economic revitalization and renewal, it is crucial that
their performances be assessed as thoroughly as possible.

Although its applicability to Canadian higher education may be limited, it is interesting to conclude the discussion of accreditation by commenting upon an initiative developed recently in New Zealand. This initiative is designed to set and monitor standards of performance by program and institution (Moorhouse 1994). The New Zealand Qualifications Authority (NZQA) is a Crown-owned entity, created in 1990, which is responsible for developing and implementing a comprehensive and coherent framework of standards for all nationally recognized qualifications offered by postsecondary institutions.

The National Qualifications Framework focused upon the specific skills, knowledge, and competencies which were to be offered to students should their institutions be accredited. This process is mandatory for all programs, whether academic or vocational, offered by both public and private colleges and universities. Standards are set by the NZQA in partnership with providers, teachers, students, industry, and other user groups. The intent is to assure employers, government, the public, and students that, if graduates are awarded credentials (i.e., national certificates [levels 1-4], national diplomas [levels 5-6], or degrees [levels 7-8]), then they have met acceptable national standards of performance. Standards are maintained through a complex monitoring process which involves initial accreditation, moderation (to verify that assessments are fair, valid, and consistent), and audit (which involves checking to ensure that standards are not being eroded). Of course, New Zealand's unitary system of government does not face the complex issues involved in setting national standards which are faced by Canada's federal/provincial system of government.

Conclusion

The title of this chapter, 'Accountability: Mission Impossible?' was chosen after a comprehensive review of the available literature. An overwhelming number of arguments testify to the importance of, the need for, and the general dissatisfaction with, current efforts to demonstrate the accountability of educational institutions. Much of the debate revolves around the university sector, where, for example, authors such as Berdahl (1990) and Peters (1992) see major threats to academic freedom arising as a consequence of government initiatives to ensure university accountability. Conversely, writers such as Grossman (1988) insist that, notwithstanding an 'array of criticisms,' the accountability movement is not only moving methodically ahead, but there is clear evidence that its effect is being realized in better assessment policies, placement rates, and instructional quality.

There is a paucity of published debate respecting accountability in the community college sector, although some US writers, such as Pilard and

Kennedy (1988), have drawn attention to the need for institutions to take action to demonstrate accountability before state legislatures do it for them. Pilard and Kennedy identified a number of critical factors (many being depressingly predictable) such as job placement and retention rates which vocational deans regard as evidence of a successful program.

As has been said, Canadian college systems have adopted a variety of approaches in order to amass evidence that their institutions are, at least in part, accomplishing either their own goals or those set by government. But the inevitable conclusion, after reviewing numerous efforts to establish accountability, is that no truly comprehensive and systematic process has been tested in Canada, although the proposal in Québec is a beginning. The reason for this is fairly clear: Accountability is in the eye of the stakeholder, each of which may demand different services, performances, and outcomes. While there may be superficial agreement upon performance indicators, they are usually so impractical that they cannot be measured. Provincial government ministries appear to be frustrated by a perceived gap between colleges as agents of socioeconomic change and colleges as educational institutions.

Ultimately, the future of community colleges in Canada will rest upon how well they address current challenges, the most prominent of which are restructuring, entrepreneurship, and accountability. With regard to accountability, there must be a meeting of minds in order to determine just what the primary purposes of colleges are, and, perhaps more important, to determine just how their achievements may be clearly measured. Until this is done, demonstrating accountability will remain a 'mission impossible.'

References

Astin, A.W. 1985. *Achieving Educational Excellence: A Critical Assessment of Priorities and Practices in Higher Education*. San Francisco: Jossey-Bass Publishers

Berdahl, R. 1990. 'Academic Freedom, Autonomy and Accountability in British Universities.' *Studies in Higher Education* 15 (2):169-180

Bowen, H.R. 1977. *Investment in Learning: The Individual and Social Value of American Higher Education*. San Francisco: Jossey-Bass Publishers

British Columbia. 1992. *Human Resource Development Project (1992): Report of the Steering Committee*. Vancouver: Human Resource Development Project

British Columbia. 1993. *Report 2: Ministry Role in the College System*. Victoria: Office of the Auditor General

Canadian Association of University Teachers (CAUT). 1993. *Governance and Accountability: Report of the Independent Study Group on University Governance*. Ottawa: Canadian Association of University Teachers

Canadian Comprehensive Auditing Foundation. 1993. *Reporting on Effectiveness in Colleges and Institutes: A Proposed Accountability Framework for the British Columbia Public System*. Ottawa: CCAF

Chickering, A.W., and Z.F. Gamson. 1991. *Applying the Seven Principles for Good Practice in Undergraduate Education.* San Francisco: Jossey-Bass Publishers

College Standards and Accreditation Council. 1992. 'Report of the CSAC Establishment Board to the Minister of Colleges and Universities,' Toronto

Conrad, C.F., and R.T. Blackburn. 1985. 'Program Quality in Higher Education.' In *Higher Education: Handbook of Theory and Research.* Vol. 1. New York: Agathon Press

Council of Regents of Colleges of Applied Arts and Technology of Ontario. 1990. *Vision 2000: Quality and Opportunity.* Toronto: Ministry of Colleges and Universities

Cutt, J. 1988. *Comprehensive Auditing in Canada: Study and Practice.* New York: Praeger

Cutt, J., and R. Dobell. 1992. *Public Purse: Public Purpose.* Halifax: Institute for Research on Public Policy

Elton, R. 1988. *A Funding Allocation System for the Colleges and Institutes of British Columbia.* Vancouver: Price Waterhouse

Glendenning, D. 1990. 'Program of the Annual Conference of the Association of Community Colleges of Canada,' Charlottetown, PEI

Grossman, R.J. 1988. 'The Great Debate over Institutional Accountability.' *College Board Review* Spring 147:38-42

Mayhew, L.B., P.J. Ford, and D.L. Hubbard. 1990. *The Quest for Quality: The Challenge for Undergraduate Education in the 1990s.* San Francisco: Jossey-Bass Publishers

Moorhouse, R. 1994.'The New Zealand Experience: Restructuring Vocational Qualifications.' *Canadian Vocational Journal* 29 (2):21-6

Nadeau, G., J. Donald, A. Konrad, J.-C. Lavigne, and D. Laveault. 1993. 'Criteria and Indicators of Quality and Excellence in Canadian Colleges and Universities.' Report distributed at the Conference of the Learned Societies, May-June 1993, Ottawa

Peters, M. 1992. 'Performance and Accountability in Post-Industrial Society: The Crisis of British Universities.' *Studies in Higher Education* 17 (2):123-39

Pilard, W., and L. Kennedy. 1988. 'Vocational Education Accountability Reports: Preparation and Use.' *Community/Junior College Quarterly* 12:127-36

Skolnik, M. 1988. 'How Academic Program Review Can Foster Intellectual Conformity and Stifle Diversity of Thought and Method in the University,' Paper, Ontario Institute for Studies in Education, Toronto

–.1991. 'Odd Country Out: A Speculative Commentary on Possible Causes and Consequences of the Absence of a National Policy toward Higher Education in Canada.' Paper presented at the Annual Meeting of the Association for the Study of Higher Education

Task Force on University Accountability. 1993. *University Accountability: A Strengthened Framework.* Toronto

Tuchman, B. 1980. 'The Decline of Quality.' *New York Times Magazine* 2 Nov., 38

9

The DACUM Technique and Competency-Based Education
Charles W. Joyner

Introduction
The DACUM (Developing a Curriculum) technique for developing curricula and the application of competency-based education (CBE) methodology are Canadian innovations now shared with many nations seeking solutions to the continuing challenge of providing education and training opportunities relevant to current social needs. Through twenty-five years of development, application, evaluation, and modification, the fundamental concepts and principles which focus on learner needs, personal goals, and career aspirations have remained unchanged. When effectively applied, the DACUM technique and CBE methodology result in an efficient and flexible system of instruction, providing maximum accessibility to a broad spectrum of learners.

Despite the irrefutable logic and the theoretical merits of competency-based education, there has been mixed acceptance of both the concept and the process in Canadian institutions. Perhaps the greatest obstacle to successful application of the DACUM technique and CBE methodology is that resistance to modifying the values, customs, and practices of traditional education has been exacerbated by an insufficient understanding of the intricacies and complexities of introducing CBE as a non-traditional learning paradigm. Canadian institutions which have made the transition to CBE have identified its strengths and weaknesses. The knowledge gained from CBE will likely influence future human resources development models both inside and outside Canada.

Paramount among the issues influencing education in the next decade is how much the government will contribute to the cost of educating and training a capable labour force. Canada, like other developing nations, realizes the need for an effective and efficient system of delivering education, training, and retraining in order to support national economic development. Increasing access to quality instruction at the lowest possible cost will lead to new approaches and systems that will address such issues as the recognition of prior learning, the relevance of curricula, learner diversity, access to learning opportunities, quality standards, mobility, and accreditation. The realization that learning is a lifelong process, and is no longer limited to young people in traditional educational institutions, results in an even greater demand for educators to become managers of the learning process rather than simply traditional purveyors of information.

This chapter will provide a brief review of the context in which the DACUM technique and competency-based education were developed. It will introduce issues regarding the delivery of instruction in Canadian colleges, describe the relationship between DACUM and CBE, and provide an analysis of present applications and future prospects.

Historical Context
Prior to 1970, education in Canada, as in most countries, was very traditional. Curricula were determined by educators and were imposed on a system-wide basis by the appropriate provincial education authorities. In predominantly Roman Catholic regions, the church played a key role in determining what was taught and how teaching and learning would take place. Primary education provided the essential foundation in languages, arts, and sciences, while secondary education emphasized mastery of academic subjects as prerequisites for admission to university programs. With few exceptions, access to postsecondary education was limited to an elite group which possessed the social, economic, and intellectual capacity to adapt to the formal customs of academia. Access to education was difficult, if not impossible, for a growing majority of people seeking employment which was dependent on training and/or retraining.

The magnitude of the impact of technological change in Canada is illustrated by the fact that mechanization in mining, forestry, fishing, and agriculture reduced the required labour force in the primary resource sector from about 50 per cent of the workforce in 1891, to 27 per cent in 1961, and to 6.2 per cent in 1991. A corresponding demographic shift accompanied this change: in 1921, 50 per cent of the population consisted of urban dwellers; in 1961, it was 70 per cent; and in 1991, it was 77 per cent (Kerr, Holdsworth, and Laskin 1990; Statistics Canada 1991).

While technological sophistication was increasing in quantum leaps, educational practices and training methodology remained virtually unchanged. Escalating demand for skilled labour, combined with a lack of educational opportunity, created an intolerable situation for employers, employees, and educators alike. By the early 1960s, issues underpinning the need for educational reform in Canada could be summarized as follows:

(1) a desire to shift national economic development priorities from an agrarian-based to an industrial-based economy
(2) a mismatch between educational programs and labour force needs exacerbated by rapid escalation in technological sophistication, creating a need for higher levels of scientific and technical knowledge and skills
(3) rigid provincial education structures inhibiting access to educational programs relevant to the changing needs of industry and society
(4) lack of access to educational opportunities for the unemployed, early school leavers, and adults wishing to upgrade skills for enhanced employment opportunities
(5) inefficiency and redundancy of costly education and training programs offered in institutions operated by various ministries and government departments whose primary purpose was something other than education

The 1960s was also a decade of questioning and probing social norms, customs, and behaviour. It was a time of increased recognition of individual rights and freedoms, consumer protection, and citizen advocacy. It was the dawning of the information age, and it was accompanied by an increase in demand for electronic technologies. Traditional education methods and school systems (born in the era of the Industrial Revolution) were being questioned. Searching for ways to improve both teaching and learning were educators and authors such as Robert Mager (1962; 1967) and Malcolm Knowles (1970; 1973) in the United States, while James Robbins (Roby) Kidd (1959; 1963; 1970) at the University of Toronto promoted fundamental concepts describing the way people learn and what motivates adult learners. Finally, the 1960s was a decade of economic prosperity and growth in all sectors, including education.

In Canada, the infusion of substantial amounts of money between 1960 and 1967 through the federal Technical and Vocational Training Assistance Act of 1960 provided an incentive for provinces to develop innovative approaches to increasing the efficiency and relevance of education and training programs (Glendenning 1964). Paralleling program development initiatives were major educational reforms which led to the creation of vocational institutes and community colleges. With the exception of those in Québec, Alberta, and British Columbia, the primary mission of the new institutions was to provide employment-related learning opportunities for anyone beyond the legal age of compulsory school attendance. Thus, the role of the colleges was to educate, train, and retrain a labour force in order to support Canada's shift from an agrarian-based to an industrial-based economy (Dennison and Gallagher 1986).

The euphoria of administrative reorganization, the excitement of designing physical facilities, and the thrill of hiring the most competent and qualified staff did not alter the fact that program relevance and instructional delivery were linked to the task of revising curricula. It was in this fertile environment that new concepts and techniques for program design and delivery emerged.

The Origin of DACUM and CBE

In 1967, the federal Department of Regional Economic Expansion (DREE) established a series of private, non-profit organizations for the purpose of developing and demonstrating new approaches to solving problems of low employment from a training or training-related perspective (Adams 1972). The new organizations were known by the generic term NewStart Inc., which was generally preceded by the name of the province or city in which they were located. In May 1968, representatives of various NewStart corporations were called to Vancouver by Howard Clement (of the Experimental Projects Branch, Canada Department of Manpower and Immigration) to discuss innovative approaches to occupational training programs. Oliver Rice (of General Learning Corporation, a division of Time Life Books) presented a model describing an occupational program developed for the Women's Job Corps in Clinton, Iowa. The Vancouver meetings concluded that the Iowa job corps model involved little more than a change in format with respect to the presentation of traditional course content and was thus not applicable to their needs. The NewStart group was seeking an analytical technique to conduct occupational analysis as the first step in developing a curriculum (DACUM). The acronym DACUM, which came out of the Vancouver meeting, was adopted as a generic label for a yet-to-be-described process.

Robert E. Adams from Nova Scotia NewStart Inc. was motivated by the Vancouver meeting and, upon returning to Yarmouth, designed a graphic analytical technique to represent job-related skills as described by experienced workers. Within three months, more than ten occupations had been analyzed and as many DACUM charts completed. In August 1968 in Montague, Prince Edward Island, Robert Adams presented his work, which led to a clear understanding that 'DACUM was an analysis of the occupation rather than a curriculum evolving from an analysis. The result is an independent specification of each of the skills [behaviours] that collectively enable an individual to perform competently in the occupation' (Adams 1972).

While Adams continued developing the DACUM technique in Nova Scotia, David Conger of Saskatchewan NewStart Inc. focused on the need to provide innovative, non-threatening instructional opportunities for adults deficient in literacy skills and basic education. The Saskatchewan program featured a teaching/learning concept called individually prescribed instruction (IPI). 'The purpose of IPI was to plan, provide, and conduct a battery of learning situations tailored to a trainee's characteristics as a learner. The process adapted instruction to the individual in an integrated scheme of evaluation, development and training' (Conger 1970). Introduced in Prince Albert, Saskatchewan, in January 1970, IPI provided learners with a truly individualized learning opportunity based on personal goals, strengths, weaknesses, and learning styles. For the first time, the role of the teacher shifted from authority figure to coach; from being the sole source of knowledge to being the manager of a student-centred learning process – a process in which the use of many forms of instructional media became a key feature (Conger 1970). These principles formed the basis for the development of self-paced, competency-based learning.

Convergence of Concepts
In 1968, Prince Edward Island underwent educational reform which culminated in the creation of a new postsecondary institution (Dennison and Gallagher 1986). The new institution, Holland College, had a mandate to provide employment-related learning opportunities to a broad range of learners. The time was opportune for Donald Glendenning, the first president of Holland College, to blend innovative curriculum-development techniques and instructional delivery methodology on a scale not previously considered possible. (Robert Adams was recruited to assist Glendenning and Lawrence Coffin, director of program and staff development, in the designing and implementing of these new programs.) This blending of concepts produced a model which merged the DACUM technique with a form of instructional delivery which had integrated IPI, thus creating a new learning process known as the Self-Training and Evaluation Process (STEP) (Coffin 1974). The merging of DACUM and CBE was key to the further exploration and development of systems models for what has generally become known as competency-based education.

The DACUM technique and CBE are frequently referred to as one concept or process. It is important to distinguish between the various procedures and techniques commonly grouped under the titles DACUM and CBE. In simple terms, the distinction between the two is that the DACUM technique identifies *what* students should learn, while competency-based education describes *how* students should learn. It is possible to modify curriculum using the DACUM technique without altering the mode of instructional delivery; however, this defeats its purpose and limits learning effectiveness.

A Description of DACUM

The DACUM technique is an effective method of determining quickly, at relatively low cost, the tasks and duties expected of anyone employed in a given job or occupation. The premise is that people employed in various occupations are capable of describing the knowledge, skills, and attitudes required to work in them. For each occupational specialization there are four distinct phases in the complete DACUM process.

The first phase is called job or occupational analysis. This phase relies heavily on a group of eight to twelve people brought together to form the DACUM committee. Members are recruited directly from business, industry, or the professions in which graduates of the educational program will eventually be employed. Committee members are selected for their credibility, experience, and expertise in their respective occupations. There are no teachers on the committee. A facilitator, knowledgeable and trained in DACUM technique, shepherds the committee for one to three days in the development of a comprehensive list of duties and tasks typically performed in the occupation under analysis. Tasks identified by the committee are arranged in horizontal bands on a DACUM chart. Each group or band of tasks is arranged according to various competencies typically required of people working in these particular occupations. Information contained on the chart may be extended to include equipment and materials used on the job, attitudes and qualities of successful workers, frequency of tasks performed, degree of difficulty, and other details associated with the occupations. When an occupation profile is developed using the DACUM technique, the relevance of its curriculum to industrial and commercial labour force needs is assured.

In the second phase, the DACUM chart is given to qualified educators familiar with the occupational specializations in order to conduct a task analysis. Each task identified in phase one is analyzed, and a description of the knowledge, learning, skills, and attitudes required to attain mastery of it is prepared. The third phase is the instructional analysis phase of the DACUM process. This phase requires a team of educators with a fundamental knowledge of the respective occupational specializations, a thorough understanding of pedagogical principles as applied to youth and adult learners, and familiarity with instructional technology, media, and resources. This phase will produce a detailed description of program content.

The fourth phase consists of instructional design and materials development. It is during this phase that various forms of instructional media will be used to prepare learning modules conveying the information, skills, knowledge, and attitudes required by the learners. Development and production of instructional materials is a time-consuming and costly phase of the DACUM process. Administrative factors such as budget, educational philosophy, government policies, and many others determine what the final product will be. When the four phases of the DACUM process are complete, the program is ready for trial implementation.

Competency-Based Education (CBE)

CBE is a systematic learning process in which the primary concern is the learner's attainment of the knowledge and skills relevant to his or her selected occupational goal. The time required to learn theoretical concepts and practical skills is secondary to the demonstrated accomplishment of objectively verifiable learning outcomes. In traditional education, the focus of attention and learner dependency is on the teacher and is set in an administrative framework bounded by rigid class schedules, facilities, the academic calendar, and other time-based concerns. In contrast to traditional education, CBE is learner-centred, focusing on individual strengths, needs, and learning styles. When fully implemented, CBE is a personalized learning system in which students progress at their own rates. The learner starts at a level of skill and knowledge based on his or her demonstrated competency.

In a self-paced CBE environment, the teacher's role shifts dramatically from that of the traditional authoritarian holder of knowledge to that of the learning process manager and resource person. The dual role of instructors in a CBE system requires competence in the subject and familiarity with the administrative process for monitoring and managing individual student progress. For the system to function effectively, the instructor must be accessible and available to individuals or small groups of students in a learning resources centre, workshop, or laboratory. Traditional classes or lectures are replaced by individual or small group consultations and/or tutorials. The teacher monitors and verifies student progress through a written evaluation of their demonstration of theoretical knowledge and of practical skills.

Because competency-based programs are self-paced, learner centred, and task-specific, students must be sufficiently mature, motivated, and determined to pursue studies on their own. Students accustomed to regimentation and authoritarianism frequently have difficulties adjusting to the freedom of competency-based education. Transition from the traditional education programs to the non-traditional CBE format may be facilitated by an orientation program and continuing support from instructors, guidance counsellors, and others. Provision for learner-support mechanisms must be included in the organization and management of CBE programs. A comparison of the characteristics of traditional programs with those of competency-based programs is given in Table 9.1.

Table 9.1

Comparison of programs

Process or issue	Conventional/ traditional	Competency-based/ non-traditional
Admission (application)	Once a year	Any time during the year
Registration	Once a year; in some cases biannual	Once a month prior to the start of the program
Scheduling	Fixed starting date for all students Rigid schedule to be maintained throughout the semester Schedules set by school	Flexible schedule based on the availability of facilities and instructors Students must maintain a minimum rate of progress throughout the program
Teaching methodology	Teacher centered Lecture method to large groups of students Students copy notes written on the board by the instructor Quality of learning largely depends on the quality and commitment of the teacher Demonstration of practical skills may be effectively seen by few students in large classes	Student focused Teacher serves as a resource when students require clarification of learning materials or demonstration of skills Quality instructional materials provide basis for student learning; individual or small groups of students receive assistance from teacher when such help is required
Evaluation	Normative according to class averages and group performance Regardless of evaluation results the teacher proceeds to the next topic in the program	Objective Criteria-based Written examinations Demonstrated competence Students must prove competency in each module before proceeding to new learning
Certification	Awarded annually to successful students	Awarded when students complete all competency requirements for the program

Introducing CBE in Traditional Institutions

Introducing competency-based education has proven to be a very complex process of change, particularly in schools having a history of traditional educational philosophy, methodology, structure, and administration. Deeply rooted organizational attitudes and values, based on time and tradition, serve as a barrier to shield faculty, staff, and administration from the upset and insecurity associated with change. Introducing CBE is further complicated when dealing with centrally controlled educational governance systems, in which a ministry or department has ultimate responsibility for the accreditation of institutions and programs, the allocation of funds, academic calendars, curricula, examinations, and certification of studies. System-wide implementation of CBE requires significant advance preparation and a sincere commitment to change. A thorough understanding of the implications of introducing a non-traditional learning methodology is essential to gaining complete support. Careful consideration must be given to issues such as the changing role of the instructor, the cost of developing programs, and the introduction of new administrative practices such as admissions, scheduling, and fee collection. Changing to CBE is a very complex undertaking, and it has implications for everyone associated with the institution in question. Failure to consider the impact on various stakeholders will ultimately lead to system failure.

In institutions where competency-based, self-paced education has been fully implemented, it is well received by students, the community, and the faculty. Three such institutions were cited in a study conducted by Watson (1991). The CBE approach is especially useful in situations where learners are widely divergent with respect to ability as well as to previous and concurrent experience. The self-pacing aspect of CBE, moreover, appears to develop independence and self-reliance, which learners generally enjoy. CBE also provides flexibility in attendance and enrolment patterns, which both employers and mature learners appreciate.

The most frequently cited example of the successful implementation of a CBE system is Holland College in PEI. Reasons for its success are:
- genuine commitment and support for change from the provincial government, board of governors, and senior administrators
- inclusion of stakeholders at the onset of planning for change
- province-wide implementation of the new system
- training and development of staff concerning their role in CBE
- information dissemination and consultation with the community
- adjustment of labour agreements and workload norms
- design, construction, and/or renovation of facilities based on instructional needs of CBE methodology

- adequate preparation and procurement of instructional resources
- orientation of students to new CBE methodology
- routine review, evaluation and adjustment of programs.

On the other hand, BC's attempt to implement CBE was fraught with difficulty. One of the reasons for its rejection in BC was that the initial concept was a government-imposed education initiative which had been developed with little community consultation and in virtual isolation from the corps of program implementers. Insufficient time and resources were provided to introduce the concepts to the staff of traditional institutions, thus causing confusion and a lack of understanding. Implementation difficulties escalated to the political level, where the sensitivity of the electorate superseded the enthusiasm for change, thus causing the process to grind to a halt.

Between the two ends of the spectrum exemplified by PEI and BC, respectively, are several Canadian institutions which have planned, designed, and presently operate competency-based, self-paced education programs based on curricula developed through the DACUM technique. For example, selected programs at Humber College, Toronto; the Commerce Court Campus of Canadore College, North Bay, Ontario; the Wascana and the Woodland campuses of the Saskatchewan Institute of Applied Science and Technology (SIAST); the Northern Alberta Institute of Technology and the Southern Alberta Institute of Technology (NAIT and SAIT, respectively); and many trades training programs in BC use self-paced CBE methodology.

Issues and Trends

Approximately twenty-five years after the establishment of the network of postsecondary colleges and institutes in Canada, most provinces have conducted major system reviews. For example, in 1990 Ontario released *Vision 2000: Quality and Opportunity* (Ontario 1990), while in April 1993, Québec released *Colleges for the 21st Century* (Québec 1993). The findings of such studies and reports highlight key issues to be addressed in the few remaining years of the twentieth century. A review of various provincial, national, and international reports reveals several key issues in postsecondary education, all of which having been addressed in some detail in various chapters of this book. In summary, however, the five key issues in all regions of Canada which need to be resolved in the immediate future are:

(1) The need to establish system-wide standards to increase the consistency, quality, and mobility of credentials. This issue has been articulated primarily by employers concerned that graduates from various institutions, while bearing the same formal certificates and diplomas, display differing skills and competencies. Furthermore, graduates follow employment possibilities, and this often necessitates crossing

provincial boundaries (the problem being that employers are often unsure of credentials earned in other provinces). Given the mobility of the workforce and the regional variations in job opportunities, greater standardization of designated credentials must become a priority for education and training institutions.

(2) Improving access to learning opportunities for a diverse range of learners living, working, and learning in areas other than urban centres. Given the continuing constraint upon education and training budgets, it has become unrealistic to expect to duplicate conventional programs available in many institutions, particularly in regions of limited population. While distance education offers a potential solution, it is in an early stage of development in most provinces. While portability of students is not feasible, portability of self-paced learning and assessment packages is.

(3) A need for mechanisms to objectively assess and formally recognize prior and concurrent learning on the job, at home, or elsewhere. The broad concept of prior learning assessment has been discussed at some length in Chapter 3 of this book. For several reasons (e.g., time, cost, and overall efficiency), the development of a viable and acceptable method of retraining, which avoids the duplication of previous relevant learning and which recognizes the accomplishments of the individual learner, is an immediate priority for institutional managers.

(4) Increase the relevance of curricula to the needs of learners and their employers. Relevance is a continuing challenge for curriculum designers in conventional educational institutions. In many fields of employment, it is virtually impossible (both administratively and financially) for colleges to keep up to new technology and advanced techniques. Again, a current priority is to create a system which will ensure that curricula are highly adaptable. One method of doing this is to consistently upgrade and redefine the competencies needed in order to keep pace with technological changes in the workplace.

(5) Increase learning efficiency and effectiveness without increasing their cost. Increasing productivity has become a major challenge which governments have directed at postsecondary systems in the past few years. This challenge implies that more students can be educated and trained at lower unit cost without compromising program quality or reducing instructional time. Given the decrease in faculty morale and the rise in faculty activism, it appears that larger classes in conventional shops and laboratories are not the answer to the problem; nor are increased teaching and contact hours. A more creative method of instruction which can accommodate more students, while, at the same time, placing the teacher in a less traditional role (i.e., that of a manager of learning) is urgently needed.

It is quite apparent that a system of instruction which utilizes individualized competency-based learning has the potential to address each of the four priorities described above. At the same time, it would be unrealistic to claim that such a system would resolve all problems without introducing others. As indicated earlier, students from conventional instructional systems often have extreme difficulty in assuming the responsibility required to adapt successfully to a self-paced methodology. Instructors trained in traditional methods do not always adjust quickly to a role which is far less teacher-dominated but which, nonetheless, requires careful monitoring of student progress and selective counselling. Curriculum designers are constantly being challenged to keep their learning modules current.

It is also important to recognize that competency-based learning has its share of critics; these people are primarily concerned with ideological aspects of the policy. Jackson (1988) produced a detailed critique which, inter alia, argued that:

> For instructors, the competency approach limits the use of educational theory as the basis of curriculum decisions and replaces it with a form of systematic empiricism, lodged in a set of ideological procedures for constituting 'needs' and 'requirements' related to job performance. It also reorganizes and limits the use of instructors' knowledge of workplace requirements as the basis for their instructional practice. A new process of organizational decision-making is created which displaces authority over such curriculum decisions from instructors to the institution itself, thus constituting the 'objectivity' of curriculum for organizational purposes. (p. 243)

Nevertheless, while acknowledging the criticisms which accompany major changes in instructional methodology and the inherent problems of implementation, the DACUM technique and CBE methodology must be considered as viable alternatives to many of the crucial challenges which confront community colleges and institutes as they attempt to adapt to the changes which will characterize education in the third millennium.

References
Adams, Robert E. 1972. *DACUM Approach to Curriculum, Learning, and Evaluation in Occupational Training.* Ottawa: Department of Regional Economic Expansion
Blank, William E. 1982. *Handbook for Developing Competency-Based Training Programs.* Englewood Cliffs, NJ: Prentice Hall

Burleigh, Adrienne R. 1986. *The DACUM Trail and Other Intersecting Paths.* Columbus, OH: Ohio State University

Cameron, Ralph. 1972. 'The STEP System: A Step in the Right Direction.' *Canadian Vocational Journal* 8 (2):19-21

Coffin, Lawrence. 1974. 'In Step with Holland College.' *Canadian Vocational Journal* 10 (3):14-17

Conger, D.S. 1970. 'Saskatchewan NewStart: One of Six Experimental Training Projects.' *Canadian Vocational Journal* 6 (3):4-12

Connor, Thomas R. 1971. 'Prince Edward Island New Start's Comprehensive Manpower Development System.' *Canadian Vocational Journal* 7 (1):2-8

Dennison, John D., and Paul Gallagher. 1986. *Canada's Community Colleges: A Critical Analysis.* Vancouver: UBC Press

Glendenning, Donald E. 1964. 'Impact of Federal Financial Support on Vocational Education in Canada.' Ph.D. thesis, School of Education, Indiana University, Indianapolis, IN

Jackson, N. 1988. 'Competence as "Good Management Practice": A Study of Curriculum Reform in the Community College.' Ph.D. thesis, Department of Social and Educational Studies, University of British Columbia, Vancouver, BC

Kerr, Donald, Deryck Holdsworth, and Susan L. Laskin. 1990. *Historical Atlas of Canada: 1891 to 1961.* Vol. 3. Toronto: University of Toronto Press

Kidd, James Robbins. 1959. *How Adults Learn.* New York: Association Press

–.1963. *Learning and Society.* Toronto: Canadian Association for Adult Education

–.1966. *Implications of Continuous Learning.* Toronto: Gage

–.1970. *Handbook of Adult Education.* New York: Macmillan

Knowles, Malcolm. 1970. *Modern Practice of Adult Education: Andragogy versus Pedagogy.* New York: Association Press

–.1973. *Adult Learner: A Neglected Species.* Houston, TX: Gulf Publication

–.1975. *Self-Directed Learning: A Guide for Learners.* New York: Association Press

Mager, Robert F. 1962. *Preparing Instructional Objectives.* Palo Alto, CA: Fearon

–.1967. *Developing Vocational Instruction.* Palo Alto, CA: Fearon

–.1972. *Goal Analysis.* Palo Alto, CA: Fearon

Matijevic, Bonita. 1992. 'Improving the Quality of Vocational Education and Training: The Australian Experience.' Paper delivered at the Asia Pacific Economic Cooperation (APEC) Conference on Quality Workforce through On-The-Job Training, Singapore, November

Norton, Robert. 1985. *DACUM Handbook.* Columbus, OH: National Centre for Research in Vocational Education

Ontario. 1990. *Vision 2000: Quality and Opportunity.* Toronto: Ministry of Colleges and Universities

Québec. 1993. *Colleges for the 21st Century.* Québec City: Ministry of Higher Education and Science

Sinnett, William E., John D. Hart, and Frederick A. Embree. 1990. 'A Systems Approach Model for a Total, Competency-Based Technical Vocational Education Process.' Paper, Humber College, Toronto

Watson, Anthony. 1991. 'Competency-Based Vocational Education: Is This the Answer?' *The Vocational Aspect of Education* 42 (114):133-45

10
Promise Fulfilled, Promise Pending
Paul Gallagher

In the more than quarter century that community college systems have operated in Canada, there has been continuing debate about the internal and external issues affecting them and their institutional components. A review of recent issues of the *Canadian Journal of Higher Education* indicates that some members of the Canadian higher education research community have also taken a more active interest in the community college phenomenon.[1] The argument presented here is that, although most of this debate and research has been devoted to interesting dimensions of the Canadian community college experience, the fundamental distinctiveness of these systems and institutions has not received the attention it deserves.

One objective of this chapter is to encourage a refocusing of attention on two characteristics that distinguish college systems and institutions from other components of the postsecondary education sector in Canada: (1) their role in the implementation of social and economic policy and (2) their commitment to teaching excellence. This chapter first comments on the degree to which Canadian community colleges have lived up to their original promise. It suggests that, if these systems and institutions are to remain responsive in a future that will be quite different from the immediate past, they must develop a common agenda for renewal. It proposes five key elements of a future-oriented renewal agenda: (1) the enhancement of institutional collaboration across Canada, (2) moving beyond access to success, (3) developing learner independence, (4) adopting a strategic approach to personnel development, and (5) preparing for new forms of institutional leadership.

Common Characteristics
As Dennison's chapters on recent developments in the Canadian community college sector reveal, one cannot speak accurately of a Canadian community college system; Canada has twelve different community college

systems, one for each provincial and territorial jurisdiction. All of them were established with the clear purpose of broadening access to postsecondary education. Across the country, it was expected that community colleges would concurrently address the needs of young people fresh out of secondary school, of adults wishing to return to full-time study to acquire new employment skills, and of a broad range of mature Canadians interested in expanding their intellectual horizons or in upgrading their work, citizenship, or recreational skills.

To address these multiple learning and training needs, our community colleges quickly appreciated that it would be necessary for them to provide a more comprehensive range and variety of instructional programs than was available at other postsecondary institutions. Accordingly, community colleges offered short-term vocational training courses as well as more extended technical and para-professional programs. Almost all such institutions became active in apprenticeship training. Many offered specialized programs with an advanced technological orientation. Programs and courses that paralleled those offered in the first two years of university study were part of the curriculum basket in several provinces. Developmental studies for people without sufficient general and academic skills to be able to cope successfully with postsecondary studies were introduced. A rich variety of continuing education courses and activities, outreach and extension services, community development programs and initiatives, and recreational and cultural activities commonly contributed even more to the comprehensiveness of community college instructional offerings.

This curriculum comprehensiveness was complemented by a broad range of instructional formats: traditional instruction and training practices were widespread, but many institutions also gave considerable emphasis to open learning systems, distance education delivery, self-paced learning, cooperative education and work-study arrangements, and similar non-traditional instructional practices.

Community colleges also quickly recognized that, given such a broad spectrum of students and instructional programs, student support services should be seen as parallel to, and as important as, instruction (Dennison and Levin 1989). As a result, academic advising services, counselling, financial aid, peer group activity, and similar student services became more central to the work of community colleges than they did to the work of other postsecondary institutions. Nevertheless, these characteristics are shared with universities, technical institutes, and vocational centres in that all institutions are now expected to increase access to opportunity, to broaden the base of their programming, to engage in non-traditional instructional activity, and to provide support services for learners.

Distinguishing Characteristics

Two other characteristics of community college systems and institutions, however, set them apart from other sectors of public postsecondary education. First, college systems were expected to serve as instruments for the implementation of provincial or territorial economic or social policy, while still retaining some degree of operational independence (Dennison and Gallagher 1986). Second, they were expected to serve as models of high-quality teaching (Dennison and Levin 1989).

How each of these characteristics can be considered to be distinguishing features of community colleges deserves some clarification. As instruments of social and economic policy implementation within the various political jurisdictions in Canada, colleges were clearly intended to be different from universities, which, as Cameron (1991) pointed out, placed such a high premium on being autonomous. Similarly, they were to differ from technical institutes and vocational centres, which originally had very little operational independence and which were considered by governments to be training institutions. As institutions intended to give priority to teaching (Dennison and Levin 1989), colleges were distinguished from other postsecondary institutions. Canadian technical training institutions at the postsecondary level usually emphasized the rigour, intensity, and relevance of their instructional programs, while Canadian universities, as Smith (1991) observed, have emphasized balancing research and teaching roles.

Topics for Debate and Research

Colleges could have been expected to devote considerable attention and energy to developing their defining characteristics. For example, scholars might well have been expected to explore issues associated with how college systems might best play out their role as instruments for public policy implementation as well as issues related to the improvement and enhancement of teaching. Most of the debate and research related to community colleges has not, however, emphasized these themes. Rather, the college literature in Canada suggests that issues related to governance, labour/industrial relations, funding, articulation with other components of postsecondary education, organizational models, and questions of centralization/decentralization have dominated the debates and preoccupied the research community.[2] Critical though these issues are, they do not include the two that make our college systems unique: colleges as instruments for public policy implementation and colleges as teaching centres.

College Systems as Instruments for Public Policy Implementation

Community college systems originally came into being as a result of provincial and/or territorial legislation (Campbell 1971). In every case, the legislation and public debate made it clear that the institutional compo-nents of these systems were not to have the same degree of autonomy as did universities. In some cases, such as in Manitoba, New Brunswick, and the Yukon, the community colleges were really no more than government field operations and could be expected to respond without challenge to government interests and priorities. But even in jurisdictions where col-leges were to have their own governing boards, it was made clear that they were to serve one or another public purpose (Dennison and Gallagher 1986). No one argued that colleges needed a degree of institutional autonomy analo-gous to that possessed by universities in order to achieve their purposes.

A review of the performance of college systems across Canada can lead to no conclusion other than that they have been remarkably active as agents of public policy change. The outstanding illustration of success is in Québec, where the community colleges (Cegeps) were specifically called upon to play a leadership role in the democraticization of education by making themselves accessible to a broad spectrum of the Québec popula-tion. Few would dispute that the Québec colleges have played a central role in the implementation of policies and practices aimed at massive so-cial reform. The several restructurings of college systems in Saskatchewan, Newfoundland, and New Brunswick, over relatively short periods of time, suggest that some provincial governments have felt free to require a scale and frequency of organizational change that would have caused tremen-dous social unrest had it been proposed for any other sector of post-secondary education.

In provinces and territories where the development of college systems has been more gradual and evolutionary (e.g., the Northwest Territories, Prince Edward Island, Alberta, British Columbia, and Ontario), there have been good working relationships between government officials and col-lege officials, although strains have been evident in recent years. However, in no case have the strains been prompted by disagreement about the ear-lier government decisions that college systems should operate as public, Crown corporation-like entities rather than as aggregations of self-con-tained institutions (such as universities). A move to greater institutional autonomy has not characterized the community college movement in Canada.

Indeed, as Dennison has already noted, provincial governments have expressed consistent confidence in their college systems, sometimes after painful and prolonged evaluation, as in the recent reviews of college activ-ity in Ontario, Québec, and Saskatchewan. Different federal governments, however, have questioned the social and economic relevance of commu-nity college systems and the effectiveness of the training they have pro-vided (Canada 1985).

It seems fair to conclude, on the basis of consistent *qualitative* evidence, such as annual reports of government departments in almost all provinces, that college systems have been successful and increasingly respected instruments for the implementation of provincial/territorial social and economic policies. Indeed, after more than twenty-five years without cries for greater autonomy for college systems and institutions, it seems accurate to say that the identification of college systems as instruments for the implementation of public policy is now an integral part of the political culture of this country.

Colleges as Teaching Centres

When colleges were first established, there was universal reference to the need for them to excel as teaching institutions. This call was, in part, a plea that they not attempt to imitate our universities, which have not had a successful history of attempting to reconcile their teaching and research functions (Smith 1991). But it was also a recognition that the diversity of college students and programs compelled much greater attention to teaching than was the case at universities and technical institutes. Canada has not escaped some of the most dramatic features of the evolution of higher education in the US (Sykes 1988), which, among other things, has come to adopt the position that it is the responsibility of students to cope with mediocre teaching ('they shouldn't need to be spoonfed!') rather than the responsibility of teachers and trainers to hone and refine their teaching skills. In contrast, from the earliest days of the community colleges, it was made very clear that instructors should be excellent communicators, professionally masterful, and content-current. In some colleges, the expectation was that the emphasis on teaching would be so pronounced that they would soon be widely recognized as centres for research into postsecondary teaching and learning (Gallagher and MacFarlane 1977), and that all community college systems would invest in determining the extent to which they were measuring up in this regard.

There is, however, almost no *quantitative* evidence with regard to the quality of teaching in Canada's community colleges. In part, this due to the difficulty inherent in attempting to quantify quality. It is also a consequence of the fact that, at a system level, excellence in teaching has not been given the attention and support that was originally anticipated. Nevertheless, individual colleges do have indicators that their teaching is frequently, though not uniformly, of high quality. As well, there have been many initiatives across the country to focus even greater attention on the need for excellence in community college teaching.

Many community colleges survey their graduates regularly to determine their level of satisfaction with their college experience. The Saskatchewan Institute for Applied Science and Technology does a thorough annual graduate follow-up, the entire New Brunswick system has a well-established program, and BC's Student Outcomes Project is impressive – and these are but a few examples of Canadian college practice. Community colleges have consistently scored very well on graduate satisfaction with teaching. Surveys of employer satisfaction with the calibre of college graduates – a matter of particular concern in Ontario – have also tended to yield encouraging results.

Almost all community colleges maintain a professional development office or committee with some resources to support instructors who wish to improve their teaching performance. Several colleges, most notably in Ontario, provide a rich array of on-campus development opportunities for their personnel. The professional atmosphere that these opportunities create also tangibly contributes to the maintenance of an environment supportive of high-quality teaching. The BC college system has developed a sophisticated, internationally recognized instructional skills program, while Alberta has shown national leadership in staging regular Great Teacher Seminars.

But the most dramatic reinforcement of the importance of high-quality teaching has been provided by the Association of Canadian Community Colleges, which established a national teaching awards program in the mid-1980s. This program annually draws nominations from all parts of the country, spotlights outstanding teaching achievements, and provides a national public reminder that excellence in teaching must remain at the core of the community college mission. In sum, though the evidence is usually anecdotal, community colleges can legitimately assert that they are known for the high-quality of their teaching and for the support and encouragement they have given to its development.

A Need for Renewal
Former successes, however, should provide little comfort to Canadian community college personnel, because it is evident that the future will not be a mere linear extension of the past. If these institutions and systems are to continue serving as instruments of public policy implementation and as centres of teaching excellence, they, like all other social institutions, need to develop the capacity to respond effectively to circumstances quite different from those of earlier days.

Canada's community colleges have already had to renew themselves in a period of less than twenty-five years. Until the late 1970s, the real task of these institutions was to manage growth in times of relative plenty. This era was followed by a period in which scarce resources called for restraint and led to the need to lay off personnel, to reduce services, and, generally, to 'do more with less' – all of which required qualitatively different leadership skills from those valued in the earlier days of growth and expansion.

These colleges and systems now enter a third era, which is fundamentally different from either of the two preceding ones. Canada is in the throes of a major restructuring of its economy (it is not experiencing just another recession), the public debt continues to grow, and both federal and provincial governments are still attempting to justify operating deficits which can only increase the accumulated debt. There is now a global economic environment, and developing the ability to compete within it is fundamental to the maintenance of a standard of living and quality of life to which Canadians have become accustomed. This is a knowledge-based world of rapid technological change, and Canada's traditional dependence upon the richness of its natural resources must be augmented by adding value to those resources. Canada is experiencing some of the highest levels of unemployment and involuntary part-time employment in the industrialized world. Despite a relatively highly educated population, there is a mismatch between the knowledge and skills that adult Canadians possess and the knowledge and skills now required for economic prosperity.

Direct consequences of these new circumstances on the community college environment are numerous and profound. Some of the more significant are a changing college student population (with a growing proportion of more mature, part-time, non-traditional, highly motivated and career-focused students); a shrinking and unpredictable labour market that is likely to prompt, in the not too distant future, a redefinition of work; and an emerging set of social values and priorities which call for new opportunities for people who have previously been disadvantaged physically, economically, culturally, or socially.

A Renewal Agenda

The leadership of the Association of Canadian Community Colleges was astute enough to recognize that these new circumstances should prompt its member institutions to reconsider their missions, policies, and activities as quickly as possible.[3] The association also recognized that it would be more efficient for all its members to reflect on their new needs and circumstances together rather than on an institution by institution, or province by province, basis. Accordingly, in 1990 this association proposed to Employment and Immigration Canada (EIC) that community colleges and technical institutes be thought of as a distinct sector of the Canadian economy, and that their human resource needs become the focal point for a reappraisal of their effectiveness. This would be analogous to the re-examination of the human resource needs of other sectors of the Canadian economy then under way.

Price Waterhouse (1993) was commissioned to coordinate this study, which commented on a broad range of issues to be addressed by the college sector in the years immediately ahead. The balance of the study draws attention to some of the issues pertaining to the historically distinguishing character-istics of Canadian community colleges and which call for new levels and kinds of responsiveness to emerging economic and social needs.

National Collaboration
Most of Canada's community colleges have encouraged the shared use of equipment and facilities, cross-departmental deliberation on issues of com-mon concern, and the development of an institutional, rather than a de-partmental, perspective on responding to student and community needs. As well, on specific issues of common concern (such as governance issues in Manitoba, academic planning in Québec, and new program approval poli-cies in Alberta), colleges within the same political jurisdiction have mani-fested admirable levels of cooperation.

The new environment within which community colleges now work sug-gests that traditional levels and kinds of intracollege and intercollege col-laboration will not be sufficient to enable them to remain effective instru-ments of public policy implementation. Rather, in a globally interdependent world, it is imperative that our colleges think and act in even more collabo-rative ways. New kinds of service to employers, communities, and students will be possible only with increased intersystem collaboration. For exam-ple, more specialized training in a variety of fields will certainly be required in the future, and no provincial or territorial system, by itself, will be able to provide that training at reasonable cost. Some provinces have already dem-onstrated the potential of intersystem collaboration by agreeing to have only one institution in a region provide certain kinds of specialized train-ing (e.g., that provided by the Police Academy of Holland College on Prince Edward Island or by the medical technology programs provided by the Brit-ish Columbia Institute of Technology). However, even higher levels of co-operation will be required in the future.

The merits of intersystem collaboration can be seen from another perspec-tive. Many industries in Canada have been struggling to establish nation-wide training standards to enable them to operate on national and interna-tional levels. In the main, Canadian community colleges and college systems have stood apart from these efforts. It would now be prudent for them to collaborate fully with initiatives to develop nation-wide training standards and to design programs and activities that increase the employment mobil-ity of their graduates. Similarly, community colleges are continually evalu-ating a broad range of their initiatives. The results of these assessments should be shared with other institutions and systems in an organized fashion, so that there will be no 'reinvention of the wheel.'

The Council of Ministers of Education Canada, sometimes in association with the Department of the Secretary of State or what is now called Heritage

Canada, has traditionally taken a very cautious approach to nation-wide collaboration. Indeed, at times its approach has had the effect of obstructing proposed national initiatives. The Association of Canadian Community Colleges and the Canadian Vocational Association have been more forceful and far-sighted advocates for national collaboration, but they have not had, and should not have, the power to effect change.

The real message is that, to be effective in this new environment, Canada's community colleges must raise their sights and function more frequently as units of a national postsecondary network. Canadian educators and policymakers have commonly shied away from what have been proposed as 'national' initiatives in education. It is now time, however, to think and act in new ways. What we need now is a truly national effort – a general initiative (coming from people, institutions, and all levels of government) to address common issues in collaborative rather than separate ways whenever and wherever this would be in the public interest.

Opposition to national efforts in postsecondary education based strictly on constitutional grounds is no longer acceptable in most of Canada. Narrow constitutional opposition is now widely perceived by ordinary Canadians, even in Québec and Alberta (where people have always been particularly sensitive to constitutional issues), as a political tactic rooted in the past – a tactic that has contributed significantly to the current level of cynicism about political processes and politicians. Surely we have reached the point, many Canadians in all parts of the country would insist, where the public good must take precedence over political sparring.

Access to Success

Canada's community colleges richly deserve their reputation as institutions that opened up postsecondary education to new segments of the Canadian population. The new circumstances of the 1990s, however, suggest that increasing access is no longer a sufficient objective. It is now necessary for our community colleges to pay considerably more attention to student success as well as to student access. From another perspective, the success of our institutions and systems should be judged not by the number of students accommodated but by the number of students who have achieved their learning objectives and by the degree to which community and employer expectations have been met.

The practical implications of shifting the emphasis from access to success are significant. The practice of admitting students to programs for which the likelihood of success is remote has not completely disappeared, but most colleges now know that they do their applicants no favour by opening them up to what can only be discouraging experiences. It is important that they draw a distinction between open admission to an institution and irresponsible admission to a specific program (which merely sets a student up for failure). Community colleges need to devote more of their energies to understanding the changing demand and need for postsecondary educational opportunity and to identifying those student characteristics which contribute to success. Admitting students to college programs on the basis of a broader set of considerations than have been used traditionally, and creating new programs to meet the needs of a broader base of students, would be constructive.

Student success, however, is far more than a matter of admission standards. Virtually all college students need varying kinds of support if they are to realize their learning potential. Advocates of increased emphasis on student success frequently conclude that postsecondary institutions need to invest more of their resources in student support services. Apart from the fact that appeals for additional resources can only fall on deaf ears in these times, we may not be talking about a simple, incremental need. Rather, the whole organization of student support services in each college merits review, if only to determine whether the need is for more of what is already provided or for something quite different. For example, the way in which students use libraries today is quite different from the way they used them five years ago; it may well be that the provision of library services should be completely reorganized rather than simply augmented. Similar observations could be made about all other traditional student support services.

The most profound change likely to influence college student success has little to do with traditional admission practices or support services but much to do with the role of the community college instructor/trainer. College instructors/trainers have traditionally been expected to instruct, but their roles have already changed quite dramatically. Increasingly, college personnel on the cutting edge of their profession have recognized that their jobs should involve managing and supporting learning processes in which students play active roles. The college instructor/trainer role, with access to new technologies, now involves much more than mere 'professing.' Rethinking the role of the instructor has become essential to any strategy focused on quality of learning, and it should centre on the need to place increased emphasis on excellence in learning rather than on excellence in instructing.

Towards Learner Independence

Formal education generally (which would include most of the activity of Canada's community colleges) has tended to encourage student dependence upon teachers and institutions. Certainly, given that the roots of most mass education initiatives were firmly planted in the mass production processes of an industrial age, it should not be surprising that almost all formal schooling has become highly regimented, that young students expect to learn at the feet of older instructors, and that teaching receives greater attention than learning.

Yet, teaching and formal education of any kind entail artificial interventions into natural processes of learning. Although these interventions have become widespread and standardized over the years, it seems evident that they should change with circumstances. Interventions in learning appropriate to an industrial age are not the same as those appropriate to the current postindustrial era of rapid change, dramatic expansions of information bases, and improved learning technologies.

When Canadian community colleges were first established, it was legitimate for students to depend upon trainers to ensure that they acquired a set of skills that would stand the test of time and ensure employment. The notion of having multiple careers throughout one's employment lifetime was just beginning to surface, and the implications for education and training were only vaguely appreciated by most Canadian educators. It was at that time appropriate to think of education and training as full-time tasks, primarily focused on the young, to be followed by the more serious task of earning a living. All of this has changed, as the day of a globally interdependent and competitive world of knowledge and technology dawns.

Though full-time, formal education may still be largely focused on the young, learning is a task that all people can pursue. As well, any set of employment skills and knowledge now has a limited life, so that the acquisition of new knowledge and skills is a challenge that will always have to be faced by those who seek economic success and/or personal fulfilment. Indeed, many young people in Canada, including the well-educated, may face a life of interrupted employment. The employability of those who do not seize available learning opportunities may well be very limited. Fortunately, there are now many sophisticated agencies and technologies available to support the learning quests of people of all ages.

The current state of access to educational opportunity through distance education and open learning systems is only the initial step in a potentially dramatic revolution vis-à-vis access to a broad range of resources in support of independent learning. Community colleges on the educational frontier are already recognizing the implications of home-based learning and community learning centres, which have the potential to deinstitutionalize many aspects of formal learning through breakthroughs in telecommunications and computer technologies. In summary, formal educational institutions, including community colleges, certainly are no longer the primary agencies available to people who wish to create their own learning opportunities.

Successful adaptation to these new circumstances requires that people accept personal responsibility for their own learning. Correspondingly, educational institutions need to reorganize themselves to support and encourage student self-reliance and to give full recognition to previous learning acquired outside formal educational institutions. Community colleges, like other formal educational institutions, now need to realize that transmission of specific knowledge, skill, and attitude is far less important than is helping students to acquire those abilities that will allow them to continue to educate themselves and to adapt to a variety of constantly changing work environments.

It is not accidental that organizations such as the Conference Board of Canada and the Steering Group on Prosperity have placed such strong emphasis on the need for Canadians to acquire 'the new skills' required to make Canadian business more competitive.[4] It should be reassuring that these new skills are essentially the same as those that are commonly advocated by people who value education for its own sake. There have been several formulations of these skills, but each seems to be reducible to the following broad sets: acquisition of proficiency with the tools necessary for independent learning (reading, writing, numeracy, computer use, information collection and classification); interpersonal skills (listening, speaking, working in group settings, respecting the views of others); thinking and problem-solving skills (organizing information, analyzing, synthesizing, weighing and evaluating choices); personal management skills (exercise of initiative, integrity and ethical conduct, sense of responsibility, creativity, adaptability); and specialized technical or professional skills required for specific employment roles. It is commonly observed that, in the past, our educational institutions have devoted their attention almost exclusively to one or another of these skill sets; that is, either to quite specific technical/professional training or to liberal studies. A real challenge to community colleges will be to assist students to translate the rhetoric of lifelong and independent learning into practice and to rebalance a master-student relationship that is inappropriate to a self-managed learning context.

Personnel Development

Community colleges, as major providers of education and training services, should commit a significant level of their resources to the development of their own employees. Yet the direct and indirect investment in professional, technical, and general development of community college employees does not appear to have been aggregated on any provincial- or nation-wide basis. A conservative estimate is that 3 per cent to 5 per cent of the total annual operating costs of each institution are assigned to valuable development initiatives. The Price Waterhouse (1993) study of the human resource needs of the community college sector pinpoints what has become a major limitation of community college employee development. The survey results indicate that, all too often, employee development resources are used to meet needs which are determined by individual employees; to serve objectives established by specific departments or other college subunits without reference to the institution as a whole; to address unanticipated and short-term crises in support service areas; to provide some constructive break from the more stressful daily activity of some employees; and/or to reward faithful service.

While all these interests are legitimate, the Price Waterhouse report observes that community colleges, like other complex organizations, do not receive optimal returns on their investments in employee development through taking a scatter-gun approach to this aspect of college activity. The fundamental point made in this report is that employee development funds need to be used strategically if they are to have the best results for employees, colleges, and the students and communities served by colleges. The strategic use of employee development funds involves the development and implementation of long-term systematic plans for employee development – plans that are analogous to those for instructional development, institutional budgeting, facilities development, and other core activities.

Three specific areas of employee development now require strategic attention in the community college environment. The first area is concerned with development for part-time and short-term personnel. Traditionally, community colleges have employed more part-time than full-time instructors and trainers. They have done so on the grounds that institutions of this kind need the program flexibility that results from employing people on a short-term and/or part-time basis, and that part-time instructors and trainers who are also employed in the field in which they teach have the opportunity to remain abreast of trends and patterns in the industries in which their students will later be employed. More recently, many community colleges have also employed more support staff on a part-time and on an 'as-required' basis as a cost-saving measure. This is consistent with the more general pattern in the Canadian workforce of decreasing the number of full-time jobs and increasing the number of part-time ones. In effect, over the years, many community colleges have become part-time rather than full-time oriented institutions.

While being a student on a part-time basis is clearly the way of the future, community colleges need to re-evaluate the impact of continuing with policies which encourage the maintenance of a high percentage of part-time employees. Anecdotal evidence would suggest that involuntary part-time employees have often felt marginalized in community college settings, regardless of the length of time they have served in such a capacity. The status of part-time instructors has frequently been an issue in some Ontario colleges, and the part-time instructor issue was the focal point of a recent labour dispute in a BC college. Part-time instructors have not usually been hired at the culmination of a rigorous recruitment process, as have full-time personnel; they have not had equitable opportunities to participate in college decisionmaking processes; they have often been low on the priority list for access to equipment, supplies, and work space; and they have not had access to employee development opportunities.

Circumstances of recent years indicate that continuing the marginalization of part-time college employees would be bad policy from virtually all perspectives, except short-term cost saving. Because part-time work is now the common, albeit indirect, avenue of entry into full-time college employment, it would be good business practice for colleges to pay much more careful attention to recruitment and hiring practices vis-à-vis part-time employees. Because they have as much impact on students as do full-time employees, performance evaluation standards should apply equally to both full-time and part-time personnel. And, if community colleges really wish to decrease the marginalization of part-time personnel, the most positive initiative they could take to foster institutional loyalty and to demonstrate a new respect for the contributions of such people would be to incorporate them and their development needs into the their strategic plans for employee development.

The second area of strategic employee development is the creation of more career advancement opportunities for college support staff. Such employees frequently sense that their contributions to the common institutional good are not as well recognized as are those of faculty members and administrators. While second-class institutional citizenship may be too harsh a term to describe the feelings of many community college support staff, 'parity of esteem' for support personnel in colleges is rarely felt. This difference in recognition and status is frequently revealed by employee development policies and practices which address long-term governor, administrator, and faculty professional development needs but neglect those of support staff. It is reinforced when community colleges do not provide career development opportunities for their own support personnel, while to their constituencies and potential students they preach the gospel of continuous learning, adaptability in the workplace, and the need to prepare for multiple jobs and several careers.

Employee development plans must include strategies for career development for support personnel. While this may be difficult, particularly in smaller institutions where the number of different support positions and career opportunities is limited, there are two workable strategies. The first is to promote the cross-training of long-term support personnel, so that all such employees are able to perform more than one role within their respective colleges. This is not to imply that support staff should be trained so that they become mutually replaceable, but to indicate that the acquisition of a broader range of skills and experience will normally enhance the career prospects of any working person. The second strategy is for community colleges within the same system to address support staff career development on a system or subsystem basis rather than only on an institutional basis. A system or subsystem approach to career development opportunities would operate as though support personnel (and such a plan need not be limited to support personnel) were system employees rather than institutional employees. Thus, for example, four or five community colleges within commuting distance of one another (or all the colleges within a provincial system) could pool their support personnel career opportunities and offer them to employees in any of the institutions that might choose to become part of the pool.

The third area of personnel development that needs strategic attention concerns providing support to employees so that they may properly use new instructional, communication, and information processing technologies. With rapid technological change being a dominant force in contemporary life, it would be ironic if community colleges were not to show themselves adept at applying new technology (especially given their promise to students that they will educate them for the future rather than for the past). To become institutions that can demonstrate to corporate clients, for example, that they are credible suppliers of relevant employee training, most colleges need to begin by ensuring that they themselves are comfortable and adept with applied technology. Having employees who are cutting-edge users of technologies appropriate to their particular tasks and roles would be a legitimate target for the strategic personnel development plans of many of Canada's community colleges.

Redefinition of Leadership
The term 'leadership' generally conjures up visions of college boards of governors or presidents issuing orders and making decisions of sweeping impact. Not infrequently, it also suggests that people in leadership positions should be held accountable for their decisions and actions to a far greater extent than are other people in the community college environment. Accordingly, despite the very broad range of activities which come under the general umbrella of leadership development, this term is still generally believed to refer to the induction of board members and senior administrators into the myths and mysteries of institutional decisionmaking, opinion-shaping, and development.

Yet even a cursory examination of contemporary popular management literature reveals that such perceptions of leadership and leadership development should be associated with the past rather than with the future (Beck 1992; D'Cruz and Rugman 1992; Handy 1989; Kanter 1989; Peters 1987). Of even greater significance, any analysis of conflict in Canada's college systems would support the view that traditional perspectives on leadership within the community college environment are no longer appropriate.

Much conflict can be attributed to the fact that community colleges have attempted, on the one hand, to be collegial, participatory, and consultative, while, on the other hand, maintaining quite traditional, hierarchical structures for administration and institutional governance. In a very real sense, many colleges and college systems have tried to marry the corporate sector's established methods of management with the university sector's sophisticated and subtle approaches to collegial operation. The seemingly never-ending labour relations tensions in Québec, Ontario, and BC college systems are as much a consequence of efforts at this kind of marriage as they are of anything else. Conversely, the relatively tranquil labour relations environment of Alberta can be attributed in large part to finding acceptable terms for this marriage through separate labour legislation for the postsecondary sector of education.

If our colleges are to cope with the future, it is imperative that they learn to operate in new ways. This implies the onset of an era of shared leadership along with the development of leadership skills on the part of a broad range of community college people. Most feminist literature provides us with excellent examples of the successful application of shared leadership principles (Anderson 1991; Kanter 1989; Neilson and Gaffield 1986), and aboriginal peoples have always emphasized shared leadership (Cassidy and Dale 1988). If our colleges are to fulfil their promise, it is imperative that they move from formal adversarialism to cooperative governance and management (resulting in an authentic 'social contract' rather than in a 'collective agreement'), that they emphasize common zones of activity and shared interests rather than restrictive job descriptions and rigidly separate areas of jurisdiction, and that they cultivate shared accountability for results rather than finger-pointing or scapegoating.

New forms of institutional leadership will not just happen. They need to be considered thoroughly, planned carefully, and implemented sensitively. As Levin concludes in Chapter 2, 'Effective leadership will be that which leads Canada's colleges into an environment of trust.'

Summary
While Canada's community colleges and college systems share many characteristics with other sectors of postsecondary education, they do have two

characteristics that they do not share equally with their postsecondary colleagues. These two distinguishing characteristics are (1) a mission to serve as instruments for the implementation of social and economic policy and (2) a commitment to excellence in teaching. For more than twenty-five years, this mission and commitment have remained paramount in the Canadian community college culture. While the community college environment has not been conducive to the collection and analysis of nation-wide empirical evidence to support the view that colleges have lived up to their original promise, there is considerable anecdotal evidence which indicates that they have remained faithful to their historical roots, despite the social and economic changes that have occurred during the last quarter century.

However, the scale of change now being experienced, and the pace of change projected for the immediate future, are of a far different order than anything that occurred in the past. Globalization, interdependence, the pace of technological innovation, the growing pre-eminence of knowledge-based economies, and the urgent need to address the sustainability of our planet are just some of the factors that require Canada's community colleges to adjust to new circumstances if they are to continue to fulfil their original promise. These institutions and systems need to renew themselves if they are to remain relevant and responsive.

The renewal agenda would see them function more as a nation-wide network or system, call for a shift from a preoccupation with access to a drive for success, support independence and personal responsibility on the part of adult learners, take a more planned and comprehensive approach to personnel development, and develop new forms of institutional leadership calculated to restore a sense of trust and shared community. Pursuing such an agenda should result in a Canadian community college movement poised to achieve its potential.

Notes

1 John D. Dennison of the University of British Columbia and Michael Skolnik of the Ontario Institute for Studies in Education have been the most active scholarly analysts of Canadian community colleges and college systems. A new generation of scholars, including John S. Levin and Glen A. Jones, is now engaged in research developed in the Dennison-Skolnik tradition.
2 The *Canadian Journal of Higher Education* has served as the major medium of communication among scholars in the field of Canadian higher education.
3 The *Association of Canadian Community Colleges* has recently relocated to Ottawa, in part to have more immediate access to federal initiatives pertinent to the work of community colleges. The executive director, Thomas Norton, has been particularly adept at identifying how federal departments work and where the interests of the association and the federal government converge.

4 The Conference Board of Canada, based in Ottawa but operating across Canada, has been particularly active in fostering business-education partnerships. Its Corporate Council on Education developed an *Employability Skills Profile* in 1992 that has become widely accepted as the best comprehensive presentation of the 'generic skills, attitudes and behaviours that employers look for in new employees and that they develop through training programs for current employees' (Bloom 1994).

The Steering Group on Prosperity was an ad hoc national committee established by the federal government to animate nation-wide discussion and action related to ensuring the continued prosperity of Canada in a world of fast-paced change. In many respects, it operated in conformity with sound community development principles. Its final report, *Inventing Our Future: An Action Plan for Canada's Prosperity*, was first distributed in October 1992 as a call to action.

References

Anderson, Doris. 1991. *The Unfinished Revolution: The Status of Women in Twelve Countries*. Toronto: Doubleday

Beck, Nuala. 1992. *Shifting Gears: Thriving in the New Economy*. Toronto: Harper Collins

Bloom, Michael. 1994. *Enhancing Employability Skills: Innovative Partnerships, Projects, and Programs*. Ottawa: Conference Board of Canada

Cameron, David M. 1991. *More Than an Academic Question: Universities, Government, and Public Policy in Canada*. Halifax: Institute of Research on Public Policy

Campbell, Gordon. 1971. 'Community Colleges.' Reprint from *Handbook of the Association of Universities and Colleges of Canada*. Ottawa: Association of Universities and Colleges of Canada

Canada. 1985. *Canadian Jobs Strategy*. Ottawa: Employment and Immigration Canada

–.1991. *Profile of Higher Education in Canada*. Ottawa: Department of the Secretary of State

Cassidy, Frank, and Norman Dale. 1988. *After Native Claims? The Implications of Comprehensive Claims Settlements for Natural Resources in British Columbia*. Lantzville, BC: Oolichan Books

D'Cruz, Joseph R., and Alan M. Rugman. 1992. *New Compacts for Canadian Competitiveness*. Toronto: Kodak Canada

Dennison, John D., and Paul Gallagher. 1986. *Canada's Community Colleges: A Critical Analysis*. Vancouver: UBC Press

Dennison, John D., and John Levin. 1989. *Canada's Community Colleges in the Nineteen-Eighties*. Willowdale, ON: Association of Canadian Community Colleges

Gallagher, Paul, and Gertrude MacFarlane. 1977. *A Case Study in Democratic Education: Dawson College*. Montreal: Dawson College Press

Handy, Charles. 1989. *The Age of Unreason*. Boston: Harvard Business School Press

Kanter, Rosabeth Moss. 1989. *When Giants Learn to Dance: The Definitive Guide to Corporate America's Changing Strategies for Success*. New York: Simon and Schuster

Neilson W.A.W., and G. Gaffield. 1986. *Universities in Crisis: A Mediaeval*

Institution in the Twenty-First Century. Montreal: Institute for Research on Public Policy

Peters, Tom. 1987. *Thriving on Chaos: Handbook for a Management Revolution.* New York: Harper and Row

Price Waterhouse. 1993. *Human Resource Study of the Canadian Community Colleges and Institutes Sector.* Ottawa: Human Resources and Labour Canada

Smith, Stuart L. 1991. *Report of the Commission of Inquiry on Canadian University Education.* Ottawa: Association of Universities and Colleges of Canada

Sykes, Charles J. 1988. *ProfScam: Professors and the Demise of Higher Education.* Washington: Regenery Gateway

Conclusion
John D. Dennison

In the account of contemporary developments in community college systems across this nation, and in the subsequent analyses of those common issues which seem destined to dominate their future, two themes arise with remarkable regularity. The first theme is the challenges which colleges must address if they are to maintain viability and relevancy. This requires finding new styles of leadership; maintaining competitiveness within a dramatically different economic reality and a growing private sector; realizing and documenting their values; being full and effective partners in a complex postsecondary system; changing an operating style which is no longer effective; and, above all, ensuring that student development remains at the heart of their operation.

But if the first theme is disconcerting, the second theme, opportunity, is encouraging. In responding to each challenge, colleges have an opportunity to re-establish themselves as flexible institutions which contribute to economic renewal; to accommodate the needs of society's most disadvantaged members; and to regain public confidence and government support. However, as a good deal of the discussion in this book has demonstrated, the path to the future will not be easy and the stakes will be high.

Part of the difficulty which Canada's colleges face in seeking and implementing change is a lack of constructive and systematic criticism. Although the American literature is rich in studies by scholars from sociology, psychology, political science, history, public administration, and organizational behaviour (all of whom critically examine both the mission of the colleges and the means by which they conduct their affairs), there is no corresponding Canadian literature.

There are, of course, several explanations for the lack of scholarly discourse in Canada. The size of the academy provides for only a very small number of scholars who view higher education, let alone the community college sector, as a fit subject for specialization. The sparse list of professional journals in Canada offers few opportunities for debate or the dissemination of ideas. But while all this may be obvious, a close review of community college development in both countries could lead to a more subtle conclusion. In spite of the difference in the size of the two multifaceted college systems, it may be argued that those in Canada are the more diverse. The dominant critical themes which focus upon US colleges are, in general, broadly applicable. For example, issues such as the transfer function, the state of vocationalism, and the education of minorities sound a common chord in virtually all regions of the country. However, it is optimistic in the extreme to attempt to apply the same dominant issues to college systems in Ontario and Alberta, and even more optimistic to apply them to either Québec or Saskatchewan. Nevertheless, there are some values which do apply to all Canada's college systems.

It is useful to review some of the most prominent critical analyses of US community colleges. These will demonstrate the scope of the topic and also reveal some themes which have limited application to Canada's institutions. In several provinces, the concept of the community college drew largely upon US experience and, hence, there is some basis for comparison.

McGrath and Spear (1987) assert that community colleges, rather than ensuring equal opportunity for all, have actually channelled graduates into the same lower-class jobs occupied by their parents. While so doing, colleges have insulated universities from non-traditional students. Dougherty (1988) directed his attention to a comparison between the functionalist and the class reproductionist views of college roles. The functionalist approach (Cohen and Brawer 1982; Monroe 1972; Medsker 1960) applauds the college concept as a path to social and economic advancement for working-class and minority populations. Conversely, the class reproductionist advocates (Karabel 1986; Zwerling 1976, 1986; Bowles and Gintis 1976) argue that 'economic and political elites have fostered community college growth in order to reproduce existing class relations by hindering the social mobility of disadvantaged students and by meeting the economic elite's need for publicly subsidized labor training' (Dougherty 1988:352). Dougherty concludes that neither position fully explains the growth of the college idea in the US; rather, government officials have promoted college expansion in their own interest.

Can the class reproductionist argument be sustained in Canada? Anisef, Ashbury, and Turritten (1989) bring a sociological perspective to the issue in Ontario. These researchers conclude that, based upon job status returns, direct entrants to universities earn twice the amount than do direct entrants to college. (However, for female students, community colleges do a relatively more effective job in producing positive job status returns than do universities.) Ultimately, they concur with the class reproductionist position. Whether Anisef et al.'s results would be sustained beyond Ontario is a moot point. That province's colleges provide no formal transfer function, unlike BC and Alberta; while in Québec all high school graduates must follow the college route to either university or the workforce. A recent study conducted by Bellamy (1992), and involving over 5,000 high school graduates in BC, revealed that several factors contributed to a student's choosing to enter either college or university. The three most powerful were grade-point average, kind of program, and level of education expected, all of which related to sociocultural influences. However, with the transfer opportunities which exist in that province, large numbers of college students continue on to university. In 1991, students who began their postsecondary studies in a BC community college constituted approximately one-third of all university enrolments (British Columbia Council on Admissions and Transfer 1994).

Several US scholars (Bernstein 1986; Eaton 1986; Raisman 1990) advocate the need to reinvigorate the academic or collegiate aspect of the college function, which they regard as having been suppressed in the interests of remedial education, workplace training, and programs aimed at raising enrolment and generating fiscal support. Again, this issue has limited relevance to the Canadian experience. Transfer programs in BC and Alberta continue to flourish. In Alberta, the numbers of university transfer students have consistently increased (Alberta Council on Admissions and Transfer 1993), while in BC, recent research indicates that students from the college sector obtain baccalaureate degrees in proportions comparable to those who enter university (British Columbia Council on Admissions and Transfer 1994), although they may take longer to do so. Pressures from the wider community for access to academic credentials have translated into expanded opportunities in colleges in Newfoundland, Saskatchewan, and Manitoba, the extension of degree-granting authority to some colleges in BC, and similar attempts to do the same in Alberta.

Finally, vocational education in US colleges has also earned its share of critics, Pincus (1974, 1980, 1986) and Bowles and Gintis (1976) being among the more prominent. Pincus (1986) concludes that

> by and large, there is no good evidence that vocational education delivers on the promises of secure employment, decent pay, and ample career opportunities. In fact, most of the evidence suggests that while a few relatively privileged workers can make use of community colleges to upgrade their skills, most students would be better advised to get a bachelor's degree, if they can. (p. 50)

Sentiments such as these would receive mixed reactions in Canada. As described in Chapter 1, most provinces can produce data to indicate that a high percentage of college graduates have gained employment, and that employers have been generally satisfied with them. Systematic follow-up studies conducted by the federal government also indicate that community college graduates enjoy levels of employment comparable to university graduates, although there are considerable variations depending on the field of study (Employment and Immigration Canada 1990). Nevertheless, in 1985, the conclusion – not dissimilar to Pincus's – of Abt Associates of Canada (1985), an independent agency, led the federal government to introduce the Canadian Jobs Strategy, which had the effect of diverting funds from the public colleges to the private sector in an attempt to support vocational training. Parenthetically, it is also worth noting that direct access to degree programs in Canada has grown more limited as universities impose ever more restrictive quotas and raise admission standards. To many unemployed citizens and other disadvantaged people, getting a bachelor's degree is financially, academically, geographically, and, in some cases, emotionally, unrealistic.

While the systematic and constructive criticism of Canada's colleges may not be comparable to what is found in the US, there have been some notable attempts to evaluate their contributions to the social and economic life of this nation, the most recent being the Price Waterhouse (1993) study. Another review of colleges and college systems, from a quite different ideological perspective, has been prepared by Muller (1990). In this work, Muller and other critics examine the implications of corporate management practices upon college culture. Muller and his associates deplore the trend towards state control of curricula, management practices, working conditions, competency-based instruction, and job training policies, all of which they regard as compromising the educational mission of the colleges and making them instruments of capitalist corporate management. Notwithstanding these limited examples, comprehensive evaluations of Canada's colleges have been rare. However, it is appropriate to reflect upon some of the common expectations which accompanied the birth of the Canadian community college movement and to comment upon attempts to honour these expectations.

One major challenge which was levelled originally at the college sector and which has continued unabated throughout three decades of development has been that of providing access. Colleges were, and still are, expected to open their doors to those who have been denied the opportunity for further education by sociocultural, economic, academic, geographic, and other such barriers. As a result, numerous social groups, multicultural organizations, immigrants, First Nations peoples, individuals on social assistance, and the physically and mentally disadvantaged continue to challenge colleges to provide programs tailored to their unique backgrounds and specific needs. Each of these groups have a legitimate claim to college services, just as do those citizens of all ages who seek a second, and often a third or fourth chance to improve their educational qualifications and, hence, to facilitate both their social and economic mobility.

The evidence from across Canada indicates that colleges are fulfilling their promise. They continue to admit large numbers of applicants with weak or incomplete academic records. Often referred to as high-risk or marginal students, many fail to complete their programs, withdraw, re-enter, and withdraw again (Dietsche 1990). While some critics, particularly those in government bureaucracies, may question the financial consequences of high attrition rates, the more disturbing issue is that colleges may not provide a learning environment which promotes student success. Clearly, access is not enough. Having admitted students, albeit in the high-risk category, a college has an obligation to provide the instructional support necessary to enable them to accomplish their goals. The issue of student success has become a matter of considerable concern in several provincial college sectors. Numerous techniques designed to overcome this problem have been tried, with limited success (Morin 1993). In spite of the temptation, to apply the conventional approach of simply raising the requisite level of prior academic achievement is inconsistent with the community college mission.

Even the term 'student success' is not uncontroversial. Although often equated with 'retention,' 'reducing dropout rates,' and 'accountability,' the literature on student development indicates it is a most complex concept and that it must be considered in relation to individual goals, aspirations, and objectives (Cope and Hannah 1975; Tinto 1987; Terenzini and Pascarella 1980; Corman, Barr, and Caputo 1990). In fact, Tinto proposed that a student's decision to withdraw is the product of a longitudinal process of interaction between his or her pre-entry attributes (e.g., family background, learned skills and competencies, and motivation) and the social and academic environment of the institution. Studies of college students in BC (Dennison, Forrester, and Jones 1982) reveal that there are numerous reasons for enrolling in a college program, and that success, in the sense of goal attainment, must be judged accordingly.

Not only do many college students bear the stigma of previous educational failure, they are often the victims of social trauma. Many who enrol in college programs are single parents, long-unemployed, disillusioned, frustrated with barriers to progress, financially impoverished, and/or otherwise disadvantaged. All of these conditions affect their ability to learn and magnify the challenges they face. Colleges provide support services of various kinds (e.g., counselling, study skills, learning assistance, etc.), but they are neither qualified nor equipped to deal with the complex personal problems which bear upon student performance in courses and programs. Although the community, government, and students themselves might regard colleges as agencies for social rehabilitation, this is simply not their mandate, and it would be improper to claim otherwise.

Yet another expectation, and one which has become increasingly prominent in recent years, relates to the role colleges should play in economic renewal. Much of the literature from government sources, and often from colleges themselves, suggests that, through job-entry training and retraining, colleges can revitalize national, provincial, and regional economies. In periods of extraordinary unemployment, when the future of displaced workers is high on political agendas, governments turn to colleges to educate and retrain people so that they may re-enter the workforce; but in periods of economic downturn, no simple relationship can be expected to exist between training (no matter how carefully crafted) and employment. Colleges can produce skilled graduates, but they cannot produce jobs. It is quite unreasonable, for example, to base the success of colleges upon the employment rate of their graduates without considering the overall state of the economy. It is equally unfair to expect colleges to successfully retrain large numbers of displaced individuals from such sectors of the workforce as fishing and logging, when a sufficient number of jobs in those specific areas simply do not exist. It is, on the other hand, quite appropriate to expect colleges to produce graduates who can communicate effectively, think independently, be sensitive to human relationships, and have reasonable confidence in their ability to compete in the workforce.

A somewhat related challenge to the college sector stems from the current demand for advanced credentials in many fields of employment (Pitman 1993). There is little doubt that certificates, diplomas, advanced diplomas, associate degrees, and degrees have become the currency upon which status, advancement, and financial rewards are based. Para-professional organizations are quick to recognize that their members' formal credentials present a convincing case for improved status and, ultimately, higher fees for service. Community colleges, as accredited public institutions largely unhampered by the traditions regarding what constitutes a conventional program of study, are obvious targets for demands for a variety of new and often non-traditional para-professional programs. This is not to imply that advanced training or education, whether or not it results in the awarding of formal credentials, is not necessary for many professions. Numerous factors (e.g., advances in technology, expanded fields of knowledge, and the growth of organizational models involving more sophisticated human relationships) make advanced training essential for an increasing array of jobs. The point is, diplomas or degrees per se do not designate status; only improved performance can ensure that. But in their haste to develop new diploma and degree programs, colleges may compromise quality and, ultimately, the reputations of both themselves and of their graduates.

Colleges in many provinces are under pressure from students, employer groups, professional associations, and society at large to expand their credentials. Indeed, many institutions are strongly sympathetic to that demand. The issue of college degree-granting authority in Alberta and BC and the report on advanced training in Ontario are examples of this trend. But while much can be said in support of this expanded role for community colleges, it is important to remind its advocates that the quality of an institution rests not upon how much it does but upon how well it does the things it claims to do.

Yet another challenge is presented in Chapter 6 by Janet Knowles. She reports upon extensive endeavours by colleges to conclude contractual arrangements with business and industry, Crown corporations, and governments at various levels in order to deliver instructional programs and other college services. Furthermore, there is a rapidly expanding international market to which many Canadian colleges have been quick to respond. There is every indication that declining government support will require colleges to explore these kinds of entrepreneurial activities and to become more financially independent if they are to survive in a more competitive marketplace. At the same time, these enterprises contribute to the stature of the colleges, raise their profiles, and demonstrate the relevance of the college sector to the wider community. However, there is also a price to pay, in that external contracts make considerable demands upon an institution's human and material resources and can divert attention away from the needs of its traditional clients. Again, the challenge to leadership is to balance conflicting demands.

All of the foregoing challenges/expectations translate into a new and, in many respects, a fundamentally different future for Canada's colleges. At the same time, those colleges which embrace these challenges with vision and commitment have a golden opportunity to confound their critics, demonstrate their viability, and prove themselves to be the educational institutions most able to accommodate the sociopolitical and economic realities of the next decade. Having said this, however, it is appropriate to conclude with a word of caution. In the excitement and euphoria of change, it is crucial that Canada's community colleges never lose sight of their most fundamental and important task – to optimize the development of each individual student through an effective teaching-learning process.

In an article published in 1977, Arthur Cohen argued eloquently that US community colleges must cease responding to their many critics by rationalizing the charges made against them or apologizing for their perceived failures. Rather, college leadership should state firmly and unequivocally what their mission really is. As Cohen notes, colleges cannot, will not, and should not try to overturn the class structure of society. Similarly, colleges cannot make learned scholars of people who have been disadvantaged for so long and in so many ways. What colleges *can* do is maintain an environment in which learning is revered and in which opportunities for personal advancement abound.

Cohen concluded his essay with a powerful admonition to community college leaders in the US: 'The universal obligation is not to be social revolutionaries, humanity modifiers, educational agency brokers or the purveyors of certificates of ever-lower value that give people the illusion that they have learned. It is to teach' (p. 81). A similar warning to Canada's colleges is expressed by Paul Gallagher in Chapter 10, where he argues cogently for revitalizing the teaching role. The continuing challenge to leadership will be to ensure that, with all of the pressures to respond to a multitude of additional roles and to provide innumerable new services, instructional quality is never compromised. This book has documented many important issues which will dominate the agenda for Canada's colleges as they approach the twenty-first century. But none is more critical than the original and still most demanding responsibility: the optimal development of this nation's most valuable resource – its people.

References

Abt Associates of Canada. 1985. *Evaluation: National Instructional Training Program*. Ottawa: Employment and Immigration Canada

Alberta Council on Admissions and Transfer. 1993. *Eighteenth Annual Report*. Edmonton: Council on Admissions and Transfer

Anisef, P., N. Okihiro, and C. James. 1982. *The Pursuit of Equality: Evaluating and Monitoring Accessibility to Post-Secondary Education in Ontario*. Toronto: Ministry of Education

Anisef, P., F.D. Ashbury, and A.H. Turritten. 1989. 'Educational Diversity and Occupational Attainment: Are Community Colleges Fulfilling Their Promise?' Paper presented at Learned Societies Conference, University of Laval, Montreal

Bellamy, L. 1992. 'Paths on Life's Way: Destinations, Determinants and Decisions in the Transition from High School.' Ph.D. thesis, Department of Educational Studies, University of British Columbia

Bernstein, A. 1986. 'The Devaluation of Transfer: Current Explanations and Possible Causes.' In *The Community College and Its Critics: New Directions for Community Colleges*. Vol. 54, edited by L.S. Zwerling. San Francisco: Jossey-Bass Publishers

Bowles, S., and H. Gintis. 1976. *Schooling in Capitalist America*. New York: Basic

British Columbia Council on Admissions and Transfer. 1990. *University Articula-*

tion and Degree Completion, 1986-1989. Victoria: Council on Admissions and Transfer

–.1994. *Some Perspectives on Transfer Effectiveness in the BC Post-Secondary System.* Vancouver: Strategic Information Research Institute

Cohen, A. 1977. 'The Social Equalization Fantasy.' *Community College Review* 5 (2):74-82

Cohen, A.M., and F.B. Brawer. 1982. *The American Community College.* San Francisco: Jossey-Bass Publishers

Cope, R., and W. Hannah. 1975. *Revolving College Doors: The Causes and Consequences of Dropping Out, Stopping Out, and Transferring.* New York: John Wiley

Corman, J., L. Barr, and T. Caputo. 1990. 'Unpacking Attrition: A Change of Emphasis.' *Canadian Journal of Higher Education* 22:14-27

Dennison, J., G. Forrester, and G. Jones. 1982. 'A Study of Students from Academic Programmes in British Columbia's Community Colleges.' *Canadian Journal of Higher Education* 12 (1):29-36

Dietsche, P. 1990. 'Freshman Attrition in a College of Applied Arts and Technology of Ontario.' *Canadian Journal of Higher Education* 20 (3):65-84

Dougherty, K. 1988. 'The Politics of Community College Expansion: Beyond the Functionalism and Class-Reproduction Explanations.' *American Journal of Education* (May): 351-94

–.1991. 'The Community College at the Crossroads: The Need for Structural Reform.' *Harvard Educational Review* 61 (3):311-36

Eaton, J. 1986. *The Failure of Humanities Education at Community, Technical and Junior Colleges.* Washington, DC: American Association of Community and Junior Colleges

Employment and Immigration Canada. 1990. *Outlook: Class of '86.* Ottawa: Employment and Immigration Canada

Karabel, J. 1986. 'Community Colleges and Social Stratification in the 1980's.' In *The Community College and Its Critics: New Directions for Community Colleges.* Vol. 54, edited by L.S. Zwerling, 13-30. San Francisco: Jossey-Bass Publishers

McGrath, D., and M. Spear. 1987. 'The Politics of Remediation.' *New Directions for Community Colleges* 15 (1):11-21

Medsker, L.L. 1960. *The Junior College.* New York: McGraw Hill

Monroe, C.R. 1972. *A Profile of the Community College.* San Francisco: Jossey-Bass Publishers

Morin, L. 1993. *Student Success in Post-Secondary Education/Training.* Victoria: BC Council on Admissions and Transfer

Muller, J., ed. 1990. *Education for Work, Education as Work: Canada's Changing Community Colleges.* Toronto: Garamond Press

Pincus, F. 1974. 'Tracking in Community Colleges.' *Insurgent Sociologist* 4:17-35

–.1980. 'The False Promises of Community Colleges, Class Conflicts and Vocational Education.' *Harvard Educational Review* 50:332-61

–.1986. 'Vocational Education: More False Promises.' In *The Community College and Its Critics: New Directions for Community Colleges.* Vol. 54, edited by L.S. Zwerling. San Francisco: Jossey-Bass Publishers

Pitman, W. 1993. *No Dead Ends: Report of the Task Force on Advanced Learning to the Minister of Education and Training.* Toronto: Ministry of Education and Training

Price Waterhouse. 1993. *Human Resource Study of Canadian Community Colleges and Institutes.* Ottawa: Association of Canadian Community Colleges

Raisman, N. 1990. 'Moving into the Fifth Generation.' *Community College Review* 18 (2):15-22

Small, J., and A. Konrad. 1986. *Transfer Study: Final Report.* Edmonton: Department of Educational Administration

Terenzini, P.T., and E.T. Pascarella. 1980. 'Toward the Validation of Tinto's Model of College Student Attention.' *Research in Higher Education* 12 (3):271-82

Tinto, V. 1987. *Leaving College: Rethinking the Causes and Cures of Student Attention.* Chicago: University of Chicago Press

Zwerling, L.S. 1976. *Second Best: The Crisis of the Junior College.* New York: McGraw Hill

–.1986. 'The Community College and Its Critics.' In *The Community College and Its Critics: New Directions for Community Colleges.* Vol. 54, edited by L.S. Zwerling. San Francisco: Jossey-Bass Publishers

Index